Religion or Belief, Discrimination and Equality

Also Available From Bloomsbury

European Muslims, Civility and Public Life: Perspectives on and from the Gülen Movement, edited by Paul Weller and Ihsan Yilmaz

Religious Diversity in the UK: Contours and Issues, Paul Weller

A Mirror for Our Times: The 'Rushdie Affair' and the Future of Multi-Culturalism, Paul Weller

The Muslim World and Politics in Transition: Creative Contributions of the Gülen Movement, edited by Greg Barton, Paul Weller and Ihsan Yilmaz

Religion or Belief, Discrimination and Equality

Britain in Global Contexts

Paul Weller, Kingsley Purdam, Nazila Ghanea
and Sariya Cheruvallil-Contractor

BLOOMSBURY

LONDON • NEW DELHI • NEW YORK • SYDNEY

Bloomsbury Academic
An imprint of Bloomsbury Publishing Plc

50 Bedford Square   1385 Broadway
London   New York
WC1B 3DP   NY 10018
UK   USA

www.bloomsbury.com

Bloomsbury is a registered trade mark of Bloomsbury Publishing Plc

First published 2013

© Paul Weller, Kingsley Purdam, Nazila Ghanea and Sariya Cheruvallil-Contractor, 2013

British Library Cataloguing-in-Publication Data
A catalogue record for this book is available from the British Library.

ISBN: HB: 978-1-44116-620-3
ePub: 978-1-44118-131-2
ePDF: 978-1-44116-530-5

Library of Congress Cataloging-in-Publication Data
Weller, Paul, 1956-
Religion or belief, discrimination, and equality : Britain in global contexts /
Paul Weller, Kingsley Purdam, Nazila Ghanea.
pages cm
Includes bibliographical references and index.
Summary: 'Benchmark publication on religion, discrimination and equality,
which contributes to international and global debates by using empirical data
from the UK as a case study'– Provided by publisher.
ISBN 978-1-4411-6620-3 (hardback) – ISBN 978-1-4411-8131-2 (epub) –
ISBN 978-1-4411-6530-5 (epdf) 1. Equality–Religious aspects. 2. Equality–Great Britain.
3. Religious discrimination–Great Britain. 4. Religious tolerance–Great Britain. 5. Religious
pluralism–Great Britain. I. Purdam, Kingsley. II. Ghanea-Hercock, Nazila. III. Title.
BL65.E68W44 2013
305.60941–dc23
2013029936

Typeset by Newgen Knowledge Works (P) Ltd., Chennai, India
Printed and bound in Great Britain

To respondents and participants who contributed to this research and also to Lesley Sawley, the project's administrator at the University of Derby, in thanks for her commitment to supporting the organization of the project's research.

Contents

Illustrations

Tables

Boxes

Acknowledgements

Research funding, research team and authors

Funding support

The 2010–12 research project (AH/H016074/1) on 'Religion and Belief, Discrimination and Equality in England and Wales: Theory, Policy and Practice, 2000–2010' that informs this book was financially supported by the Arts and Humanities Research Council and Economic and Social Research Council through their jointly sponsored Religion and Society programme (www.religion-and-society). More information about the project and its outputs than can be included in this book can be found on the project website at: www.derby.ac.uk/religion-and-society.

Researcher and author team

The book draws on research conducted by an interdisciplinary team. This includes Paul Weller (Cert Ed, MA, MPhil, PhD, DLitt) who researches in the study of religion and was Principal Investigator of the research. He is Professor of Inter-Religious Relations at the University of Derby and Visiting Fellow in the Oxford Centre for Christianity and Culture at Regent's Park College, University of Oxford. He was (2010–11) a member of the former Faith Advisors Panel advising Ministers and Civil Servants in the Department of Communities and Local Government and has been a member of Office for National Statistics working groups on the religious affiliation questions for the 2001 and 2011 national Censuses.

The project co-investigators were Nazila Ghanea (BA, MA, PhD) and Kingsley Purdam (BA, MA, PhD). Dr Ghanea teaches International Human Rights Law at the University of Oxford and was previously Director of Human Rights Law at the University of London's Master's in Understanding and Securing Human Rights. She was Founding Editor of the *Journal of Religion and Human Rights*. She serves as a member of the Organization for Security and Co-operation in Europe (OSCE) Advisory Panel of Experts on Freedom of Religion or Belief. Dr Purdam is a Research Fellow in the Cathie Marsh Centre for Census and Survey Research at the University of Manchester. He has over a decade's experience in conducting high-profile social research and teaching research methods. His main area of interest is in public consultation and policy-making.

The Project Researcher, Sariya Cheruvallil-Contractor (BSc, PGDBM, PhD), is Postdoctoral Researcher in Sociology of Religion at the University of Derby. In other relevant work, Dr Cheruvallil-Contractor has researched Muslim women's engagement in inter-religious dialogue and has taken part in a study of Muslim leadership training for the Department of Communities and Local Government.

The project researchers worked together with the project administrator, Ms. Lesley Sawley, and the project studentship holder, Ms. Lisa Taylor-Clarke, whose doctoral research conducted on 'Religious Freedom and Sexual Orientation: Compatibility, Contestation and Convergence: The Case of Church-related Adoption Agencies' has itself been a microcosm case study of the broader range of intersecting issues with which the project and the book is concerned.

General acknowledgements

Respondents to the survey and participants in the fieldwork

The most important acknowledgments must go to the individuals, groups and organizations that gave of their time freely to complete the questionnaire, participate in fieldwork interviews and focus groups and to contribute to the research in other ways that informs this book.

University of Derby

Acknowledgements are also due to the University of Derby, and a range of its staff are acknowledged below, together with Dr Rebecca Barnes, previously of the University's Social Studies subject area and now of the University of Leicester, who acted as second supervisor of Lisa Taylor-Clarke's doctoral research.

Christina Watson and Vicki Lomas from the Marketing Team of Faculty of Education, Health and Sciences assisted in the promotion of the project Knowledge Exchange Workshops, assisted by Daisy Henesy. General assistance to the project was provided by Claire Purdy, Catherine Pooley, Julia Pooley, Carol Otter, Julie Eley and Helen Lord of the Faculty Administrative team, and Madeline Bridges as a volunteer. Thanks are also due to Matt Cartwright in Design and Tony Walkington in the University's Print Unit for the design and production of various publicity and other materials used in the project. The Centre for Society, Religion and Belief's Graduate Assistant, Frauke Ullenbruch assisted in organizing the workshops, while the following were engaged to transcribe the project fieldwork interviews and Knowledge Exchange Workshops. For the interviews this included Sue Jeffels, Eileen O'Sullivan, Stephen O'Sullivan, Becki Peace, Julia Pooley, Fiona Raistrick, Louise Samson, Peter Samson, Pippa Thomas and Michelle Wood. For the workshops this included Donna Franklin, Michelle Wood and Lydia Brown. Acknowledgements are also due to Professor Alison Scott-Baumann, Professor of Society, Philosophy and Belief, for her 'critical friend' reading and feedback on some draft material for this book.

Universities of Manchester and Oxford

Acknowledgements are also due to the Universities of Oxford and Manchester. At the latter, a range of graduate student volunteers from the Cathie Marsh Centre for Census and Survey Research shared in supporting telephone follow-up of initial non-respondents within the questionnaire survey sample, while others undertook survey data entry into the SPSS social science statistical software. Anonymous readers at the Cathie Marsh Centre also provided some 'critical friend' feedback on some of the draft materials for this book. The Department for Continuing Education at the University of Oxford contributed financially to the telephone follow-up work and supported the costs of the project's workshop held in Oxford.

Multi-Faith Centre at the University of Derby

The Multi-Faith Centre at the University of Derby was a formal collaborative partner in the project. Its staff, Eileen Fry and Luke Foddy, worked with Lisa Weller, Josh Henry and Michelle Wood, who were engaged to undertake telephone follow-up work on the survey. The Centre was also formal co-sponsor for all the Knowledge Exchange Workshops, including the first one held at the Multi-Faith Centre (19 September 2012). It contributed the administrative resource of Jo Thornewill to a number of workshops, while the Centre's Director, Phil Henry, helped in facilitating some of the workshop breakout groups.

Other organizations

Other organizations collaborated with the project in its workshops. This included, at Rewley House, Oxford (5 October 2012), the University of Oxford's Department for Continuing Education and the Oxford Centre for Christianity and Culture and Regent's Park College at the University of Oxford; at Luther King House, Manchester (11 October 2012), the University of Manchester's Cathie Marsh Centre for Census and Survey Research and the Luther King House Educational Trust; at the University Hall, Cardiff (25 October 2012), the Cardiff Third Sector Council/Cyngor Trydydd Sector Caerdydd, People Can (Wales) and the Cardiff Interfaith Steering Group; at Senate House, London (9 November 2012), the Human Rights Consortium and the Institute of Advanced Legal Studies, School of Advanced Study, University of London.

Finally, acknowledgement is due to the United Kingdom Government Home Office, which commissioned from the University of Derby a 1999–2001 research project on 'Religious Discrimination in England and Wales', which Paul Weller directed and on which Kingsley Purdam also worked – the results of which were taken as a baseline for comparison with the results of the research that informs this book.

Copyright permissions

The vast majority of the book is formed from new primary research findings. But it also draws upon and reworks some already published writing, in relation to the permission of relevant publishers and copyright holders. In particular, acknowledgement is due under Crown Copyright by kind permission for quotations made from the report by Paul Weller, Alice Feldman and Kingsley Purdam et al. (2001), *Religious Discrimination in England and Wales*, Home Office Research Study 220, Research Development and

Statistics Directorate, Home Office, London; as well as to the University of Derby, for drawing upon Paul Weller et al. (2000), *Religious Discrimination in England and Wales: An Interim Report. January 2000*, University of Derby, Derby; and to the Equality and Human Rights Commission (EHRC) for permission to draw on material from Paul Weller (2011), *Religious Discrimination in Britain: A Review of Research Evidence, 2000–10*, Equality and Human Rights Commission Research Report 73, Equality and Human Rights Commission, Manchester.

The authors also wish to acknowledge many others from whose work we have either quoted within the generally recognized provisions for 'fair dealing . . . for the purposes of criticism or review', or to whose work we have been referred. Every attempt has been made to identify any copyright material appearing in this book that may go beyond the generally recognized permissions for 'fair dealing . . . for the purposes of criticism or review'. If, in error, we have failed specifically to identify and/or acknowledge such or have by mistake inaccurately or not fully represented or referenced any material originally written by anyone than ourselves or the authors of the chapters, then we offer our sincere apologies. If any such copyright holders were to bring the matter to our attention, we are committed to rectifying any such failure in any future editions of this book that may be published.

Personal and professional thanks

The authors also wish to record their professional thanks to colleagues who supported them in their work on this book and the research that underlies it, including Helen Langton, Guy Daly and Andrew Shacknove; and their personal thanks for the support of their families and friends including Margaret Preisler-Weller, David Weller, Lisa Weller, Katrina Weller and Marie Adenau; also Robert, Amelia and Layli Ghanea Hercock; and Murtuza Ali Contractor, Sayira Cheruvallil, John Thomas Cheruvallil, Sadaqat Cheruvallil and Sanaa Cheruvallil.

Thanks are also due to colleagues at Bloomsbury and at Newgen for all their work in bringing this book to publication – and in particular to our editor at Bloomsbury, Lalle Pursglove, for her patient support.

The Book, the Research and Key Concepts

Focus of the book

This book sets out to make a benchmark contribution to research, policy, law and practice in relation to religion and belief, discrimination and equality by drawing lessons from, and building upon, the key findings of unique research completed in 2012 in England and Wales. It is concerned with the challenging and controversial issues of religion or belief, discrimination, equality and human rights as they have come to the fore in public debate during the decade 2000-10, with a specific focus on England and Wales within Britain and the United Kingdom of Great Britain and Northern Ireland (UK), but also the wider context of Europe and globally.

These issues include the question of the nature and extent of discrimination and unfair treatment on the basis of religion or belief, as well as debate about how far the law should be involved in this area and, if so, on what basis. For example, to what extent is it possible, in law, to protect a person's religion or belief identity and practice? If so, can this be done in the same or a similar way as in relation to someone's sex, ethnic identity or sexual orientation? These are sensitive and highly contested matters. They touch on the nature of religious believing and belonging. They involve individual freedom of conscience and speech in community and public life; the organization of corporate religion or belief activity in which individuals come together to practice and express their religion or belief; and wider responsibilities among employers and service-providers.

When overlapping and interacting with other issues of rights and responsibilities, conflicts between different rights and laws and questions about whether there are any hierarchies of rights come to the fore. Are some aspects of identity seen as more important than others, by whom, and if so why? What about gender as compared with religion or belief, or disability as compared with ethnicity? In the United Kingdom, many of these debates turn upon the role and development of law especially over the last decade. Thus, during 2012 the UK's Equality and Human Rights Commission (EHRC) intervened (see Chapter 4) to question and test before the European Court of Human Rights (ECtHR) some of the ways (especially related to sexual orientation and religious symbolism) in which equality and human rights law relating to religion or belief have been interpreted and applied by domestic tribunals and courts.

Informing our consideration of these questions are data and insights derived from the 'Religion and Belief, Discrimination and Equality: Theory, Policy and Practice (2000-2010)' research project conducted during 2010-12. In part, this followed up on the 1999-2001 Home Office commissioned 'Religious Discrimination in England and Wales' research project (Weller et al., 2001), which provided a comparative baseline.

In order to simplify the presentation and discussion of the data, results from the 2010-12 project's survey (that took place in 2010-11) and fieldwork (that took place in 2011) will be referred to as 'the survey completed in 2011' and 'the fieldwork completed in 2011', or sometimes in summary together as 'the 2011 research'. The results of the previous 1999-2001 project survey (that took place in 2000) and fieldwork (that took place in 1999-2000) will be referred to as 'the survey completed in 2000' and 'the fieldwork completed in 2000', or sometimes in summary together as 'the 2000 research'.

The 2011 research was a mixed methods study of the reported experiences and attitudes of religion and belief groups, organizations and individuals, both religious and non-religious, including the perspectives of individuals working in the public, private and voluntary sectors in England and Wales. It included a national survey of religious organizations (including a follow-up survey of organizations that participated a decade previously) and fieldwork interviews conducted in Blackburn, Cardiff, Leicester, Newham and Norwich, where people working in the public, private, voluntary and community, and religion or belief sector organizations were also interviewed. As an innovation compared with the 2000 research, focus groups (held in each of the fieldwork locations) were also held with participants who understand themselves as 'non-religious' (see Bullivant and Lee, 2012).

The 2011 research has also been informed by a systematic collation and analysis of relevant key domestic legal cases as well as other relevant research evidence from the past decade. Finally, it includes the contributions of participants in five Knowledge Exchange Workshops held in Cardiff, Derby, London, Manchester and Oxford, which involved a wide range of people from the public, private, voluntary and community, religion and belief, and legal sectors.

The book sets the findings from these methods within the context of a broader consideration of the impact of legal and policy developments on religion and human rights in which, over the last decade, the category of religious discrimination has become more widely accepted, but also challenged and modified by reference to the category of 'belief', and in relation to shifting policy foci around shared values and social cohesion. In doing so, it takes cognizance of the global impact of 9/11 and the domestic impact of what Weller (2008: 195) calls the 'social policy shock' generated by the 7/7 London transport bombings and their impact on the discourses, policies and practices of multiculturalism and how these work through into people's lives, including initiatives to prevent violent extremism and to counter religiously justified terror.

In conclusion, this book aims to inform public and policy debates around equality and discrimination in relation to religion and belief and to equip opinion-formers and policy-makers in public, private and voluntary and community sector organizations (including among religion or belief groups themselves) to develop their understanding, policy and practice on equality and discrimination in relation to religion and belief in a more evidence-based way. Therefore, drawing upon disciplinary perspectives from

Religious Studies, Law and the Social Sciences and engaging with research findings, the book highlights recommendations concerning the most appropriate and effective ways to tackle unfair treatment on the basis of religion or belief and outlines a distinctive approach to the future development of relevant policy, law and practice.

Looking back: 'Religious Discrimination in England and Wales' (1999-2001) project

In April 1999, the Home Office commissioned the University of Derby to conduct research on religious discrimination in England and Wales. Through systematic review of the existing available evidence and application of qualitative and quantitative research instruments, this project's aim was to identify new primary research evidence relating to the nature and extent of religious discrimination. It was conducted by two of the current book's authors (Weller and Purdam) together with Alice Feldman, who led the fieldwork. Its terms of reference were: to assess the evidence of religious discrimination in England and Wales, both actual and perceived; to describe the patterns shown by this evidence, including, its overall scale, the main victims, the main perpetrators and the main ways in which the discrimination manifests; to indicate the extent to which religious discrimination overlaps with racial discrimination; and to identify the broad range of policy options available for dealing with religious discrimination.

That project's *Interim Report* (Weller et al., 2000) can be accessed via the 2011 project website at: www.derby.ac.uk/religion-and-society; its final report (Weller et al., 2001) provided, for the first time, an empirical evidence base for the position with regard to religious discrimination at the start of the 2000s. The *Summary Findings* of that project, including an outline of the research methods used can also be found on the website.

'Religion and Belief, Discrimination and Equality' (2010-12) project

Brief overview of aims and methods

Ethics, survey, fieldwork, focus group and Knowledge Exchange Workshops

The 2000 research provided the baseline for a unique opportunity of comparison and contrast with the position by the end of a decade of continuity and change. The detailed original aims of the 2011 project can be found on the project website at: www.derby.ac.uk/religion-and-society.

Research ethics approval was sought and given (at the University of Derby) for each distinctive phase of the project. The survey and fieldwork research methods used generally replicated those of the 1999-2001 project. Exceptions to this are given in Chapter 5, where details of the research methods used in the 2011 research are set out.

Systematic review of relevant legal cases

Looking across the decade under review, the 2011 research identified 130 relevant legal cases (using search engines, legal directories and press reports). These were coded according to categories reflecting different aspects of people's lives and were systematically reviewed and analysed within the following thematic codes: abuse – physical and/or sexual; accommodation/exemption, etc.; adoption; arbitration; assets of religion/belief community; child – cases involving a child; continued existence of a church; customary law; doctrinal issues; discrimination; direct discrimination; indirect discrimination; diversity; dress (head dress, hair); employment; employee definition; equality; freedom of expression; religion or belief, definitions of; observations; school; and suicide. Many of the cases consisted of more than one element highlighting the complex nature of religion and belief, discrimination and equality.

A list of these cases and their references can be found in the Appendix. Many of them had initial judgements in domestic courts and tribunals that were then appealed, sometimes resulting in different outcomes. That some of these appeals have also gone beyond the domestic system to the ECtHR is an important reminder that the interpretation and application of the law is itself subject to continuity and change through case law and the role within it of the judiciary as well as through legislative change initiated by political process. Chapter 4 of this book therefore explores some of the key legal developments, locating the domestic changes of the past decade in the wider continuity of international law obligations and unpacking some key illustrative cases.

Systematic review of other relevant research

Because of the richness and extent of the primary research data presented and discussed, there is no space in this book to review and discuss in detail other relevant research and associated literature. However, in parallel with the research undertaken within the framework of the project itself, a further systematic review of other relevant research evidence from the decade 2000-10 was undertaken, the results of which were also reflected in a review (Weller, 2011) of evidence on religious discrimination undertaken for the EHRC and to which the reader is referred. The project has also created an annotated bibliography on the project themes covering the period 2000-10, which is accessible from the University of Derby Online Research Archive at: http://derby.openrepository.com/derby/. In future, the present authors (and hopefully also other scholars), might be able further to contribute to the field by bringing the specific contributions of this book and the findings and analysis of other relevant research into critical interaction.

Doctoral research case study

A doctoral research study (not yet completed at the time of writing) took place under the title of 'Religious Freedom and Sexual Orientation: Compatibility, Contestation and Convergence. The Case of Church-Related Adoption Agencies'. Its topic has therefore been a microcosm of the wider project's concern with the tensions and possible clashes between different 'protected characteristics' in the equalities laws.

The project research evidence

Intentionality in commissioning research and positionality in its conduct

Research undertaken into matters which are subject to political contention cannot be viewed as entirely neutral. First, the source of the funding for and/or the commissioning of the research has an impact upon its nature, wider perceptions of it and its potential impact. The 2000 research was conducted within constraints from the terms of reference determined by the UK Government's Home Office while the 2011 research was funded by two of the UK's Research Councils on the basis of research aims, objectives, outcomes and potential impacts proposed by the researchers themselves.

Second, the individuals who conduct research and write about it have a positionality that is affected by their disciplinary background – which among the authors of this book encompasses human rights law (Ghanea), social science (Purdam), sociology of religion (Cheruvallil-Contractor) and the study of religion (Weller). Furthermore, regardless of how far the researchers and authors have managed to 'control' for the possibly skewing effects of their own personal and group self-understandings and/ or affiliations, the epistemological presuppositions and social understandings of the researchers entail both benefits and limitations.

Finally, the individuals and groups who provide research evidence are not providing comment in a detached way. Especially in as hotly a debated area as religion or belief, discrimination and equality, contributors to the research are themselves actors in a political process in which they are seeking to advance views, interests and perspectives. However, it is the 'raw' nature of the contributions made by survey respondents, interview and focus group participants that brings a particular power to more analytical consideration of the issues and their implications for policy, law and practice.

A 'mixed methods' approach

In the 'mixed methods approach' (Creswell, 2003) to social research, quantitative and qualitative methods complement and augment each other, and it is this approach that was adopted by both the 2000 and 2011 research projects.

Our questionnaire survey constituted the quantitative aspect of the research. Quantitative results are generally informed by random (or, as in the case of the previous survey and in our project survey) purposive selection of respondents within a sampling frame constructed by reference to transparent criteria. Especially when the same questions are asked over a period of time such data can help to identify areas of continuity and change. While the research reported on here cannot be described as a time series, the fact that it can make comparisons between answers to questions, many of which were the same in both 2000 and 2010-11, and some of which were provided by the same organizations, offers a unique insight.

In the interviews and focus groups of the fieldwork completed in 2011, research participants were 'given voice' directly. This emphasized their collaborative role in the research process (Schratz, 1993; Schratz and Walker, 1995) reassuring them that their 'voice' will be reflected in the 'voice' of the research (Creswell, 2003). By giving participants greater 'control' in the research process their different voices – as individuals, as representatives of a religion or belief group and as members of a plural society – can be heard and are used to inform the research findings. Therefore, such a process captures nuances of participants' personal contexts, and multiple and overlapping identities (Hall, 1996), as well as of the linkages and relationships that they share in their wider communities.

In the 2011 research this was achieved using semi-structured narrative interviews that, through participants' stories, collated evidence of underpinning cultural milieux, social contexts and personal attitudes (Riessman, 2002; Rubin and Rubin, 1995; Wengraf, 2001). Focus groups (Krueger and Casey, 2000; Stewart and Shamdasani, 1990) were also used as a methodological tool to explore and discuss the views, opinions and experiences of participants who consider themselves 'non-religious'.

Key concepts and terminologies

'Religion': Contested and working definitions

When the possibility of passing law on religion or belief discrimination for the first time in the United Kingdom outside Northern Ireland was first being discussed, an objection often raised was, as Hepple and Choudhury (2001: 25) put it: 'The difficulty of defining religion is regarded as a key obstacle to legislation prohibiting religious discrimination.' Nevertheless, in other areas of equalities and human rights, the imperfection of any likely working definition has not constituted an impediment to the making, application and development of law. For example, the meanings understood and ascribed to 'race' and 'ethnicity' have a history of contestation (see Bacal, 1981) in people's everyday lives, in community politics and in social theory. Thus, when Parliament originally passed legislation on 'race' or ethnicity it did not attempt to define meanings in a comprehensive way. Rather, it set out some key parameters, the interpretation and application of which were expected to evolve in line with Parliamentary intent. This was based on recognizing that the issue at stake was not one of abstract definition but of adequacy in assisting the law to address a specific kind of discrimination.

In the academic study of religion there has been a vast range of what might be called 'working definitions' of religion, each of which has tended to reflect particular disciplinary traditions and approaches – from the anthropological (for a classical definition, see Geertz, 1966) and the sociological (see Durkheim, 1947) to the theological. In the study of religion, there are scholars who have criticized the utility of any distinctive concept of 'religion'. An early example of this was the theologian and historian of religion Wilfred Cantwell Smith (1978) who, in his classic book on *The Meaning and End of Religion* argued that 'religions' are better understood as historical constructions superimposed upon the diverse experiences of people of 'personal faith' who live within 'cumulative traditions'. More recently, Timothy Fitzgerald (2000, 2007) has argued not only that the category of 'religion' has been 'essentialized' but also that it is a deeply ideologized construction which entrenches what he argues is a socially constructed division between 'religion' and 'the secular'.

Beyond academia the notion of religion has often been assumed according to one or more of its popular senses. A number of polities have attempted to develop a list of religions that are formally recognized by the state; are administered by an office of state; have explicit criteria; and have a defined process for achieving recognition. While having the benefit of relative clarity, such an approach has often led to religions that are historically not so embedded in a society encountering serious difficulties in achieving recognition.

In Britain, apart from specific areas such as the Prison Service, there is neither a generally applicable list of recognized religions, nor a single legal definition of what constitutes a religion. Thus, in charity law (from which can flow a range of privileges) there is no list of 'recognized religions'. In this, historically, 'religion' was often considered to be related quite closely to a belief in God or a divine being. However, it gradually became clear that such an understanding is very culturally limited since, not only did it not fit the beliefs of newer movements such as Scientology and others – concerning which some (see Lewis, 2009) have questioned the degree to which they should be understood as religions – it also did not fit the instances of Buddhism or Jainism that are 'a-theistic' but are generally considered to be 'world religions'. Therefore, in contemporary charity law, the emphasis is less on defining the nature of religion than on evaluating the nature of the activities (see Chapter 4) of organizations that present themselves as religious, and in which the question of their contribution to 'the public good' is an important criterion.

It is important, however, also to note that, although our survey focuses on organized religious groups, the category of religion more broadly is not limited to *organized* religion. Thus, the sociologist of religion, Grace Davie (1994) classically argued that there is a phenomenon of 'believing without belonging' – which means that identification with a religion is likely to be considerably wider than active involvement in a religious community or the 'orthodox' affirmation of what may be deemed to be the central tenets of a religion. Evidence for this can be seen in the quite substantial difference – even after the fall in the 2001 and 2011 Census of the numbers of self-identifying Christians – between those who in some sense identify as Christian and those who actively participate in the regular worshipping Christian community (see Chapter 3).

A further aspect of this is the notion (Berger et al., 2008) that there can be a vicarious aspect to religion where a more active minority is directly involved in a religion with the tacit support and approval of the wider population. At the same time, there are those (see Bruce and Voas, 2010) who critique such an approach, although David Voas (2009) argues that there is a broader identifiable phenomenon of 'fuzzy believing' in which individuals have a looser uncommitted connection to religion but are also not self-consciously non-religious (see also Arweck, 2013 and Vincett et al., 2012, for a recent discussion of research on how young people including young Christians, see their identities).

It can also be argued that definitions which operate largely in relation to religious ideas, beliefs and doctrines locate the significance of belief more centrally than would be the case in some traditions. Thus, in contrast to much of Protestant Christianity in which intellectual beliefs predominate, among Catholic and Orthodox Christians there is often a greater emphasis on performativity. Even more, Weller (2005: 9) has described a possibility of 'belonging without believing' (which can, for example, be found among many Hindus and Jews) in which identification with a community can be as much or more significant than an individual's particular beliefs (or sometimes even their practices) and may be expressed in terms of 'my culture'.

However, the relationship between religion and community, culture and religion and ethnicity is not straightforward. Many religious communities are ethnically diverse, and just as one religious tradition may embrace many ethnicities, so also one national or regional origin can be shared by people of several religions. In both commonsense terms and to some extent at least within the religious perspectives of the more 'universal' traditions of Christianity, Islam and Buddhism, religion, culture and ethnicity can be distinguished. However, separating out these dimensions in the lived experience of actual populations is not always possible.

Within the social sciences, the historically dominant academic tradition has tended to understand religion as a dependent variable of ethnicity and/or culture (Clements, 1971). To varying degrees, within this tradition religion has been seen as a functional and sometimes an almost instrumental reinforcement of a primary category of ethnicity. At the same time, there were others (Gill, 1975) who, even some years ago, argued that religion and ethnicity should be seen as much more clearly distinct, or in a reciprocal relationship and this more careful evaluation is now more common..

In drawing this discussion to a close, it is worth noting that it is likely that there will be significant differences between a more general and abstract consideration of the concept and definition of 'religion' in comparison with the use of the concept in the specific contexts of discrimination, unfair treatment and equality. In this, both religion and ethnicity can together be a part of how people are treated. There are also overlaps with other aspects of identity or what, in terms of equalities and human rights law, are called 'protected characteristics' (see Chapter 4). Therefore, when considering evidence in relation to discrimination and unfair treatment of any kind, including religion or belief discrimination, it is important to keep in mind the phenomenon known as 'intersectionality' which was first coined by the legal scholar Kimberlé Crenshaw (1989), and is now used in critical theories (especially in Feminist critical theory) when discussing how various oppressions are interconnected and cannot be examined separately from each other.

In the light of these conceptual and practical issues, the 2011 research proceeded on the basis that, when it is understood that any definition can only be a 'working' one, then the 'self-definition' of religious groups is the least problematic approach to take. There can clearly also be problems with such an approach – such as the possibility of tendentious claims being made in order to try to secure the advantages that accrue to such recognition. But in such a highly problematic and controversial area, the development of law, policy and practice in relation to self-definition perhaps represents the most practical way forward. For all its problems, such an approach at least allows policy, law and practice to connect with 'where people are at'. It can also link with legal definitions through the concept, in international law, of an individual's freedom of religion or belief being absolute, while limitations to its 'manifestation' are legally justifiable in only quite restricted circumstances (see Chapter 4).

'Belief' and its contestations

The 2011 research also examined the discourse and practice surrounding the concepts of 'belief' and the 'non-religious'. The 2000 research did not utilize the specific terminology of 'belief' because at that time it had not come into general legal or policy use in Britain. But as Woodhead with Catto (2009) note, because of equality and human rights laws that relate to religion or belief, a new legal and conceptual space has been created within which the category of belief can apply to those with no religion, but who also live by reference to specific philosophical and/or ethical perspectives and values.

In the *Employment Equality (Religion or Belief) Regulations*, 2003, the definition of religion or belief initially referred to 'religion, . . . religious belief, and . . . similar philosophical belief'. However, in the context of the development of integrated equalities law this was subsequently changed, with a specific reference to lack of 'belief' being added and the word 'similar' being removed from the reference to 'belief'. This has added complexity to an already difficult area. In the light of this, as explored by Woodhead and Catto (2009) the notion of 'belief' in legal contexts relating to discrimination and equality has been at least as much contested and problematic as that of religion. This has been especially so following the case of *Grainger Plc and other v. Nicholson*, 2009, in which 'environmentalism' was deemed to be a philosophical belief. At the same time, this Employment Appeal Tribunal case held that for belief to be recognized it needed to:

> be genuinely held; be a belief and not an opinion or viewpoint, based on the present state of information available; be a belief as to a weighty and substantial aspect of human life and behaviour; attain a certain level of cogency, seriousness, cohesion and importance; and be worthy of respect in a democratic society, compatible with human dignity and not conflict with the fundamental rights of others.

While extended in this way, support for a political party has not been deemed to be philosophical belief in a legal sense, although a belief in underlying political philosophies such as socialism, Marxism, communism or free-market capitalism might be deemed to qualify. However, as in relation to religion, while operating within the overall territory constituted by new law, policy and practice in relation to religion or belief, the 2011 research did not restrict itself to investigating these matters with reference only to the legal definitions of belief. Thus, in relation to the fieldwork completed in the 2011 research and its focus groups with the non-religious, the standpoints expressed by participants reflect positions that would fall within these legal definitions, as well as some that go beyond them, such as the view that a non-religious stance is purely and simply something rational rather than being grounded in values or beliefs.

Religion or belief discrimination and equality: Their varied meanings

As compared with the more contested concepts of religion and belief, the concepts of discrimination and equality might appear to offer something more stable. However, as argued by Hepple and Choudhury (2001: 33-40, 67-9), legal definitions of discrimination are 'system-specific'. Thus, while discrimination law in countries such as Canada, New Zealand and Australia often has a historical and often continuing case law connection with English law, the operative legal definitions of discrimination can and do differ.

In the United Kingdom alone, the relatively piecemeal evolution of discrimination law over the past decade means that a variety of legal and policy definitions have been operative at different times and in relation to different grounds of discrimination. At the same time (and as will be explored in Chapter 4), one of the achievements of the *Equality Act*, 2010 has been the, in principle, broad integration into a common legal definition and understanding of what were separately developed bodies of legislation in relation to 'protected characteristics' such as sex, age and race, but also including others (religion or belief, sexual orientation, gender reassignment) that have not had such a long legal history in Britain.

The chequered developmental history of the individual 'equalities strands' means (as also discussed in Chapter 4) that perhaps too much was assumed in relation to the 'sameness' of these 'protected characteristics' and, in particular, how they might be integrated. But even clear legal definitions do not settle this matter, since the kind of social research that also informs this book is not concerned simply with identifying and recording instances in which the outcome of legal process has found that discrimination has occurred. Rather, it seeks to capture what might more accurately be called the perception and/or reported experience of religion or belief discrimination, which may differ from legal definitions, and certainly from legal outcomes.

Finally, 'religion or belief discrimination' is perhaps best understood as shorthand terminology for 'discrimination on the basis of religion or belief'. In other words, it is descriptive of those attitudes, actions, circumstances and dynamics in which, in relation to factors concerned with religion or belief, an individual or group is treated less favourably than another individual or group either of a different religion or belief, or of no religion or belief. It is because of this that, when conducting the survey and talking with fieldwork participants, both the 2011 research and the 2000 research framed data collection with reference to the broader concept of 'unfair treatment'. As explained in the report (Weller, 2001: 7) of the 2000 research, 'The questionnaire deliberately referred to "unfair treatment" in order to be as inclusive as possible and to capture any sort of grievance.'

Related to this, in Chapter 9, the project's concept of an analytical spectrum for understanding discrimination and unfair treatment on the grounds of religion or belief is introduced and used for interpreting and evaluating the primary research data, as well as in offering a basis for identifying appropriate signposts for policy, law and practice in tackling such discrimination and unfair treatment. Implicit in the notion of 'unfair treatment' is the opposite notion of 'fairness'. Thus, although its formal title speaks of 'equality', the 2011 research conceptualizes this not in terms of an impossible to achieve abstract position of mathematical equality of outcomes, but in relation to the perhaps more modest and achievable aim of equitable treatment.

Structure of the book

The book begins with dedication, acknowledgements and contents pages, followed by this introduction. This is followed by Chapter 2 on 'Historical Perspectives, the Law, Rights and Religion or Belief Discrimination' which argues that aspects of the (especially nineteenth century) historical experience of Free Church and Roman Catholic Christian minorities, of Jews and of atheists can offer a prefiguration that, through both similarity and difference, might help to illuminate relevant contemporary issues in policy, law and practice.

Chapter 3 is on 'Contemporary Context of Religion and Belief, State and Society' and locates what is at stake in the debates about religion or belief discrimination in a portrait and understanding of the principal contours of the contemporary religion or belief landscape of Britain, including the positioning of religious groups relative to the state and the institutions of the wider society.

Chapter 4 is on 'The Law: A Decade of Continuity and Change'. It describes the main changes in the domestic legal landscape that have taken place during this period, informed as they have been by EU policy and international law, culminating in the *Equality Act*, 2010, which integrated previously diverse legal provision across the range of 'protected characteristics'.

Chapter 5 on 'Religion or Belief Discrimination, Claims, Evidence and Methods' sets out how the research at the heart of this book was planned and implemented, including how the samples of survey respondents and fieldwork participants were constituted, and the planning and conduct of the project's Knowledge Exchange Workshops.

Chapters 6, 7 and 8 report the evidence gathered from the project's structured questionnaire, its fieldwork interviews with a range of people working in the public, private and voluntary sectors and from religious groups, its focus groups with 'non-religious' people and some aspects of the contributions of its Knowledge Exchange Workshop participants. Within this, Chapter 6 focuses on 'Experience of Unfair Treatment in Education, Employment and Media'; Chapter 7 focuses on 'Experience of Unfair Treatment in Criminal Justice and Immigration; Housing; Health Care; Social Services; Planning and Other Services; and Funding'; and Chapter 8 focuses on 'Experience of Unfair Treatment from, between and within Religious Groups' and from 'Political, Community and Other Pressure Groups'. The data provides first-hand insights into the lived experience of individuals, organizations and groups.

Chapter 9 on 'An Analytical Spectrum for Understanding the Evidence' brings together the historical, contemporary and legal contexts set out in Chapters 2-4 and the findings presented and discussed in Chapters 6-8, into engagement with an analytical spectrum developed by the project in order to achieve a more nuanced understanding of the varied nature of unfair treatment and discrimination on the basis of religion or belief.

Finally, the closing Chapter 10 of the book is on 'Evidence-Based Signposts for Future Policy, Law and Practice'. This connects the project's empirical findings with discussion about what might be the most appropriate measures for tackling discrimination and unfair treatment on the grounds of religion or belief. It does this by summarizing the key findings of the 2011 research and considering further findings from respondents and participants about the extent to which legal, policy and practice developments had proved helpful or unhelpful, along with their evaluation of various measures for tackling unfair treatment on the basis of religion or belief.

These overall findings are then discussed in the context of policy developments over the past decade, leading into a conclusion in which we argue for a 'three-dimensional' approach to future policy, law and practice which takes full and balanced account of each of the elements of the Christian, secular and religiously plural dimensions of the religion and belief landscape of England and Wales, in Britain, and also globally.

The book then closes with an Appendix listing selected legal cases identified in the course of the 2011 research. This is followed by the Bibliography and Index.

Historical Perspectives on Law, Rights and Religion or Belief Discrimination

Religion and belief, discrimination and equality in global historical context

In Europe, matters relating to religion and belief, discrimination and equality have again emerged into vigorous and often heated public debate. In the first instance, this followed the re-entry into public life of religious communities, groups and organizations following the end of the Cold War and the dismantling of the states of Central and Eastern Europe that had previously been organized with reference to Marxist-Leninist political philosophy, which had severely restricted the space for religious belief and believers in terms of the public sphere (Beeson, 1975). At the same time, and especially in the European Union, the growing ethnic and religion and belief diversity of the populations of its member states, including as a result of migration, have resulted in attention increasingly being paid to the implications of such diversity in relation to the significance of notions of European identity and the place of religion or belief within that.

In the wider world, the continuing and often turbulent significance of religion or belief has become apparent, including in the continuing conflicts around Israel/ Palestine and in the emergence of phenomena such as the 'Christian Right' in the United States. However, it has been seen most clearly in the struggles of the predominantly Muslim world that emerged out of the end of the binary polarization of the world during the Cold War, from the Iranian Revolution (1979) through to the emergence of Al-Qaeda out of the conflicts in the Gulf region and the invasion of Afghanistan (2003). This has, in turn, led foreign affairs specialists such as Samuel Huntington (1993) to articulate a thesis that in place of the previous Cold War between the capitalist and communist political, economic and military blocs, there has instead emerged a 'clash of civilizations'. At the same time this thesis has been strongly criticized by those who point out that it is more accurate to identify a clash within and across civilizations (Sengaas, 1998).

Historical roots

Experiences and claims of discrimination and unfair treatment in relation to religion or belief did not begin only with the large-scale labour and refugee migrations of the modern era. In addition, neither did the aspirations, projects and mechanisms for greater equality in relation to religion or belief begin only with the development of modern human rights and equalities laws.

For large parts of at least recorded human history, little social space was accorded to religious diversity or to the place and rights of the individual in matters of religion or belief. This was, among other things, because religion was seen to play a key role within the unity of the family, and within tribal and ethnic groups and/or as a kind of 'social glue' that bound 'subjects' to their overlords within the structures of hierarchical and feudal societies (Toynbee, 1956). Such patterns reached their apex in what were widespread understandings of the person of a kingly ruler imbued with a sacred unity of person and role. This resulted in loyalty to a particular religious tradition or community becoming aligned with loyalty to a ruler, with the consequence that religious minorities often became at least disadvantaged, if not actively persecuted.

In relation to the Christian inheritance that, together with Roman law and Greek philosophy, has so strongly shaped both wider European and British history, for a number of centuries following its emergence as a minority predominantly Jewish sect in the Middle East, Christianity had been seen in the dominant Roman Empire as a 'new religion'. Within this status, its followers were, among other things, charged with cannibalism and incest – due to the affirmation in the Christian Eucharist that believers partake in the Body and Blood of Christ, while 'brothers and sisters' in the Christian faith greeted one another with a kiss.

However, despite general prejudice and disadvantage, and occasional systematic persecution, the Christian religion spread within a Roman Empire composed of peoples of many religions and ethnicities until the 313 CE promulgation of the Edict of Milan and then the adoption of Christianity as the official religion of the Empire appeared to offer to the Empire a socially cohesive force to match the military cohesion of the Roman legions (Fox, 1986). What is known as the 'Constantinian settlement' (Kee, 1982) resulted in a coming together of inheritances from Roman law and the (then still relatively new) Christian religion. Since then, this model for religion, state and society relationships has, in many ways, been the dominant pattern in European history and societies, including the later secularizing reactions to this.

After the adoption of Christianity by Constantine, the previously persecuted minority Christian religion itself started to restrict the social space of other religions and, ultimately, also began to persecute their followers. Such disadvantaging and persecuting of the religiously 'other' occurred first in relation to those of different Christian theologies who became defined as 'heretics' (in other words, those who were seen as having separated themselves from the Catholic Church), such as the Cathars. External to Christianity, Pagan temples began to be forcibly closed, and there were attempts at the suppression of Pagan practices, although parts of Europe (such as what is today Lithuania) were only 'Christianized' as late as the eleventh and twelfth centuries (Jones and Pennick, 1995). In the later Middle Ages the outbreak occurred of what contemporary Wiccans refer to as 'the burning times', in which thousands of people (mainly women) were hunted down and burned at the stake on the basis of seeing pre-Christian religious traditions as, in one form or another, associated with so-called devil worship (Cohn, 1973).

The nexus between theological perspectives and temporal power and its consequence for the social space of individuals and groups outside of that nexus can also clearly be seen in the experience of Jews in Europe. Following the advent of Constantinian Christendom, Jewish people saw their social space reduced on the basis of a theological perspective that, following the advent of Jesus as the Messiah, the Jewish people should no longer exist as a separate group. From time to time, as a more extreme expression of this denial of theological legitimacy, violent anti-Jewish pogroms ensued that were an attempt at what, in echo of the contemporary language of 'ethnic cleansing' might be called attempts at 'religious cleansing'. These outbreaks were often, but not always, connected within the phenomenon of 'Crusading' in which Christian rulers and their armies sought, as they saw it, to recover for Christendom the holy sites of Christian origins from the new religion of Islam and the rulers associated with the early Muslim empires (Wheatcroft, 2004).

Against the background of the inheritance of the religio-political entity of Catholic Christendom, the historical eruption of Protestantism into the west of the continent resulted in tensions that issued into the savage and bloody religious bigotry of the European Wars of Religion that raged within the Holy Roman Empire from around 1524 until the 1555 *Peace of Augsburg*, which ended the armed conflict between military forces aligned with Protestantism and Catholicism. It did so by establishing within the Empire the principle of *cujus regio, ejus religio* (Latin for: 'whose realm, his religion'). While bringing about the cessation of armed conflict, the *Peace of Augsburg* was made at the price of linking the religion of the people to the religion of the ruler of a particular territory. In many ways it therefore solidified new forms in the relationship between religion(s) and the state(s) that were based upon territorial belonging, which the contemporary Anglican Bishop and critic of established forms of religion Colin Buchanan (1994) has characterized as those of a 'nationalized monopoly'. The forms of these 'nationalized monopolies' varied throughout Europe, but in each case they reflected the outcome of struggles for power and influence between different versions of Christianity as well as the espousal of these by rulers and politicians for diverse motives.

In various ways these 'institutionalized monopolies' of religion and state were responsible for centuries of discrimination on the basis of religion. When combined with moral reaction to the suffering and destruction associated with religiously informed violence, this led to a growing religious indifference, scepticism and the desire to confine religion to the private sphere. Such developments, in turn, mapped onto other broader social, political and economic developments that, when coalescing with a growing distinction between the spheres of the church and the world, started to prefigure the later emergence of the modern idea of the secular. Eventually, when combined with the impact of the Enlightenment on both moral and political philosophy, this reaction led to the development of the notion of a state that would avoid the historical exclusion, disadvantage and discrimination against individuals or groups based on their religious identity. In the context of the disintegration of the old European Empires, a new European map of nation states emerged inspired by the new 'imagined communities' of nationalism (Anderson, 1983). Following the Soviet Revolution in the old Russian Empire, a different form of the secular emerged in the shape of an ideological 'secular*ism*' rooted in a Marxist-Leninist political philosophy. Following the end of the Second World War, for much of the second half of the twentieth century, in the central and eastern parts of the continent having governments led by Communist Parties, there was a state-enforced separation of religion and state, informed by the promotion of state-sponsored atheism, more or less vigorously pursued according to specific national contexts (Beeson, 1975).

Religion and belief, uniformity, the state and the law

Introduction

Turning then to the specific religion or belief history of the geographical territory now known as England and Wales, for large parts of history there were attempts to impose varying degrees of uniformity in the public profession of religious belief and worship. Especially in rural areas, while the pre-Christian indigenous Pagan traditions lived on, they were subject to discrimination, eventually resulting in the 'witch-hunts' and burnings. There were also, of course, Jewish communities in England who, from early on, experienced discrimination and unfair treatment, culminating in their 1290 CE expulsion by King Edward I in connection with a 'blood libel' allegation, in which Jews were falsely accused of murdering children in order to use their blood in religious rituals (Almog, 1988).

From the seventeenth century until the middle of the eighteenth century, as reported by Rosina Visram's (1986) book, *Ayahs, Lascars and Princes: Indians in Britain, 1700–1947* and Michael Fischer et al.'s (2007) *A South Asian History of Britain: Four Centuries of Peoples*: Indians in Britain, 1700–1947, there were (as were described in the language of the times) 'Moormen and Gentoos' (in other words, Muslims and Hindus) in Britain numbering in the hundreds. However, as summarized by Peter Bishop (1991: 33): 'From the seventeenth century until the 1820s the notion that to be fully and properly English it was necessary to be a member of the Church of England was reinforced by law as well as by custom.' Nevertheless, in considering the implications of this it is important to understand (as is explained in the following sections) that this related at least as much, if not more so, not only to other than Christian religious minorities, but also to Free Church and Roman Catholic Christians.

The struggle for religious liberty

Dissenting and Nonconformist Christians

Evaluating the overall development of religious liberty in England, the legal academic St John Robilliard (1984: ix) argued, in a succinct statement, that:

The early story of the struggle for religious liberty is one of sects establishing an identity of their own, with their members being freed from the obligation of supporting a faith they did not hold. From the struggle for existence we pass to the struggle for equality, in many important fields, with the Established Church.

In England and Wales, the origins of the distinctive and continuing (albeit adapted and evolved) form of relationship between the Established Church of England, the state and key institutions within the wider society go back to the special connection created between the Church of England and the Monarchy during the sixteenth century rupture between King Henry VIII and the Papacy, following which the reigning monarch has been the supreme governor of the Church of England.

The continuity of this pattern was then itself disrupted during the upheaval of the English Civil War, the subsequent execution of King Charles I and the ensuing period of the Commonwealth and the Protectorate (Hill, 1975). However, following the 1660 restoration of the Monarchy under Charles II, these relationships were re-established and then further entrenched in laws such as the *Acts of Uniformity* (1662), the *Test Acts* (1673, 1678) and *Corporation Act* (1661), the *Conventicle Acts* (1644, 1670) and the *Five Mile Act,* (1665), which restricted the religious freedom of Roman Catholic and Nonconformist Christians to gather together for worship according to their conscience and beliefs. In terms of participation in the wider civil society, the *Corporation Act* and *Test Act* of 1661 and 1673, respectively, made holding of civic office conditional upon taking Holy Communion according to the rites of the Church of England and an Oath of Supremacy acknowledging the sovereign's right to be Supreme Governor of the Church of England, of allegiance to the sovereign and of denial of Catholic doctrine of transubstantiation at the Eucharist.

Because of their broad alignment with the Parliamentary Revolution, after the restoration of the Monarchy, Dissenting Protestant Christians were seen as a potential threat to the social order. This changed only gradually (Jordan, 1936). Thus, the popularly called *Toleration Act* of 1689 was, in fact, only *An Act for Exempting their Majesties' Protestant Subjects Dissenting from the Church of England from the Penalties of Certain Laws.* Therefore, what the Act produced was legal toleration for Trinitarian Protestant Christians who adhered to the 39 articles of the Church of England – with the exception of Articles 34, 35 and 36 that concerned matters of ritual and, for Baptists, part of Article 20 which concerned infant baptism – rather than religious liberty for all.

For much of the nineteenth century, issues concerned with the civil and political rights and disabilities of Nonconformist and Roman Catholic Christians (Bebbington, 1982; Larsen, 1999), Jews (Salbstein, 1982), Humanists, Freethinkers and other groups outside of the established religious tradition of Anglican Christianity, were at the forefront of social, religious and political debate.

Eventually, the 1846 *Religious Disabilities Act* removed the last legal restrictions on Nonconformists, while allowing Jews the same rights as Nonconformists in respect of education, charities and property. Even so, it was only in 1871 that the *University Tests Act* removed religious tests for all degrees except Divinity and for all official posts except the Professorship of Divinity. But church rates (to support the Church of England) continued to be charged on non-Anglican Christians, and births were registered by Anglican clergy who were the only ones able to conduct legal marriages (Bebbington, 1982).

Discrimination and Roman Catholic minorities

Through their allegiance to the Pope as the Supreme Pontiff, Roman Catholics were seen by most Anglican (and also a majority of Free Church) Christians as having political implications that threatened British sovereign rights and were thus seen as potentially treasonable fifth columnists in ways similar to how Muslims, as part of the global *Ummah* (or Muslim community) are sometimes seen today (see Nye and Weller, 2012: 45–47). Thus 1688 had seen the so-called Glorious Revolution in which William of Orange took the throne from the Catholic Monarch James II in a move understood by its supporters at the time to be a defence of Protestantism against what was perceived to be the threat from external and internal forces allied to Roman Catholic Christianity.

These events, coupled with the earlier so-called Gunpowder Plot, inform an historical inheritance of anti-Catholicism, resonances of which can still be found across many aspects of religion(s), state and society relationships within the United Kingdom. Symbolic of this has been the fact that, under the *Royal Marriages Act* of 1772, marriage of a successor to a Roman Catholic disinherits anyone in line to the throne. Although two-and-a-half centuries later this restriction was, in April 2013, abolished under the terms of the *Succession to the Crown Act*, it is not without significance that the former Prime Minister Tony Blair felt that he needed to wait until he was no longer Prime Minister in order to complete his process of conversion to Catholic Christianity.

In the nineteenth century, because of the deep-seated nature of this anti-Catholicism (Marrotti, 2005; Norman, 1968), while rapid advances took place in the removal of civil disabilities from other non-Anglican Christians, it was only in 1829 under the terms of the *Roman Catholic Relief Act* that Roman Catholics were admitted to Parliament. Of course, during this period the general franchise was itself limited through exclusion of all women and of men who were not property-owning. But among those who otherwise qualified for participation in formal and representational politics, differentiation on the grounds of religion or belief was a legally entrenched source of discrimination and unfair treatment. The 1846 *Religious Disabilities Act* eventually removed most of the laws restricting Roman Catholics.

Discrimination and Jewish people

The changes for Catholics outlined above in due course also had implications for other groups. As Michael Salbstein (1982: 434) pointed out in his book *The Emancipation of the Jews in Britain: The Question of the Admission of the Jews to Parliament*:

> Because the Roman Catholics, in common with the Jews, belonged to a universal religious membership which transcended national boundaries, once the problems

of dual loyalty to spiritual and temporal authority had been resolved in the case of the one group the claims of the other would be correspondingly enhanced.

Until its abolition in 1826, in order to become a British subject by naturalization it had been necessary to receive Holy Communion according to the rites of the Church of England. However, the 1828 repeal of the *Corporation Act* involved an amendment moved by the Anglican Lord Bishop of Llandaff, that a pledge before taking public office should be made 'on the true faith of a Christian' – thus excluding Jews. Therefore, for Jews, it was not until the *Jewish Disabilities Act* of 1845 that Jews could take municipal office without having to take a Christian oath, earlier attempts at change having been defeated in the House of Commons in 1830, and in Lords in 1833. In 1847, a further Bill to allow Jews to participate in the legislature was passed in the Commons, but defeated in the Lords. During the heated debates around this, Lord Ashley is recorded (in *Hansard*, XCV, 1278, 16 December 1848) as saying that, if the principle of a more inclusive legislature were followed then '. . . not only would Jews be admitted to Parliament, but Mussulmans, Hindoos, and men of every form of faith under the sun of British dominions'.

The Jewish subjects Lionel de Rothschild and David Saloman were elected to the House of Commons, respectively, in Westminster in 1847 and in Greenwich in 1851. However due to the requirement to take an oath 'on the true faith of a Christian' neither could take up their seats. It was only in 1858 that the *Jews' Relief Act* allowed Jews the same civil rights granted to Catholics in 1829, and those Jews who had been previously elected to Parliament could take up their seats.

Discrimination and Atheists, Humanists and Freethinkers

In relation to those who were of what can be termed 'no religion', atheists, humanists and Freethinkers generally speaking suffered from similar civil disabilities as non-Anglican Christians. Symbolic of their position in society was that the right for atheists to affirm rather than to swear an oath had to be contested over a considerable period. This was especially in connection with the unsuccessful attempts, from 1850 onwards, of the atheist Charles Bradlaugh to take his seat in Parliament, until agreement was eventually reached in 1855. This was followed by the *Promissory Oaths Acts* of 1868 and 1871, the *Evidence Further Amendment Act* of 1869, the *Evidence Amendment Act* of 1870 and the 1880 *Oaths Act* allowing individuals to affirm in legal matters instead of having to make religious oaths.

Wider social attitudes and Parliamentary changes

In relation to other than Christians, as Bishop (1991: 37) summarized the situation: 'The Victorians had seen great changes in law and official policy towards those who had previously been outsiders.' However, the question remained, 'to what extent at all had their attitudes towards newcomers changed?' Many people of other than Christian heritage at least outwardly conformed to the dominant laws and customs of the imperial metropolis, including in relation to Anglican Christianity as the established religion in England. However, even full and formal conversion to Christianity did not always lead to acceptance.

An illuminating example both of this issue and of wider social attitudes to other than Christian religions is the story of Shapurji Edalji, a Parsi convert to Christianity who, during the 1870s, became vicar of Great Wyrley in Staffordshire. He married an English woman and their son, George, was a brilliant law student. However, in 1903 George was arrested and imprisoned for maiming horses, of which Visram (1986: 71) records that the police and people of the area, 'were convinced that George Edalji made nocturnal sacrifices to his alien gods – and this despite the fact that the Edalji family were Christians'. The maiming carried on until after three years in prison he was eventually released but remained under police surveillance until a campaign eventually led to a Home Office established committee concluding that he had been wrongly convicted.

Rosina Visram's (1986: 75) incisive evaluation of the situation in this period for people of other than Christian or Jewish religion was: 'Whatever their profession and their contribution to British society, and despite their small numbers, their experiences of British society were in one important respect similar. Racial prejudice, indifference or at times grudging acceptance characterized their presence.' Visram's assessment of the treatment of these early other than Christian migrants could also, in fact, characterize Christian minorities of other than European background.

The large-scale migrations of the twentieth century brought different dynamics into play than the encounter with and between individuals of various religions. But it is clear that even without the dynamics associated with migration, the 'religiously other' – especially when from beyond the boundaries of the Christian tradition (but also within it) – experienced discrimination and unfair treatment. At the same time, towards the end of the nineteenth century two Parsis (of the Zoroastrian religion) – Dadabhai Naoroji and Mancherjee Bhownagree were, in 1892 and 1895 respectively, elected as members of Parliament, thus symbolically and actually taking political representation beyond the limits of the Christian and Jewish traditions, and those of atheism and freethinking, to include also people of a religion beyond the broad Judaeo-Christian spectrum.

As Peter Bishop (1991: 37) commented, 'The apparently slight changes involved in admitting people of faiths other than Christian to parliament may be seen as an official and public assent to a multi-cultural society given in Victorian times.' It is therefore possible to see this as a culminating point in a process of change that, in many ways, might be understood as prefiguring aspects of the development of Britain into a 'three-dimensional' religion or belief landscape: Christian, secular and religiously plural, as explored in Chapter 3 of this book. At the same time, in relation to these nineteenth-century developments Bishop (1991: 37) made the pertinent observation that, 'On the whole, Victorian multi-culturalism was a very middle-class affair, and middle-class interests had strongly influenced the removal of religious disabilities. Attitudes to newcomers of other cultures and religions who were not members of the middle class were rather different.'

The accuracy of this judgement can be illustrated by what happened in connection with Jewish immigration from the pogroms of Russia and Eastern Europe, in which concerns about numbers of arrivals, employment for natives, heightened consciousness of cultural and religious difference, political opportunism and the introduction of immigration controls all featured. In the 1890s, it would appear that approximately 120,000 Jewish people came as refugees, although many in the wider population perceived there to have been many more (Cohen, 1984).

In contrast to the previously settled Jewish minority, these Jewish migrants wore distinctive clothes and beards and spoke Yiddish. Much comment was made in the press (Cohen, 1984) and among the wider public about their business on Sundays and about their observance of a Saturday Sabbath. Charges were made that Jews undercut British labour costs, leading to formation, in 1901, of the British Brothers' League – in many ways a prototype of contemporary groups such as the English Defence League. Although a Royal Commission on Alien Immigration, set up in 1902, contradicted most of the myths surrounding Jewish immigration, it proposed immigration controls. Eventually, in 1905, an *Aliens' Act* was passed, bringing in the first immigration controls of the modern British state.

Religious discrimination in the twentieth century

Out of political focus but continuing for Jews and in Northern Ireland

Following the kind of public social, political and religious debates that accompanied the last major phase of Jewish settlement at the end of the nineteenth and the beginning of the twentieth centuries, issues to do with discrimination on the grounds of religion or belief, generally speaking, disappeared out of the focus of public and political attention in England and Wales until their re-emergence in the last two decades of the twentieth century. It is not that discrimination did not exist. Jewish people, for example, continued to face deeply entrenched prejudice that was exacerbated in the 1930s by the rise of such groups as the British Union of Fascists. However, by the latter quarter of the twentieth century, many – and perhaps especially among politicians in England and Wales – thought that issues of religious discrimination were no longer of relevance to public life, apart from what a 'metropolitan' and 'mainstream' perspective has often viewed as the exceptional case of Province of Northern Ireland.

Following the creation of Northern Ireland (as also in the Republic of Ireland), no religion was formally established (the episcopal Church of Ireland having been disestablished as long ago as 1871). Indeed, the 1920 *Governance of Ireland Act* associated with the establishment of the Irish Free State and the six county state of Northern Ireland proscribed the establishment of any particular religion or religious tradition. Nevertheless, until the challenge posed from the Civil Rights Movement of the 1960s, the Northern Ireland state had a 'Protestant ascendancy' built into many of its social and political institutions in ways that were identified by the Civil Rights Movement as being an expression of both an entrenched and a systematic form of discrimination. Communal identity related to (Protestant and Catholic Christian) religion was therefore a significant dimension of the conflict known as 'The Troubles' (McSweeney, 1989), with religion overlapping with other aspects of ethnic and communal identity to maintain a high degree of social and political division (Badham, 1990; Bruce, 1986; Comerford et al., 1990; Hickey, 1984; McSweeney, 1989).

Following British military intervention, the conflict redeveloped into an armed paramilitary campaign against British rule by the Provisional Irish Republican Army (PIRA) accompanied by violence from a range of Loyalist paramilitary organizations. It resulted in a substantial loss of life and personal injury until the cease-fire declared by paramilitary organizations in the context of the 1998 *Good Friday/Belfast agreement*. Throughout this period and until today, issues of religious discrimination have continued to be of major concern in the context of the wider political and national struggle between Nationalists and Unionists, Republicans and Loyalists (O'Brien, 2010).

Christian 'sects' and 'New Religious Movements'

Among other than Catholic Christian minority groups, a range of issues from time to time emerged with regard to tensions between their beliefs and practices and the policies and practices of a range of public organizations. Thus, the commitment of Seventh Day Adventists to congregational worship on a Saturday and to observance of Sabbatarianism sometimes resulted in employment difficulties for them, while Jehovah's Witnesses and Christian Scientists continued on occasion to come before both the domestic courts and European court in respect of disputes over child custody and medical treatment. Such cases highlighted complex issues in the relationship between religious commitments and individual freedom, the rights of families, the responsibilities of professionals, the interests of the wider society and the terms and interpretation of the law.

However, prior to the public re-emergence of issues of religious discrimination as connected particularly with visible religious minorities of minority ethnic community background, the highest profile political and legal debates (Barker, 1982, 1989a,b) relating to claims of unfair treatment on the basis of religion in terms of general attitudes of religion or belief prejudice occurred in relation to the so-called New Religious Movements (or NRMs). In popular perception and debate they are often referred to as 'sects' and/or 'cults', many of whom have experienced what Eileen Barker (1989b) calls 'tolerant discrimination'. Particularly in the wider context of the United Kingdom's membership of what is now the European Union, a new and high level of concern was generated around the alleged nature and activities of some of some of these groups, leading to periodic attempts to try to restrict the activities of such movements, an example of which were the European Parliament debates and proposals led by the British MEP Richard Cotterell (1984).

However, alongside issues in relation to these groupings other newer issues have emerged. Pagans, for example, were often the subject of sensationalist and distorted treatment in the media that made it difficult for them to hold employment in some contexts unless they were secretive about their own religious identity (Weller et al., 2001: 42). There have also been conflicts over the legitimacy of claims for charitable status on the part of the Unification Church and the Church of Scientology. Sexual lifestyle issues among groups such as 'The Family' and the followers of Bhagwan

Rajneesh have led, on the one hand to charges of 'brainwashing' and 'deprogramming' in matters of personal freedom, family and social rights and, on the other, to claims of biased media coverage (Nye and Weller, 2012).

Antisemitism and anti-Judaism

Despite the impact on European awareness of the Holocaust, antisemitism and anti-Judaism have remained very much a part of a common European inheritance, including in Britain. For example, as both the tone and content of debates on *schechita* slaughter, circumcision and other matters of importance to the Jewish community have emphasized – and as the Runnymede Trust's (1994) report *A Very Light Sleeper* has evidenced – the persistence of antisemitism and anti-Jewish attitudes and discrimination should not be underestimated.

There have also been continuing attacks on Jewish synagogues, cemeteries and other property as highlighted by the All-Party Parliamentary Inquiry into Antisemitism (2006) and its follow-up report (Communities and Local Government, 2010) and as documented annually by reports from the Community Safety Trust.

Minority ethnic groups and new patterns of religious discrimination

Despite the persistence of antisemitism, and some degree of political attention having been paid to it, it has been primarily as a consequence of issues raised by the migration and settlement of groups from the former British Empire that attention to issues of unfair treatment and discrimination on the grounds of religion and belief re-emerged into more mainstream social and political consciousness. In the earlier period of migrant settlement in the United Kingdom, the emphasis was more on basic economic issues related to employment and housing, and minority organizations were formed that centred more around national origins and/or ethnicity. In that context, however, Sikhs were an early example of the social, political and legal struggles that were to come, in their campaign for being allowed exemption, on religious grounds, from the general requirements of the *Road Traffic Act*, 1972, for motorcyclists to wear safety helmets.

The *Road Traffic Act*, 1988, re-enacting the *Motor-Cycle Crash Helmets (Religious Exemption) Act*, 1976, now exempts a follower of the Sikh religion 'while . . . wearing a turban' from the crash helmet requirements applicable to others. A similar exemption was granted by the *Employment Act*, 1989, to allow turbaned Sikhs to work on construction sites without a helmet or hard hat as required by new safety regulations and, in the famous legal case of *Mandla v. Dowell-Lee*, 1982, it was held that Sikhs could be considered an ethnic group for the purposes of the *Race Relations Act*, 1976, thus according to them a degree of legal protection under this law, as Jewish people also had.

From the 1980s onwards Muslims (McDermott and Ahsan, 1980), in particular, began to raise a range of issues concerned with religious identity and practice. These included (UK Action Committee on Islamic Affairs, 1993) concerns about religious patterns of work in relation to the rhythm of daily prayers; observance of the fasting month of Ramadan; the wish of many for Muslim voluntary-aided schooling; matters of Islamic personal and family law in relation to the European legal systems; and the existence of blasphemy laws protecting only one religion; and a range of other matters. In a piecemeal way Muslims gradually began to achieve some of the adjustments and accommodations that had been recognized in law for Jewish people, including exemptions from general legislation governing the protection of animals at the time of slaughter in order to fulfil religious requirements for animal slaughter, although from an animal rights perspective, controversy has continued around these exemptions.

During the 1990s in the United Kingdom an evidence base gradually began to emerge in relation to religious discrimination as being something that was not only confined to the specific circumstances of Northern Ireland. With regard to employment, as well as referring to discrimination in the employment of Roman Catholics, a research report by Yarrow (1997) noted, in particular with regard to Scotland, issues surrounding the lack of provision for Muslims to observe religious holidays. Also in relation to Scotland, O'Connor and Lewis (1999) conducted a small-scale study that noted the presence of religious discrimination with religious exclusion being 'perceived to be caused by a society firmly rooted in Judeo Christian tradition values' (O'Connor and Lewis, 1999: 18). In this report, Muslims spoke of being publicly ridiculed for their beliefs, in particular their choice of prayer times, and their abstinence from alcohol (O'Connor and Lewis, 1999: 20).

But it was Runnymede Trust's 1997 report on *Islamophobia: A Challenge for us All*, which brought about a sea-change in political and public awareness and debate both in relation to religious discrimination generally and the experience of Muslims in particular. In doing so, the report brought the concept of 'Islamophobia' from more obscure historical use into mainstream public and political debate (Allen, 2010).

'Re-recognizing' and addressing religious discrimination in law

Introduction

During the 1990s, attention began to be drawn to the inconsistency of it being illegal to discriminate on the grounds of religion or belief in Northern Ireland while it was not illegal under domestic law in three of the other countries (namely England, Wales and Scotland) of the United Kingdom (though see Chapter 4 in relation to the continuity that has existed in relation to obligations under international law).

The example of Northern Ireland

Northern Ireland had been the first part of the United Kingdom in which there had been a comprehensive attempt to address religious discrimination through legislation and social policy. The *Fair Employment (Northern Ireland) Act* of 1976 prohibited direct (but not indirect) discrimination on political as well as religious grounds, reflecting the context of sectarian conflict it was intended to address. Its aim was to promote and ensure fair participation in employment opportunities for Catholics and Protestants by providing a framework of redress for victims of discrimination based on religious belief. The Act established the Fair Employment Agency (FEA) which, in addition to having a responsibility for addressing individual complaints of discrimination, was given power to investigate equality of opportunity across the two communities.

The *Fair Employment (Northern Ireland) Act* of 1989 attempted to remedy the defects and limitations of its predecessor by providing individuals with a right of complaint against 'indirect discrimination'. It also introduced into UK law the notion of affirmative action, and divided implementation responsibilities between two new bodies: the Fair Employment Tribunal and the Fair Employment Commission. Northern Ireland's *Prevention of Incitement to Hatred Act (Northern Ireland)* of 1970 also prefigured other later related legal developments in the rest of the United Kingdom. This made it an offence if, with the 'intent to stir up hatred against, or rouse the fear of, any section of the public in Northern Ireland on the grounds of religious belief, colour, race or ethnic or national origins' a person: '(a) publishes or distributes written or other matter which is threatening, abusive or insulting, or (b) uses words of a similar nature in any public place or in any public meeting'. Of course, there both were, and continue to be, distinctive circumstances pertaining to Northern Ireland as compared with the rest of the United Kingdom. But in considering the history of discrimination on the basis of religion and belief and responses to it, it is important to note that the rest of the United Kingdom was not moving into entirely uncharted territory when consideration was eventually given to the introduction of such laws also in England, Wales and Scotland.

Religion, ethnicity and the Commission for Racial Equality

In the rest of the United Kingdom, when increasing attention was being paid to these issues in the early 1990s, strong representations began to be made from Muslims and others to the Commission for Racial Equality – whose remit was shaped primarily by the *Race Relations Act* – to undertake work in this area also. From 1992 onwards, the Commission tried to collect evidence of cases of religious discrimination, including a 1994 survey of 2,047 agencies dealing with complaints of religious discrimination. There was only a low response to the survey and the Commission's *Position Paper on Religious Discrimination* noted that: 'specific information was received about 38 cases of alleged religious discrimination', although also that, 'This was not surprising given the lack of monitoring by all the agencies surveyed, and also the lack of any direct legislation on the issue.'

In October 1995, the Commission established a Project Group to further develop work in this area, and because of continuing concerns and representations, towards the end of 1996, it agreed to carry out a consultation exercise with religious communities to explore the scope of then current *Race Relations* law and to debate whether the law needed amendment to make discrimination specifically on the grounds of religion unlawful. Of the outcomes of this exercise, the Commission reported that: 'The overwhelming majority of those who participated in the consultation believed there was a need for legislation outlawing religious discrimination.'

From the 'struggle for existence' to the 'struggle for equality'

Symbolic controversies and the rights of minority religious citizens

St John Robilliard's (1984: ix) analysis of the developments that occurred in the nineteenth-century movement for religious equality as being grounded initially in a 'struggle for existence' of those religious groups that were concerned with 'establishing an identity of their own', and then passing into the next phase of a 'struggle for equality', could be seen as being also pertinent to the situation in contemporary Britain.

During the 1950s–1980s, communities composed primarily of people with South Asian ancestral origins began with 'the struggle for existence' and 'establishing an identity of their own' in the British context. Then from the 1980s and especially 1990s, they moved into the phase of a 'struggle for equality' as religious minority citizens. In this period, a number of highly charged public controversies took place (Nye and Weller, 2012: 38–43).

The Satanic Verses controversy

In many ways, *The Satanic Verses* controversy (Asad, 1990; Weller, 2008) represented a key moment in these developments. The common law offences of blasphemy and blasphemous libel were, until the later development of the human rights and equalities laws, the one aspect of the domestic law in England and Wales, and Scotland that provided any significant protection with regard to people of religious beliefs and commitments. In England, during the twentieth century there had been only two prosecutions under these laws – the first having been *R. v. Gott*, 1922, followed by the high-profile 'Gay News' trial, formally known as *Whitehouse v. Lemon*, 1977, in the context of which the House of Lords defined blasphemy as being something scurrilous, abusive or offensive so as to outrage religious feelings.

Even before *The Satanic Verses* controversy brought them to greater prominence, the laws of blasphemy and blasphemous libel had been the subject of considerable debate with the Law Commission (1985) having examined them as part of its programme of reviewing common law provision. In its 1985 report, *Offences against Religion and Public Worship*, the majority of the Commission argued for their abolition, concluding that the impossibility of satisfactorily defining 'religion' precluded the creation of a more widely applicable offence of wounding the feelings of religious adherents.

However, abolition did not follow and cases brought in connection with *The Satanic Verses* controversy underlined the exclusivity of the protection which these laws afforded to the Christian religion in general and the rites and doctrines of the Established Church of England in particular. In *R v. Bow Street Magistrates ex parte Choudhury*, 1990, it was confirmed that legal protection from blasphemous libel extended only to Christian sensibilities, a position later endorsed by the Court of Appeal, thus underlining the perception among Muslims of a deeply rooted religious disadvantage and discrimination.

The Bhaktivedanta Manor controversy

Concerned with a different set of issues but with, in some ways, a parallel significance among Hindus in terms of religious identity and its mobilization, was the long running conflict over the use of Bhaktivedanta Manor, at Letchmore Heath in rural Hertfordshire (Nye, 2001). This house, purchased by the former member of the Beatles, George Harrison, is the centre for the 'Hare Krishna' movement (ISKCON – the International Society for Krishna Consciousness) in England. From the 1970s onwards, a small temple room was dedicated as a temple and became very popular with Hindu residents of north-west London.

However, planning permission for the centre had not included authorization for public worship, and the temple brought severe weekend traffic congestion to the lanes around the Manor and the neighbouring villages. The conflict raged for over twenty years involving the legal rights of the local authority; the wish of local residents not to be disturbed; and the claimed rights of the Hindu worshippers to freedom of expression of religious practice as full members of British society. Eventually planning permission was granted for the Manor to be used for public worship, alongside permission being given for the construction of a new access road to relieve the impact of temple traffic.

The Bezhti controversy

A similar clustering of issues in the relationship between free speech, vilification, respect and artistic expression that were at the centre of *The Satanic Verses* controversy were reprised around the play *Behzti*, written by a British-born playwright of Sikh heritage, Gurpreet Kaur Bhatti, and which opened at the Birmingham Repertory Theatre in December 2004.

The title of the play means 'dishonour' and it was the writer's intention to uncover the hypocrisy that can be found among religious people, including matters of social status, mixed-race relationships, corruption, drug-taking, domestic violence, rape, paedophilia and murder. Most controversially of all, she set the play in the precincts of a Sikh gurdwara. The reactions to it ranged from, on the one hand, a series of meetings with the theatre management on the part of the local Sikh leaders to see if some compromises could be reached about community concerns, through to a violent storming of the theatre by Sikhs who largely came from outside the local area; to threats on the life of the playwright. In this controversy, no resolution was reached. The theatre cancelled the play and the playwright had to go into hiding.

Jerry Springer: The Opera

In 2005, a controversy blew up around the musical, *Jerry Springer: The Opera*, by the British writers Stewart Lee and Richard Thomas. This occurred when the BBC2 television channel planned to broadcast it in early January 2006 despite receiving many thousands of advance complaints prior to broadcast. As with *The Satanic Verses*, the musical played with intersections between revered and loved figures of a religion and lewd sexuality with, for example, a character of Jesus being introduced who bore similarity with a previously introduced character that had a nappy fetish.

In other echoes of the *The Satanic Verses'* reversal of good and evil, the figures of Jesus and of Satan indulge in a battle of wits in which Eve is called as a witness and attacks Jesus, while Mary, the mother of Jesus, leads a general condemnation of him. The organization Christian Voice coordinated the campaign against the broadcast and tried to initiate blasphemy charges against the BBC, but these were rejected by the High Court.

New religious discrimination law for England and Wales?

Despite the impact of *The Satanic Verses* controversy, when the Commission for Racial Equality's (1992) *Second Review of the Race Relations Act* (1976) argued that: 'a law against religious discrimination should be given serious consideration', the then Home Secretary Michael Howard stated (quoted in the CRE *Religious Discrimination Position Paper*) that: 'I have yet to be convinced that legislation could be justified. So far, there is little hard evidence of discrimination against individuals on religious rather than racial grounds, but I can assure you that the Home Office remains ready to look at any evidence.'

Following the election of the New Labour Government in 1987 and the signing of the *Amsterdam Treaty* of the European Union – which committed member states to inclusion within their domestic law of a variety of provisions relating to equalities – it became clear that action in relation to religious discrimination would not be long in coming for England, Wales and Scotland. As noted in Chapter 1, in 1999 the Home Office commissioned the University of Derby to undertake research on religious discrimination in England and Wales.

The findings from this research provided an evidence base for the position with regard to religious discrimination at the start of the 2000s and are therefore also frequently referred to in the main text throughout this book, and especially in Chapters 6-10 when presenting and discussing the results of the survey and fieldwork completed in 2011. Even before this, the passage through Parliament of the *Human Rights Act* (HRA, 1998) had already signalled substantial changes in this area, although it was only to come into force in 2000 and its scope was restricted to 'public authorities' or bodies acting as such.

Nevertheless, as will be explored in more detail in Chapter 4, the HRA brought existing international legal obligations in relation to religion or belief firmly into the context of domestic law where, previously, outside of Northern Ireland, there had been very little protection for the holding or manifestation of religion or belief, and there had been no domestic legal sanction in relation to discrimination on the basis of religion.

However, before examining these developments in more detail, it is necessary in Chapter 3 to locate these matters in an understanding of the contemporary religion and belief landscape in the United kingdom, including the relative position of various religion and belief groups in relation to power in society and the state and the consequences of that for the lives of individuals and groups of various religions and beliefs.

Contemporary Context of Religion and Belief, State and Society

Religion and belief, state and society: Structural parameters and consequences

Introduction

Across the world the constitutional and legal forms in which the interface between religion(s), state and society are embodied are very much shaped by the historical and religious inheritances of the countries concerned. In relation to England and Wales within Britain and the United Kingdom, aspects of this inheritance were explored in Chapter 2. Such forms may be more or less 'adequate' to the contemporary religious landscapes and populations in which they now operate. But because of their embeddedness in either the constitutions or other legal and social structures of states and their societies, they provide broad parameters within which specific questions of religion and belief, discrimination and equality operate.

The European and EU inheritance

Citing the *Treaty of Lisbon*'s statement that the European Union: 'Respects and does not prejudice the status under national law of churches and religious associations or communities in the Member States', it is often argued that the European Union does not have any competence in matters of religion or belief and that relationships with religious and philosophical organizations are reserved to the member states. But especially following the *Amsterdam Treaty*, 1999, the *Charter of Fundamental Rights*, 2000, and the *Treaty of Lisbon*, 1999, matters of religion or belief have increasingly intersected with the European institutions.

During the work of the Convention on the Future of Europe (begun in 2004), and the original process towards a *Treaty for Establishing a Constitution for Europe*, there were significant and substantial debates about the inclusion or otherwise in the European Union's constitution of a reference to God and/or Christianity. Because the

Constitution could not be ratified by all member states, it was superseded by the *Treaty of Lisbon*, 2009, in which the relevant article states that the European Union:

> Respects and does not prejudice the status under national law of churches and religious associations or communities in the Member States; Equally respects the status under national law of philosophical and non-confessional organizations; Recognising their identity and their specific contribution, the Union shall maintain an open, transparent and regular dialogue with these churches and organizations.

The European Union's *Charter of Fundamental Rights*, 2000 – the implementation of which is monitored by the EU Agency for Fundamental Rights – includes Article 10 that affirms religious freedom in language that, in turn, reflects Article 18 of the *United Nations Declaration of Human Rights* and of the *International Covenant on Civil and Political Rights*, both of which have been ratified by all member states of the European Union and are discussed in Chapter 4. At present the European Union is not itself a Party to the Council of Europe's *European Convention for the Protection of Human Rights and Fundamental Freedoms*. However, Protocol No. 14 (2010) of the Convention amended it to provide the legal basis for the European Union's accession to the Convention, which the European Union is committed to do under the *Treaty of Lisbon*, thus bringing the EU legal system within the scope of the European Court of Human Rights.

However, prior to this, in ways that will be explored in more detail in Chapter 4, the *Treaty of Lisbon* already itself provided a legal basis for the European Union to develop directives related to discrimination. Although unevenly implemented in different member states, *The Employment Directive*, 2000, has had particularly far-reaching implications, having created an EU-wide framework of minimum expectations for legal protection against discrimination of various kinds in employment, including in relation to discrimination on the grounds of religion or belief.

In addition to the legal framework above, it is also arguable (see Sergio Carrera and Joanna Parkin, 2010: 36) that 'there is a complex and highly heterogeneous patchwork of EU normative approaches delineating the relationship between religion and the EU'. This is because Directorates General and other Commission services deal with areas such as citizenship and fundamental rights, non-discrimination, immigration and integration, social inclusion, education and culture in their interactions with religion or belief, all of which have an important bearing on how religion or belief matters play out in the lives of individuals and groups within EU member states.

Religion and belief, state and society in the United Kingdom

Turning now to the United Kingdom, both the historical and contemporary forms for the relationships between religion, state and society are shaped by the historical and religious inheritances of what is not a single 'nation state', but a multinational one including four national traditions. These forms are, in turn, related to the distinctive history of the different Christian confessions found in each of the national traditions, including their diverse relationship with their societies and the state.

Since the 1603 accession of James VI of Scotland to the English Crown as James I, Scotland has shared a monarch with England. From 1707 there was a union of Parliaments. However, Scotland has remained distinct from England and other parts of the United Kingdom, especially in matters of education, law and religion. Thus, the church that is established in Scotland is not the (Anglican) Episcopal Church of Scotland, but is the (Presbyterian) Church of Scotland, which for a long time was seen as the 'national Church' there. Because of this, as late as the 1980s it could still be written (Bisset, 1986: 3) that, 'To be a Scot is to be a Presbyterian, even though that designation may say more of cultural identity than of religious persuasion.' Indeed, it was sometimes argued (Bisset, 1989) that, until the restoration of the Scottish Parliament brought a measure of self-government back to Scotland, the elected presbyteral system acted as a kind of 'surrogate Parliament'.

In Wales, the Anglican Church was disestablished in 1920. Unlike in Scotland, there has never been a single denominational tradition that has acted as an alternative focus for national identity. Because the absorption of Wales into the English Crown took place much earlier than the union of Crowns with Scotland, Wales retained comparatively little constitutional or legal distinctiveness. However, the Churches (and especially the Free Churches) in Wales have played a significant role in preserving the distinctive social and cultural life of the country, especially including its language that, after the radical 1960s campaigns of Cymdeithas yr Iaith Gymraeg (Welsh Language Society), was more generally revived.

Although the focus of this book is on Britain rather than on the whole of the United Kingdom of Great Britain and Northern Ireland, because (as discussed in Chapter 2) of the role of religion or belief in the conflicts of Northern Ireland and the earlier adoption there of laws relating to discrimination on the basis of religion, it is important briefly to look at the context in Northern Ireland for the relationships between religion(s), state and society.

In contemporary Northern Ireland those of Roman Catholic background form the largest single population grouping, although at present the combined numbers of people of Protestant background remains larger. During 'the Troubles' the Roman Catholic community in the North was identified with broadly Nationalist, and often Republican, aspirations, while Protestants have generally been identified with a Unionist, and sometimes, Loyalist, perspective (Bruce 1986). However, despite the political border and the history of national conflict, nearly all of the Christian Churches are organized on a cross-border, all-Ireland basis.

Coming finally to England, key aspects of its historical inheritance in religion, state and society were illustrated and discussed in Chapter 2. The contemporary significance of the Church of England as the Established Church in England and its constitutionally unique status in relation to the UK state, along with its role within English society, will be discussed further below.

Establishment of religion in the United Kingdom: A 'special relationship'

Despite the national differences outlined above, although a range of other religious groups have various mechanisms to facilitate their access to the state, it is only the Church of England that has what might be described as a 'special relationship' with the UK state. As the Scottish journalist Stewart Lamont argues, although 'The British Constitution has never been formulated as a single written document', nevertheless, 'the bond of the Church of England with the Crown and the parliament of England is clearly spelt out'. Lamont argues that this bond still hangs upon 'three pegs' – namely, 'the appointment of bishops, parliamentary oversight of the Prayer Book; and the position of the sovereign' (Lamont, 1989: 183).

The nexus between these aspects can be seen in the current presence of two archbishops and twenty-four of the Church of England's other most senior bishops who sit as 'Lords Spiritual' in the Westminster Parliament's (currently) non-elected, second chamber, the House of Lords. Although other religious figures have also become members of the House of Lords, this has been on the basis of their personal/professional role and contribution rather than by virtue of office.

In their analysis of the relationship between religious bodies and the state in Europe, Madeley and Enyedi described the Church of England as being in the categories of 'indirect state aid, no control' (Madeley and Enyedi, 2003: 13) and 'limited state subsidies to churches' (Madeley and Enyedi, 2003: 16). In contrast, therefore, to the Lutheran national churches in Norway and Denmark, the Church of England is not, strictly speaking, a 'state' church, nor is it in general directly funded by the state through the tax system, as is in the case with the Catholic Church and the major Protestant Churches in Germany.

In contrast with the high watermark of historical debate about establishment during the nineteenth century, apart from the campaigns of bodies such as the National Secular Society and internal debates reflected in a number of Church of England Commissions on the relationship between church and state, the establishment of the Church of England has, generally speaking, not been a matter of intense public debate (Morris, 2008). Disestablishment has been the policy of only one mainstream political party – the Liberal Democrats. This is perhaps because, alongside its structurally privileged position relative to the state as compared with other religious bodies, in recent years the Church of England has operated what Weller (2005: 168-70) has elsewhere called a kind of 'extended establishment' model, through which it has sought to facilitate the contribution to public life of other than Christian religious groups. In addition, the current heir to the throne, Prince Charles, has suggested adapting the Crown's historic title of 'Defender of The Faith' (which, in fact pre-dates the Reformation, having been given to King Henry VIII by the Pope) so that for the future it might become a more inclusive and general role of 'Defender of Faith' in the context of a religiously plural society (Ipgrave, 2003).

Although many of both its supporters and detractors refer to the Church of England's special relationship with the UK state as a merely 'symbolic' one, Weller (2005) has elsewhere argued that the symbolism that continues to be associated with this is not 'merely' symbolic, but is 'active symbolism'. In this sense, it can be argued that established religion in England consists not of fragments of ecclesiastical and political 'archaeology', but rather that it remains at the heart of the 'hidden wiring' of the UK constitution as embedded within a complex constitutional nexus of the social, religious, cultural, legal and political strands that have together made up the ethos and constitution of the UK state and of English society since the restoration of the Monarchy (see Hastings, 1991a, 1991b).

Cumulatively these dimensions of establishment both *reflect* and *give effect* to the role of the establishment of the Church of England which, through a conjunction of its symbolic, structural and operational functions continues to be both of symbolic and operational significance in the machinery of government, the structures of the state and the monarchy, the law and the institutions of civil society. Its operational significance also still permeates large parts of the social, religious, cultural, legal and political life in England because, regardless of the future of its Bishops in the context of plans to reform the House of Lords, it continues to have a special role on special national occasions and in many ceremonial aspects of local societies. Despite the broadening of chaplaincy arrangements (see Mansur Ali and Gilliat Ray, 2012), as compared with other religious groups (including also other Christian churches) the clergy of the Church of England still have particular rights of presence in some key social institutions.

Even more significant is the Church of England's key role in the maintained system of education, within which it is responsible for a significant number of voluntary-aided and controlled (especially primary) schools. Thus, in England it has a special and legally entrenched position on the Standing Advisory Councils on Religious Education (SACREs) that rule on key aspects of the local interpretation and application of the law with regard to collective worship and the Religious Education (RE) curriculum.

Therefore, in many ways, whether positively, negatively or neutrally evaluated, the form of the Church of England's relationship with the UK state and society sets the overall framework and pattern for the nature and development of other religion(s), state and society relationships in the United Kingdom. This, in turn, has a range of significant implications for the place of corporate religious bodies and groups of other Christian traditions; for those of other religious traditions; and for the 'non-religious' groups which, together form a part of what the following section describes as the contemporary 'three-dimensional' religion and belief landscape of the United Kingdom.

A 'three-dimensional' religion or belief landscape in a 'four nations' state

Against the background of the structural frameworks for religion and belief, state and society that have so far been discussed in this chapter, there is also a reality 'on the ground' which might be described in terms of the contours of the religion and belief landscape. In *Time for a Change: Reconfiguring Religion, State and Society*, Weller described the United Kingdom's religious landscape as being something that could now be seen as 'exhibiting contours that are "Christian, secular and religiously plural"' (Weller 2005: 73) and that therefore:

> . . . the contemporary socio-religious reality of England and the UK might be described as 'three-dimensional' in contrast with a more 'one-dimensional' Christian inheritance or the 'two-dimensional' religious-secular modifications made to that self-understanding during the course of the nineteenth and early twentieth centuries.

In order to fully understand the implications of this for discrimination and unfair treatment on the grounds of religion or belief, each of these dimensions needs to be understood in the context of the other two, and in the overall context of the 'four nations state' discussed in the previous section. Indeed, over the past decade, these diverse national contexts have become even more distinctive.

Therefore, following the restoration of the Scottish Parliament that deals with some matters of devolved governance in relation to the Scottish Executive (the devolved government for Scotland), significant aspects of law and social policy are now distinctively addressed in Scotland. An example of this is *The Offensive Behaviour at Football and Threatening Communications (Scotland) Act*, 2012, that was passed with the intention of combating 'religious, racial and other forms of hatred, specifically in the context of football' in Scotland. In Wales, the National Assembly for Wales and the Welsh Assembly Government also use devolved powers to carve out distinctive Welsh approaches to a range of sectors in the society – including education and health – within which unfair treatment on the basis of religion or belief can take place. In Northern Ireland, following the *Good Friday/Belfast Agreement*, 1998, the Northern Ireland Assembly was implemented alongside devolved government by the Northern Ireland Executive. This follows a period of direct rule from London that had been in place after the closure of the former Stormont Parliament in 1973.

In England, by contrast, there is no English Parliament or Assembly. For a number of years in the past decade there were assemblies for the English regions, but only one of these (the Greater London Assembly) was elected. It is now the only Assembly to remain following the abolition in 2010, by the Conservative-Liberal Democrat coalition government, of the other regional assemblies and the transfer of their executive powers to Regional Development Agencies which were, in turn, abolished.

Thus – with the exception of Greater London, where a directly elected Mayor has been working with the Greater London Assembly – in England there have generally speaking been no structures for elected governance at either national or regional levels, but only more locally. However, elected mayors have emerged in a number of other places, such as Hull, and since 2012 the former police authorities have been replaced by elected police and crime commissioners.

Religion and belief statistics and landscape

Until the last decade in the United Kingdom, with the exception of Northern Ireland (where a religion question had been asked in the census since the inception of the

Northern Ireland state), the main focus on personal and social identity data had been in relation to ethnicity and/or country of origin and language. In general, outside of Northern Ireland and prior to the introduction of the census questions there was a relative lack of religion or belief population size information on a national and UK level, although there has been more information in comparison with a number of other European countries (such as France), in which there has been an historically strong resistance to government asking questions about religion or belief.

Relevant data sources other than the census were reviewed by Barley et al. (1987), Purdam et al. (2007) and, more recently, by Perfect (2011). These included information derived from relatively small sample surveys which, like the British Social Attitudes Survey, have been largely focused on matters of belief or practice, rather than identification with a religion or belief, and/or were based on projections and assumptions regarding the relationship between religion and ethnicity. An important exception to the general pattern was in relation to the Jewish population, where the cross-over between ethnicity and religion has historically been close, and where substantial internally organized research had been conducted by the Community Research Unit of the Board of Deputies of British Jews and by bodies such as the Institute for Jewish Policy Research.

The overall picture changed with the inclusion, for the first time, of questions on religion in the 2001 decennial census for England, Wales and Scotland. This followed considerable lobbying on the part of many religious groups, and advocacy from within some parts of government, but in a context in which there was also a lot of debate around the desirability and/or practicability of such questions (Weller and Andrews, 1998; Weller, 2004).

The questions that were eventually included were voluntary ones in a census that is otherwise compulsory for residents to complete. In England and Wales, between 2001 and 2011 there were only minor adjustments to the question asked. Quite large absolute numbers of people choose not to answer the question, although there were some other (compulsory) questions with lower rates of completion, indicating no general reluctance to answer such questions as had been suggested by some prior to the introduction of the question in 2001. However, because of the question's voluntary status, the Office for National Statistics did not impute responses where individuals did not answer the religion or belief question, and this means there are quite large numbers of people about whom we have no census data relating to religion or belief.

There are also other limitations to the data derived from these questions, some of which lead to census results on religion or belief being used in over-simplistic and misleading ways. For example, these questions do not ask about religious belief or practice (which surveys such as British Social Attitudes Survey do). Rather, they focus on religious affiliation. Similarly, the census category and response of 'no religion' may itself not be quite as straightforward as it might at first sight appear (see Cheruvallil-Contractor et al., 2013). Additionally, the fact that those completing the census are offered pre-set categories means that there is a tendency towards the dominance of a particular kind of taxonomy of religions based strongly on the notion of 'world religious' traditions and communities – albeit that it is possible for people to elect to respond by using a 'write-in' option.

Finally, in relation to the 2001 UK data, the collation of religion or belief census data from across the four countries of the United Kingdom is not unproblematic. This is because in 2001, the questions in both Northern Ireland and Scotland differentiated between current religious affiliation and the religion in which respondents were brought up. In 2011, only the Northern Ireland question did so. However, in both 2001 and 2011, the Scottish and Northern Irish questions asked about religion or belief 'belonging', whereas the England and Wales questions asked only about 'What is your religion?' The tick-box options provided for response also differed between those in England and Wales – which did not differentiate between different Christian traditions – and those in Scotland and Northern Ireland which did.

Despite these limitations, the fact that there are now some at least broadly comparable data available to inform an understanding of the religious landscape and its population size and changes is important. The first release of 2011 Census data on religion for England, Wales and Northern Ireland took place in December 2012. However, because the production and release schedule of census statistics is different in Scotland, at the time of writing religion or belief statistics for the whole of the United Kingdom were not available.

Table 3.1 therefore gives these UK statistics for 2001 only. The religion or belief results that are already available for 2011 include those for England and Wales as well as partial results for religious affiliation in Northern Ireland. Given the focus of our research on England and Wales, Table 3.2 sets out the relevant data for both 2001 and 2011, in terms of absolute numbers, for England and Wales both separately and together. Table 3.3 does the same but in terms of the percentages within these populations.

The first thing to be noted is that, since 2001, there has been considerable change, both in terms of overall population growth and also in the absolute numbers and proportions of respondents concerning religion or belief. In both the 2011 and 2001 Censuses for England, and also for England and Wales taken together, the largest religion population is Christian. After Christian, the next largest group of respondents

Table 3.1 Self-identification by religion in the 2001 Census by numbers and by percentages of the populations of the United Kingdom taken as a whole

Religion	UK (total)	UK (%)
Buddhist	151,816	0.3
Christian	42,079,417	71.9
Hindu	558,810	1.0
Jewish	266,740	0.5
Muslim	1,591,126	2.7
Sikh	336,149	0.6
Other religion	178,837	0.3
Total of all religions	*45,162,895*	
No religion	9,103,727	15.5
Not stated	4,288,719	7.3
No religion/ not stated	*13,392,446*	

Source: Census (April 2001). National Statistics website: www.gov.uk. Crown copyright, 2004. Crown copyright material is reproduced with the permission of the Controller of HMSO. Percentages may not total 100% due to the cumulative effect of decimal places.

Table 3.2 Self-identification by religion in the 2001 and 2011 Censuses by numbers in the populations of England, Wales, and England and Wales taken together

Religion	England		Wales		Total England and Wales	
	2001	2011	2001	2011	2001	2011
Buddhist	139,046	238,626	5,407	9,117	144,453	247,743
Christian	35,251,244	31,479,876	2,087,242	1,763,299	37,338,486	33,243,175
Hindu	546,982	806,199	5,439	10,434	552,421	816,633
Jewish	257,671	261,282	2,256	2,064	259,927	263,346
Muslim	1,524,887	2,660,116	21,739	45,950	1,546,626	2,706,066
Sikh	327,343	420,196	2,015	2,962	329,358	423,158
Other religion	143,811	227,825	6,909	12,705	150,720	240,530
Total religions	*38,190,984*	*36,094,120*	*2,131,007*	*1,846,531*	*40,321,991*	*37,940,651*
No religion	7,171,332	13,114,232	537,935	982,997	7,709,267	14,097,229
Not stated	3,776,515	3,804,104	234,143	233,928	4,010,658	4,038,032
No religion/ not stated	*10,947,847*	*16,918,336*	*772,078*	*1,216,925*	*11,719,925*	*18,135,261*
Total all	*49,138,831*	*53,012,456*	*2,903,085*	*3,063,456*	*52,041,916*	*56,075,912*

Source: For the 2001 and 2011 data, see the National Statistics website: www.ons.gov.uk. Crown copyright, 2004. Crown copyright material is reproduced with the permission of the Controller of HMSO.

Table 3.3 Self-identification by religion in the 2001 and 2011 Censuses by percentages of the populations of England, Wales, and England and Wales taken together

Religion	England (%)		Wales (%)		England and Wales (%)	
	2001	2011	2001	2011	2001	2011
Buddhist	0.3	0.5	0.2	0.3	0.3	0.4
Christian	71.7	59.4	71.9	57.6	71.7	59.3
Hindu	1.1	1.5	0.2	0.3	1.1	1.5
Jewish	0.5	0.5	0.1	0.1	0.5	0.5
Muslim	3.1	5.0	0.8	1.5	3.0	4.8
Sikh	0.7	0.8	0.1	0.1	0.6	0.8
Other Religion	0.3	0.4	0.1	0.4	0.3	0.4
Total	*77.7*	*68.1*	*73.4*	*60.3*	*77.5*	*67.7*
No religion	14.6	24.7	18.5	32.1	14.8	25.1
Not stated	7.7	7.2	8.1	7.6	7.7	7.2
No religion/ not stated	*22.3*	*31.9*	*26.6*	*39.7*	*22.5*	*32.3*
Total all	*100*	*100*	*100*	*100*	*100*	*100*

Source: For the 2001 and 2011 data, see the National Statistics website: www.ons.gov.uk. Crown copyright, 2004. Crown copyright material is reproduced with the permission of the Controller of HMSO.

indicating identification with a religion, were, in both 2001 and 2011, Muslim; then Hindu and Sikh; then Jewish. Following these groups, in 2001, the next largest group had been 'other religion' and then Buddhist. In 2011, it was Buddhist and then 'other religion'. In relation to Wales on its own, in both the 2011 and 2001 Censuses, the next largest groups after Christian were Muslim; then 'other religion', then Hindu; then

Buddhist. Following these groups in 2001, the next largest groups had been Jewish and then Sikh. In 2011, this was Sikh and then Jewish.

However, in addition, as compared with the 2001 Census, the 2011 results for England and Wales (both combined and separately) show a substantial rise in both the numbers of people and percentage of the population stating that they are of 'no religion', which is now the largest overall group after Christian. The rise has been especially steep in Wales, where those reporting 'no religion' rose steeply from 18.5 per cent in 2001 to 32.1 per cent in 2011. The results also show substantial drops in both the numbers and percentage of those identifying as 'Christian', together with stability or rises in the numbers and percentages of the population of all those identifying with 'other religions' than Christian. When the Scottish results become available it will be interesting to see whether they follow trends in England and Wales, and in Northern Ireland, since in 2001 Scotland had been the country of the United Kingdom with the highest proportion (27.6%) of those reporting 'no religion'. Northern Ireland continues to be the part of the United Kingdom that exhibits least diversity of religion or belief, although the 2011 Census results include some indication of a small rise in the other than Christian, but religious, population.

Implications for religion and belief, discrimination and equality

In the light of the Census data, the decade under review might be interpreted as having been one in which, taken as a whole, the society (both as a whole and in its 'four nations' parts) could be seen as having become more secular, less Christian and more religiously plural. Nevertheless, both overall and in the vast majority of local areas, respondents self-identifying as Christians remain the largest group. At the same time there is other survey evidence that points to a long-term decline in Christian self-identification, some of which may reflect the population 'shape' in terms of the age of those identifying as Christian, both in absolute terms and also relative to other religious groups (Beckford et al., 2006). In other words, as compared with the self-identifying Muslim population, the self-identifying Christian population is an ageing one.

At the time of writing what was not yet available from the census is an up-to-date comparative insight of the kind that was been developed from 2001 Census (see Beckford et al., 2006) into the multiply layered intersections of the religion or belief profile of the population when considered in relation to other aspects of personal and group identity and social position, such as ethnicity, gender, country of birth, age, occupational and educational profiles. But what does seem to be suggested by the new census data is a probable narrowing of the gap that previously existed between the (generally higher) census data on 'religion' and (lower) on 'no religion' as compared with broader social survey data, such as that from the British Social Attitudes Survey, which were framed in terms of 'belief' rather than affiliation.

Finally, it is possible that part of the difference between 2001 and 2011 may be accounted for by what Voas (2003) and Voas and Bruce (2004) suggested in relation to the 2001 data – namely that, especially in relation to England, the response of 'Christian' may have said as much, if not more, about ethnicity as about religion.

However, in the light of campaigns run by the British Humanist Association and others for people to answer 'no religion' rather than to give a 'cultural' response, more 'cultural Christians' may, in the 2011 Census, have come out as being of 'no religion'.

In addition to differences between the countries of the United Kingdom, because of the differing patterns of migration and settlement, some geographical areas within each country are characterized by a more pronounced religious diversity and others by greater religious concentrations. Thus the cosmopolitan nature of London means that religious as well as ethnic and linguistic diversity is at its broadest there, with now just less than half (48%, compared with 60% in 2001) of London's population recording their religion as Christian. The greatest concentrations of people from minority religious traditions are also to be found in London, with the exception of Sikhs, whose regional population share is at its greatest in the West Midlands. Such concentrations of minority religious populations underline the fact that, as in 2001, religious diversity is still primarily an urban phenomenon.

Seaports such as Liverpool, Cardiff and London generally have longer-established communities because trade led to the settlement of seafarers there (Fisher et al. 2007; Visram 1986). In addition, many old industrial towns and cities of the English Midlands and North, such as Leicester and Bradford, have communities of South Asian origin that were established as a result of migration from particular areas of Commonwealth countries in response to the post-Second World War labour shortages in Britain (Ballard, 1994).

The local authorities whose populations have the biggest proportions of various religious groups include: the London Borough of Barnet with 15 per cent Jews; Slough with 11 per cent Sikhs; the London Borough of Tower Hamlets with 35 per cent Muslims; the London Borough of Harrow with 25 per cent Hindus; Rushmoor with 3 per cent Buddhists; the London Boroughs of Harrow and Brent with 3 per cent using the 'other religion' write in response; and Knowsley with 81 per cent Christians. By contrast, Tower Hamlets is also the local authority with lowest proportion of Christians, at 27 per cent.

In the light of the above – and as will also be seen in the presentation and discussion of the profiles of the project fieldwork localities in Chapter 5 – it is clear that the interplay between locality and the kind, degree and variability of religion and belief diversity is important.

Towards the law in context

In the context of the United Kingdom's 'four nations' state's inherited patterns for the relationship between religion, state and society, the religion or belief landscape of England and Wales within Britain exhibits significant local variations but within an overall 'three-dimensional' picture of a rising secularity; a growing religious diversity; and a continuing, while declining, majority presence of Christianity. Bearing this context in mind, we turn now to consider the place of the law relating to religion and belief, discrimination and equality in terms of continuity and change over the past decade.

The Law: A Decade of Continuity and Change

Religion and belief: Human rights and anti-discrimination law in global context

Context

As set out in Chapter 2, in Britain (and in many other countries) until the late nineteenth and early twentieth centuries, and sometimes until much later including in some contexts until the present day, domestic law has often supported discrimination and inequality on the grounds of religion or belief with legal force and sanctions. In other words, when looking at the law in terms of continuity and change, it is important not to do so in an ahistorical way. In this regard, the promulgation of the 1948 *Universal Declaration of Human Rights* marked a watershed, both in terms of the articulation of legal support for freedom of 'thought, conscience and religion' and the internationalization of that support as standards against which domestic law, policy and practice are scrutinized.

Significantly, therefore, from the very drafting of the Declaration onwards, religious freedom has always been protected under a banner which includes both religion *and* belief. Despite the controversies pertaining to the definition of 'religion' in politics and policy-making in general, this broad inclusive definition, based largely on self-definition, has been the one upon which human rights law has long rested. It is for this reason that human rights bodies have objected to governments relying on fixed lists of 'recognized' and 'other' religions (see also discussion in Chapter 1). Nevertheless, registration processes for religions such as that operated, for example, in the Federal Republic of Germany, are not rejected outright, as long they are not excessively burdensome (OSCE, 2004: 17).

'Belief' in the context of 'religion or belief' in human rights law is to be determined by a relevant authority, as having a recognized cogency, seriousness, cohesion and importance to the holder (*Campbell and Cosans v. UK*, 1982: para. 36). This inclusivity has been reflected in regional human rights systems found in various parts of the world. Thus, this broader scope has also been adopted in Article 9 of the *European Convention on Human Rights* (ECHR; 'freedom of thought, conscience and religion').

Beyond Europe it is also found in Article 12 of the *American Convention on Human Rights* ('freedom of conscience and of religion'), Article 8 of the *African Charter on Human and Peoples' Rights* ('freedom of conscience, the profession and free practice of religion') and Article 26 of the 1994 *Arab Charter on Human Rights* ('freedom of belief, thought and opinion').

In addition to these particular freedoms for religion or belief, non-discrimination on the basis of religion or belief enjoys separate support as well, along with non-discrimination on other grounds. This 'enjoyment without distinction of any kind' has served as the nucleus of a separate track for the pursuit of 'religion or belief' freedoms through the pursuit of equality and non-discrimination. In the following discussion we consider how these two legal tracks have both been linked with changes within the jurisdiction of England and Wales. In fact, it will be seen that the emphasis over the past decade in England and Wales has shifted legal attention from freedom of religion or belief in itself to addressing anti-discrimination through a wider equalities agenda. Though many international obligations to freedom of religion or belief remain with an unchanged continuity, the new equalities legislation has brought substantial change to the domestic legal landscape.

Religion or belief and law in England and Wales

In England and Wales, set within the political context of Great Britain and the United Kingdom of Great Britain and Northern Ireland, legal questions regarding religion or belief matters are dealt with by a wide variety of laws depending on whether they relate to employment, schooling, burial, property, pensions, charity law, health, discrimination or other issues. This in part highlights the complexity of religion in terms of its role across different aspects of people's lives.

The decade 2000-10 illustrates a varied picture with regard to the law concerning religion or belief in England and Wales (see Hill, 2005; Knights, 2007). There have been changes that have stemmed from a range of different sources and objectives (political, policy-oriented and legal) and were crafted in response to domestic, regional and/or international developments or tensions. Within this period, there has been movement from a relative lack of legal clarity and some gaps regarding religion or belief laws to multiple developments, stemming from different sources and causes. These sources and causes can be divided into those primarily emerging from developments in human rights legislation and those emerging from equality legislation.

With the coming into force of the HRA in 2000, there was an upsurge in cases relating to Article 9 of the ECHR. This human rights legislation was not new, since the United Kingdom had been bound by it since it originally came into force in 1953. In 1966, the United Kingdom had also accepted the jurisdiction of the ECtHR, and UK Article 9 cases had been heard by the ECtHR in Strasbourg. However, the United Kingdom's dualist approach to international law had meant that Article 9 and other convention rights had not been directly enforceable in UK domestic law. The HRA changed this, giving 'further effect' to these rights and making Article 9 and other convention claims directly enforceable in UK domestic law. Article 9 cases could now be heard before UK judges before possible further appeal to Strasbourg.

The timing of this development coincided with a period of an increased public visibility and concern with matters of religion or belief. The legal questions being adjudicated under Article 9, both within the United Kingdom and in other European contexts, implicated the question of what might be justifiable limitations to the manifestation of religion or belief in the public sphere (see further discussion in Chapter 10). Whether in relation to wearing religious head dress, the display of symbols, the right to holidays and conscientious objection in relation to schools or employment, an increased profile for religion in the public space was at the same time paralleled by a decrease in tolerance of religious 'exceptionalism' – that is, of separate laws to cater for religion or belief persons or organizations to be 'excepted' from generally applicable laws on the grounds of their beliefs and practices.

For example, there was much polarized and public debate around the exemptions for genuine occupational requirements offered in the *Employment Equality (Religion or Belief) Regulations*, 2003 (para. 7) and in the *Employment Equality (Sexual Orientation) Regulations*, 2003 (para. 7). The former allowed the religion or belief of the applicant to be considered where being of a particular religion or belief was a genuine and determining occupational requirement; and the latter allowed organized religions to have requirements regarding sexual orientation in order to comply with the doctrines of that religion or avoid conflicting with strongly held religious convictions.

The decrease in political tolerance for religious exceptionalism was reinforced by the second development that was being brought about through equality legislation. The broadening of equality legislation to address religion or belief was a byproduct of other intentions rather than being purposeful in relation to the specific characteristics of religion or belief. The experience of equality legislation relating to women's rights and racial discrimination; the momentum for the creation of a national human rights institution; and the need to deal with EU directives relating to different areas of discrimination, first in relation to employment and later also goods, services and activities; coalesced into the proposal to combine these into one legislative package resulting in the *Equality Act*, 2006 and then the *Equality Act*, 2010. These have resulted in the 'packaging together' in the same legislation of religion or belief with a range of other 'protected characteristics' such as disability and age. These characteristics have not only been brought together in terms of the law but also in terms of their understanding and advocacy by the EHRC and now also in public perception.

The legal landscape in England and Wales has been indelibly impacted by these human rights and equalities changes, affecting not only *what* is protected but also *how* it is protected. On the one hand, because of the HRA there has been greater awareness and more active resort to the courts to test the new domestic access to the human rights protections flowing from Article 9 of the European Convention. On the other hand, religion or belief has been 'shaped' into being understood as one of numerous 'protected characteristics' within a broader range of equalities. This is due to the fact that religion or belief is now legally understood as being part of the 'package' of nine very different protected characteristics, the others of which are: age, disability, gender reassignment, marriage and civil partnership, pregnancy and maternity, race, religion and belief, sex and sexual orientation (*Equality Act*, 2010: para. 4). In the light of the findings concerning aspects of these interrelationships, as seen in both the survey and the fieldwork completed in 2011, some of the implications of this for the development of appropriate future policy, law and practice will be discussed in Chapter 10.

In what follows below, the legal commitments of the British Government covering the key international, regional and domestic perspectives on religion or belief will be tracked.

International obligations relating to religion or belief

Legally, much remains unchanged in terms of the international obligations. That is to say, the international legal commitments into which the United Kingdom has voluntarily entered, and by which it is therefore bound, have remained largely unchanged. Despite this broad continuity, it is important to examine these obligations, both because they serve as a wider legal framework within which any distinctive domestic and regional changes relating to religion or belief can be situated and understood and also because, in many broader contemporary discussions of the law in relation to religion or belief, discrimination and equality, relatively little attention has been paid to them, with the exception of reference to the ECHR.

However, the United Kingdom has been answerable to its prior legal obligations in relation, in particular, to Article 18 of the *International Covenant on Civil and Political Rights* (ICCPR, 1966). As in the case of other human rights provisions, this distinguishes between the having/holding/changing religion or belief and its manifestation. The right to have, hold, adopt, choose or change one's religion or belief (legal instruments use a number of these terms) is legally absolute. It cannot be subjected to limitations of any kind and it is considered an inner and absolute freedom known as the *forum internum*. The right to *manifest* religion or belief either alone or with others and in public or in private, however, can be *limited*. Manifestation is an outer freedom or part of the *forum externum*. Manifestation may be limited by law, but only in strictly limited circumstances. It is therefore important first to understand that manifestation of religion or belief needs to be understood very broadly before considering any circumstances where, under law, it can be limited.

Manifestation of religion or belief has been interpreted by international monitoring bodies and courts very broadly, and encompasses a broad range of acts going beyond worship, observance, practice and teaching – to include, for example, evangelism, conscientious objection to military service and operating places of worship. Article 18 of the ICCPR states that:

1. Everyone shall have the right to freedom of thought, conscience and religion. This right shall include freedom to have or to adopt a religion or belief of his choice, and freedom, either individually or in community with others and in public or private, to manifest his religion or belief in worship, observance, practice and teaching.

2. No one shall be subject to coercion which would impair his freedom to have or to adopt a religion or belief of his choice.
3. Freedom to manifest one's religion or beliefs may be subject only to such limitations as are prescribed by law and are necessary to protect public safety, order, health, or morals or the fundamental rights and freedoms of others.
4. The States Parties to the present Covenant undertake to have respect for the liberty of parents and, when applicable, legal guardians to ensure the religious and moral education of their children in conformity with their own convictions.

Other related provisions in the same Covenant which are of relevance are articles relating to non-discrimination (Articles 2.1 and 26) and minority rights (Article 27). Minority rights provisions amplify and strengthen the collective rights pertaining to religion or belief minorities and underline the positive measures required from States (Ghanea, 2011). Thus, article 27 of the ICCPR (1966) states:

> In those States in which ethnic, religious or linguistic minorities exist, persons belonging to such minorities shall not be denied the right, in community with the other members of their group, to enjoy their own culture, to profess and practise their own religion, or to use their own language.

Other binding law stems from UK treaty obligations to the UN *Convention on the Elimination of All Forms of Racial Discrimination* (CERD, 1969). As with all States Parties to these international treaties, the United Kingdom has submitted reports to the UN regarding the extent of the realization of their standards within the United Kingdom. In 2008, the United Kingdom participated in the periodic reporting to which it is bound as part of its obligations to the ICCPR. All States that have accepted to be legally bound by the provisions of the ICCPR (and all other core international human rights treaties) have to have their records examined periodically. In these periodic 'State dialogues' the State reports to a body of independent experts who are entrusted with monitoring that treaty regarding its successes and challenges in relation to realizing the human rights articulated in the treaty. These experts examine the record of each State on the basis of their own research, the submissions of the State itself, other UN documents, as well as any submitted reports by Non-Governmental Organizations (NGOs) – these being known as 'shadow reports'.

The expert monitoring body of the ICCPR is known as the UN Human Rights Committee. As with all monitoring bodies, their views are not strictly legally binding but enjoy authority. In 2008, the Human Rights Committee raised a number of issues that related to religion or belief in England and Wales. The Human Rights Committee (2008: para. 3) welcomed the adoption of the *Racial and Religious Hatred Act*, 2006; the *Criminal Justice and Immigration Act*, 2008 abolishing the common law offences of blasphemy in England and Wales (Human Rights Committee, 2008: para. 4); and the passage into law of the *Equality Act*, 2006 (Human Rights Committee, 2008: para. 5).

Another of the tasks of these monitoring bodies is that they can, in principle, receive individual complaints and claims of violation of rights in relation to treaties. However, they are only able to receive such complaints if the State has allowed for this and the United Kingdom does not allow for individual complaints under the ICCPR, so there are no resulting observations (or 'jurisprudence') on which to draw. The Human Rights Committee (2008: 6) pointed this out in the conclusion to its report ('Concluding Observations'), noting that 'the Covenant is not directly applicable in the State party' and that the United Kingdom was 'the only Member State of the European Union not to be a party to the Optional Protocol to the Covenant'. It recommended that accession to that first Optional Protocol to allow for individual complaints from the United Kingdom be considered as a matter of priority. The United Kingdom has, however, expressed reluctance to do so, arguing that these rights are already enjoyed there; their practical value to citizens is unclear; that it would incur additional costs to the public funds; and because the communications procedure cannot produce legal rulings (Human Rights Committee, 2008: 6). The Human Rights Committee (2008: para. 16) also registered its concern about 'negative public attitudes towards Muslim members of society' and recommended that 'energetic steps' should be taken

> in order to combat and eliminate this phenomenon, and ensure that the authors of acts of discrimination on the basis of religion are adequately deterred and sanctioned. The State party should ensure that the fight against terrorism does not lead to raising suspicion against all Muslims.

A further State dialogue took place in 2011 between the United Kingdom and the expert monitoring body of the CERD – the UN Committee on the Elimination of Racial Discrimination. The Committee (2011: para. 6) welcomed the enactment of the *Equality Act*, 2010 'as a landmark improvement in anti-discrimination legislation' and (2011: paras 6-7) noted appreciation of the establishment of the EHRC under the *Equality Act*, 2006 and the adoption of the *Racial and Religious Hatred Act*, 2006.

As in the case of the ICCPR the United Kingdom has not recognized an obligation to make the CERD Convention part of its domestic legal order as such. The situation is that Convention rights are not directly enforceable in UK domestic law, as was the case with the ECHR before the HRA, 1998. The CERD (2011: 10) does not support this position and it reiterated 'its continuing concern that the State party's courts may not give full legal effect to the provisions of the Convention unless it is expressly incorporated into its domestic law or the State party adopts necessary provisions in its legislation'. It also recommended that the United Kingdom reconsider its position 'so that the Convention can more readily be invoked in the domestic courts' (CERD, 2011: 10). Because the United Kingdom does not allow for individual complaints under CERD, as in the case of the ICCPR, there is no jurisprudence to review.

The above provides an idea of authoritative and expert views from the UN during the 2000-10 decade of 'continuity and change' in the United Kingdom in relation to religion or belief matters and in the context of international obligations to which the United Kingdom has continued to be bound. Though not highly detailed or close to the ground, they provide an interesting overall snapshot of critical human rights analyses of this landscape.

The United Kingdom's obligations are also informed by international normative standards within the 1981 *Declaration on the Elimination of All Forms of Intolerance and of Discrimination Based on Religion or Belief* and the 1992 *Declaration on the Rights of Persons Belonging to National or Ethnic, Religious or Linguistic Minorities.* Though these standards are not legally binding (because they are upheld in an international declaration rather than a binding treaty) their standards, agreed after decades of negotiation at the UN, represent the commitment of states regarding these issues. These are also complemented by the advisory status of UN experts who are part of the UN Special Procedures mechanisms. The UN's Special Procedures refer to independent experts (mostly referred to as 'Special Rapporteurs') who are appointed by the UN and entrusted with a portfolio of work in relation to human rights in a particular country or in relation to a particular theme. They carry forward this portfolio or mandate by producing reports for review by the UN, carrying out field missions to examine a situation first-hand for their reporting and putting any complaints of violations they receive to States for comment and, then, inclusion in their public reports to the UN.

The Special Rapporteur on the Right to Freedom of Opinion and Expression (2000) visited the United Kingdom in late 1999, just before the period under review but did not directly raise religion or belief issues. The UN Special Rapporteur on Freedom of Religion or Belief visited the United Kingdom from 4 to 15 June 2007. She welcomed the *Racial and Religious Hatred Act*, 2006 and its extension to non-religious believers, but expressed concern about the blasphemy offence which she considered discriminatory and in favour of Christianity alone (Report of the Special Rapporteur on Freedom of Religion or Belief, 2008: 2). However, as outlined above this was to be abolished in England and Wales in the subsequent year through Section 79 of the *Criminal Justice and Immigration Act*, 2008.

In her consultations with a range of stakeholders, the Special Rapporteur (2008: 27) heard concern about 'reported discrimination and violence related to sectarianism' among various Christian denominations; complaints by student Christian Unions at several universities regarding 'pressures with regard to their adherence to university equal opportunities policies'; criticism of the 'application of counter-terrorism legislation and the adverse influence on the situation of British Muslims' and 'the inflammatory tone of many media reports on issues regarding Muslims, especially with regard to the wearing of headscarves; attacks on believers and community property, concern about manifestation of religious symbols'; as well as (Special Rapporteur, 2008: 35) 'under-representation of some religious communities in the Houses of Parliament; as well as institutional and legal examples of discrimination against non-religious believers'.

The Special Rapporteur (2008: 54, 57) drew attention to the vulnerability of women and converts, and also of asylum seekers facing religious persecution in their home countries. The Special Rapporteur (2008: 69) also recommended that specific attention be given to RE syllabuses, especially of publicly funded schools, and particularly that 'a non-discriminatory membership of relevant committees preparing such syllabuses seems vital to adequately present the various theistic, non-theistic and atheistic approaches'. Three paragraphs of the report focused on RE in relation to which the Rapporteur noted 'with appreciation that parents may request that their children be wholly or partly excused from receiving religious education or attending at religious worship' and 'particularly welcomed' (2008: 70) what was described as:

> the recent adoption of opt-out possibilities for pupils in the sixth form with regard to legal requirements of taking part in an act of collective worship in maintained schools. The right to freedom of religion or belief also includes the right not to manifest a religious belief. The parents or legal guardians of the child have the right to organize the life within the family in accordance with their religion or belief and children themselves also enjoy in their own right the freedom of religion or belief.

The Rapporteur also welcomed 'the case-by-case approach by the authorities and courts' in relation to religious symbols and school uniform policies (2008: 71). She also noted the guidance of the Department for Children, Schools and Families which assured her that 'each [such] case depends on the circumstances of the particular school and that the recent judgments do not mean that banning such religious dress will always be justified, nor that such religious dress cannot be worn in any school' (2008: 71).

The United Kingdom was also reviewed by the UN Universal Periodic Review both during and subsequently to the 2000-10 decade that is under consideration – its first review being in 2008 and the second in 2012. Universal Periodic Review is a procedure that has been running at the UN's Human Rights Council since 2008, whereby in every four-and-a-half years, the overall human rights record of every UN Member State is examined in the presence of other States. Through this procedure, States make public recommendations for the improvement of each other's human rights records.

Whereas one may, rightly, consider that these recommendations are politically coloured by the State which is making the recommendations to the United Kingdom, it should be remembered that the State will be well aware of the possibility of a 'reprisal in kind', or a similarly critical recommendation by the concerned State. So although this context should not be forgotten, the recommendations again offer an interesting international State-considered human rights perspective on the human rights record of the United Kingdom in relation to religion or belief. Among the relevant recommendations made to the United Kingdom during its second Universal Periodic Review, and which were accepted, are the following (Human Rights Council, 2012: para 110):

- 110.53: Take effective measure to eliminate discrimination on the grounds of race, religion and nationality and to guarantee the rights of Muslims, Roma people and migrant workers (China).
- 110.55: Investigate allegations that stop and search orders disproportionately fall on persons belonging to ethnic, religious and other minorities and introduce adequate safeguards in this regard (Austria).
- 110.58: Put an end to the use of religious profiling in combating terrorism by inserting legal safeguards against abuse and the deliberate targeting of certain religious groups (Malaysia).

Overall then, it can therefore be observed that while both continuing concerns and new issues arose during the 2000-10 timeframe, they did not stem from *new* international obligations with regard to religion or belief. The issues raised by UN treaty bodies and mandate holders primarily not only welcomed new legal developments but also raised concern about governmental measures and policies arising out of the 9/11 crisis. These observations at the UN reflected a number of concerns that were also reported domestically, for example regarding blasphemy; school educational provision and opt outs; stop and search and profiling; religion or belief discrimination and dealing with conflicts on a case-by-case basis.

Regional obligations: The ECHR

In contrast with the trend of continuity in relation to international obligations, the regional and domestic legislation has experienced a lot of change, leading to a substantially altered religion or belief landscape in England and Wales. These changes have been such that they have even been described as having led to 'considerable policy turbulence around the human rights agenda' (Riddell and Watson, 2011: 194).

Much like its international obligations, the United Kingdom's obligations with regard to the ECHR remain largely unchanged. As noted earlier in this chapter, the United Kingdom was one of the first signatories of the ECHR in 1951. However, its 'dualist' system meant that for the subsequent 49 years the ECHR standards were not directly enforceable through UK law. In 1998 new domestic legislation was brought into force through the HRA, which allowed for the direct enforcement of ECHR standards in British courts. This had a noticeable effect on knowledge of and reference to such rights by claimants and lawyers alike and multiplied the 'importation' and testing of its standards, for example of Article 9 – freedom of thought, conscience and religion – into the domestic law. Article 9 of the ECHR (1950) states:

1. Everyone has the right to freedom of thought, conscience and religion; this right includes freedom to change his religion or belief and freedom, either alone or in community with others and in public or private, to manifest his religion or belief, in worship, teaching, practice and observance.
2. Freedom to manifest one's religion or beliefs shall be subject only to such limitations as are prescribed by law and are necessary in a democratic society in the interests of public safety, for the protection of public order, health or morals or for the protection of the rights and freedoms of others.

This allowed domestic judges to 'shape Convention law under the HRA so as to reflect our distinctive cultural and historical practices' and to 'promote an indigenous human rights jurisprudence, as the architects of the HRA originally envisaged – thereby contributing to the development of European law in this field' (Clayton, 2012: 32). Furthermore, it gave 'domestic courts the power directly to enmesh European human rights norms into the interpretation of statutes and the common law', thus bringing about 'some significant changes in the methods by which cases are determined'

(Bamforth, 2004: vi) but not having 'a "radical" or "revolutionary" effect within the domestic legal system' (Bamforth, 2004: iv). In considering the internal organization of religious groups, including when this involves intersections between religion or belief rights and other human rights, it should be noted that Section 13 of the HRA (1998) holds that if a court or tribunal's 'determination of any question arising under this Act might affect the exercise by a religious organization (itself or its members collectively) of the Convention right to freedom of thought, conscience and religion, it must have particular regard to the importance of that right'.

The HRA entered into force on 2 October 2000 – requiring of public authorities, as a matter of domestic law, to comply with the ECHR and for all legislation to be developed, read and given effect in a way that is compatible with the ECHR. 'Public authorities' have been defined in Section 6 of the HRA to include both 'pure' public authorities as well as private and voluntary sector actors when discharging a public function – for example, companies running public utility services in relation to activities previously exercised by public authorities but not in relation to their commercial activities; doctors and dentists in relation to their National Health Service (NHS) patients but not in relation to their private patients; private security companies contracted to run prisons but not in relation to its other work; and voluntary and community, and religion or belief groups, when providing a public service.

The significance and implications of complying with the ECHR when carrying out a 'public function' in the light of the HRA came into sharp focus in the case of the *Charity Commission v. Catholic Care*, 2010. This case concerned an adoption agency – Catholic Care – that received public as well as private donations, and which unsuccessfully sought permission to 'limit its adoption services to potential adoptive parents on the grounds of sexual orientation; specifically to those individuals who are heterosexual' (*Charity Commission v. Catholic Care*, 2010: para. 16). Catholic Care argued for this on the grounds that Article 14 of the EHRC would support differential treatment in favour of heterosexual couples as a justifiable differential treatment, as well as being a proportionate means of achieving a legitimate aim. However, the Charity Commission did not find 'particularly convincing and weighty reasons justifying the proposed discrimination' (*Charity Commission v. Catholic Care*, 2010: para. 110), and the applicants were unsuccessful.

The issue of 'public function' was also evident in the *Hall and Preddy v. Bull and Bull*, 2011, case in which the defendants were Christian guesthouse owners who refused a double bedroom to a gay couple on the ground of their religious beliefs. In arriving at a judgement, the judge accepted the relevance of Article 8 (private and family life) and Article 14 (non-discrimination) to both the applicants and the defendants. Article 9 was also relevant to the defendants in that the judge accepted that running a hotel along Christian principles could be described as manifesting one's religion (*Hall and Preddy v. Bull and Bull*, 2011: para. 27). The defendants wanted to manifest their religion in their home and called for respect of their private and family life. Nevertheless, the judgement found that:

> the defendant's right to have their private and family life and their home respected is inevitably circumscribed by their decision to use their home in part as a hotel.

The regulations do not require them to take into their home (that is the private part of the hotel which they occupy) persons such as the claimants and arguably therefore do not affect the article 8 rights of the defendants. (*Hall and Preddy v. Bull and Bull,* 2011: para. 52)

The judge held that enabling the guesthouse owners to discriminate on the grounds of sexual orientation because it would otherwise be inconsistent with their beliefs would create 'a class of persons (namely those who hold the views of the defendants) who are exempt from the discrimination legislation' (*Hall and Preddy v. Bull and Bull,* 2011: para. 52) and therefore found in favour of the applicants.

Domestic enforcement of EU obligations

As discussed above, although the United Kingdom's obligations with regard to the ECHR retained much continuity, their domestic effect through the HRA led to a lot of change in terms of the domestic awareness and the pursuit of these standards. It was the EU obligations that changed the legal landscape most substantially. This was primarily due to 'the decision by the UK government to draw together the equality and human rights agendas' (Riddell and Watson, 2011: 193) into a single and more comprehensive domestic legal framework, supported by integration into a single body (the EHRC) concerned with the monitoring, promotion and enforcement equality and human rights matters. This has had a notable impact on questions of non-discrimination and equality on the basis of religion or belief, and has led to changes that, as O'Cinneide (2011: 7) has argued, remain unsettled and somewhat uncertain.

It was through the EU directive – the *Framework Equality Directive 2000/78/ EC* – that direct protection against discrimination based on religion or belief in the employment field came into force in the United Kingdom through the *Employment Equality (Religion or Belief) Regulations,* 2003. Although recognizing very limited circumstances in which 'a difference of treatment may be justified where a characteristic related to religion or belief, disability, age or sexual orientation constitutes a genuine and determining occupational requirement, when the objective is legitimate and the requirement is proportionate', the *Framework Equality Directive* requires legal protection against discrimination based on religion or belief with regard to employment and occupation, including vocational training. It sets out to combat such discrimination in relation to direct discrimination, indirect discrimination and harassment.

The *Employment Equality (Religion or Belief) Regulations,* 2003 have since been revoked as a range of regulations and legislative enactments came to be established in the comprehensive legislative framework offered by the *Equality Act,* 2006, and then in the *Equality Act,* 2010 which extended protection beyond the scope of the EU Directives. Hailed as 'a major achievement for the equal rights movement' (Hepple, 2010: 11) and giving rise to the dominant changes of the decade, the *Equality Act,* 2010 will be discussed separately below at the end of the following section.

Existing and new domestic legal standards

In order to aid understanding of the references to domestic legal standards in both the survey completed in 2011 and as they are referred to (see especially Chapters 6–8) by survey respondents, fieldwork interviewees and focus group participants, the other domestic legal standards that are most directly relevant to the research are briefly outlined below before we return to a discussion of the *Equality Act*.

The *Education and Inspections Act*, 2006 built on the *Education Reform Act* of 1988 and required RE to be part of the school curriculum in the United Kingdom. Section 375 requires that the syllabus in England and Wales 'shall reflect the fact that the religious traditions in Great Britain are in the main Christian whilst taking account of the teaching and practices of the other principal religions represented in Great Britain', though sixth-form students can be excused from attending religious worship. The provisions of the *Equality Act*, 2010 also need to be mentioned here: namely the specific exceptions that apply to organizations and charities relating to religion or belief and 'faith schools' in which the Act's requirements in relation to the provision of services in relation to religion or belief-related discrimination do not apply to the school curriculum; to admission to a school with a religious ethos; to acts of worship or other religious observance organized by a school or on behalf of a school; or to the responsible body of a school with a religious ethos and so on (*Equality Act*, 2010: Schedule 3, Section 11). The legal issues involved in this became part of the focus in the case of *E, R v JFS*, 2009). This case concerned the refusal of the JFS (formerly Jews' Free School) to admit a child who was not recognized to be Jewish by the Office of the Chief Rabbi. As the case outlined:

> So long as a maintained faith school is undersubscribed, it cannot use religious criteria to allocate places. But once it is oversubscribed, it can lawfully restrict entry to children whom, or whose parents, it regards as sharing the school's faith. . . . because such schools are exempted from the prohibition of discrimination on grounds of religion or belief contained in Part 2 of the Equality Act 2006. (S. 50(1) (a), *E, R v JFS*, 2009: para. 12)

As the next paragraph goes on to note, though, 'No school, however, is permitted to discriminate in its admissions policy on racial grounds. Such discrimination is forbidden by the Race Relations Act 1976 as amended' (*E, R v JFS*, 2009: para. 13). The Supreme Court determined that JFS's refusal to admit a child who was not recognized as Jewish by the Office of the Chief Rabbi constituted an exclusion based on racial rather than theological grounds, and therefore the pupil had to be admitted.

The *Religious and Racial Hatred Act*, 2006 made the stirring up of hatred against persons on religious grounds an offence. 'Religious hatred' is defined as 'hatred against a group of persons defined by reference to religious belief or lack of religious belief' (Section 29A), while 'A person who uses threatening words or behaviour, or displays any written material which is threatening, is guilty of an offence if he intends thereby to stir up religious hatred' (Section 29B1). The offence can be committed in a public or a private place unless inside a dwelling and not heard or seen by others or if there was no reason to believe it would be heard or seen by others (Sections 29B 2 and 4).

The Act was adopted on 31 January 2006 and entered into force on 1 October 2007. It inserts a new part 3A into the 1986 *Public Order Act*. This responded to the concern that although Sikhs and Jews fell within the scope of the *Race Relations Act* of 1976 within the case law as constituting both religious and ethnic groups, other religious groups (e.g. Muslims, Rastafarians, Jehovah's Witnesses) did not. The *Race Relations Act* of 1976, as amended, made it unlawful to discriminate directly or indirectly against a person on racial grounds (based on colour, race, nationality or ethnic and national origins) in employment, education, housing and in the provision of goods, facilities and services.

The *Religious and Racial Hatred Act* created new offences in the *Public Order Act* of 1986 regarding religious hatred, that is: 'hatred against a group of persons defined by reference to religious belief or lack of religious belief' (29A), which may lead to imprisonment of up to seven years, a fine or both. It should be noted that this Act led to a lot of vigorous and very heated debate and its wording reflects the difficulties entailed in striking a balance between the interests of both expanding protection against racial hatred to religious hatred while not stifling freedom of expression. Therefore, a safeguard is provided so that there is an appropriate balance with freedom of expression and that vigorous debate in the field of religion or belief is not restricted:

> nothing in this Part shall be read or given effect in a way which prohibits or restricts discussion, criticism or expressions of antipathy, dislike, ridicule, insult or abuse of particular religions or the beliefs or practices of their adherents, or of any other belief system or the beliefs or practices of its adherents, or proselytising or urging adherents of a different religion or belief system to cease practising their religion or belief system. (*Religious and Racial Hatred Act*, 1986: 29J)

The broader territory relating to equality, religion and belief was further developed by the *Equality Act*, 2006 which established the EHRC. Hepple (2010: 11) described the Act as being 'part of the fifth generation of equality legislation in Britain'. He furthermore explains:

> The Act is a major achievement for the equal rights movement. Over the past 45 years, struggles for equality in Britain have resulted in the gradual recognition of the legal rights of a wider range of disadvantaged groups and the expansion of the law from *formal* to *substantive* equality to deal not only with individual acts of discrimination, harassment and victimisation, but also subtler forms of indirect discrimination. It has also been recognised that equal treatment does not mean identical treatment, and that full and effective equality entails accommodating differences.

> The new fifth generation, embodied in the *Equality Act*, 2010, goes even further than this. First, it is based on the principle that equality is an indivisible fundamental human right, and that there can be no hierarchy of equality. . . . Secondly, the Act recognises that members of disadvantaged groups will not have equal life chances

or enjoy respect for their equal worth unless institutions take proactive measures to ensure equality. The streamlining and broadening of the public sector equality duty and the provisions on permissible positive action are the core of the new approach to *transformative* equality. (Hepple, 2010: 21)

Sections 44-80 of the *Equality Act*, 2010 relate to discrimination on the grounds of religion or belief, prohibiting direct and indirect discrimination. Regarding service provision the Act noted:

> when providing goods, facilities and services, when disposing of premises, when admitting pupils to educational establishments, when providing schools and transport as well as when public authorities exercise a function of a public nature. Specific exceptions apply to organisations and charities relating to religion or belief, faith schools, care within family and acts justified by national security purposes.

'Protected characteristics' was the new language used to refer to the nine different characteristics of persons which may serve as grounds for discrimination against them. A number of other 'protected characteristics' were also upheld through different laws, for example *The Equality Act (Sexual Orientation) Regulations*, 2007 which made it unlawful to discriminate or subject another person to harassment on the grounds of sexual orientation. An exception was provided for organizations related to religion or belief, such that it was not unlawful for them to:

1. to restrict membership of the organisation,
2. to restrict participation in activities undertaken by the organisation or on its behalf or under its auspices,
3. to restrict the provision of goods, facilities or services in the course of activities undertaken by the organisation or on its behalf or under its auspices or
4. to restrict the use or disposal of premises owned or controlled by the organisation (*The Equality Act (Sexual Orientation) Regulations*, 14(3), 2007).

The Act goes on to specify that these restrictions can only be imposed if

1. it is necessary to comply with the doctrine of the organisation; or
2. so as to avoid conflicting with the strongly held religious convictions of a significant number of the religion's followers (*The Equality Act (Sexual Orientation) Regulations*, 14(5), 2007).

Further developments (the aims and objectives of which are explained by Hepple below) later led to the *Equality Act*, 2010 which integrated previously diverse legal provision across the range of 'protected characteristics' and came into force on 1 October 2010. Hepple (2010: 14-15) outlines the objectives of the Act in this way:

> The overriding aim of the Equality Act 2010 is to achieve harmonisation, simplification, and modernisation of equality law. This in effect expresses several

principles in the Declaration, in particular the right to equality of all human beings (principle 1), equal protection from discrimination regardless of the grounds concerned (principle 6), and the obligation on states to give 'full effect' to the right to equality in all activities of the state (principle 11). There must be no hierarchy of equality. The same rule should be applied to all strands unless there is convincing justification for an exception. To a large extent, the Act achieves this aim.

The *Equality Act* (Sections 20, 21 and 22) sets out the different ways in which it is unlawful to treat someone, such as direct and indirect discrimination, harassment, victimization and failing to make a reasonable adjustment for a disabled person. The Act prohibits unfair treatment in the workplace; when providing goods, facilities and services; when exercising public functions; in the disposal and management of premises; in education; and by associations (such as private clubs). The Act brought together the separate equality duties into a single 'mainstreamed' public sector equality duty as of 5 April 2011:

1. A public authority must, in the exercise of its functions, have due regard to the need to –
   a. eliminate discrimination, harassment, victimisation and any other conduct that is prohibited by or under this Act;
   b. advance equality of opportunity between persons who share a relevant protected characteristic and persons who do not share it;
   c. foster good relations between persons who share a relevant protected characteristic and persons who do not share it.

2. A person who is not a public authority but who exercises public functions must, in the exercise of those functions, have due regard to the matters mentioned in subsection (1).

3. Having due regard to the need to advance equality of opportunity between persons who share a relevant protected characteristic and persons who do not share it involves having due regard, in particular, to the need to:
   a. remove or minimise disadvantages suffered by persons who share a relevant protected characteristic that are connected to that characteristic;
   b. take steps to meet the needs of persons who share a relevant protected characteristic that are different from the needs of persons who do not share it;
   c. encourage persons who share a relevant protected characteristic to participate in public life or in any other activity in which participation by such persons is disproportionately low.

4. The steps involved in meeting the needs of disabled persons that are different from the needs of persons who are not disabled include, in particular, steps to take account of disabled persons' disabilities.

5. Having due regard to the need to foster good relations between persons who share a relevant protected characteristic and persons who do not share it involves having due regard, in particular, to the need to:

   a. tackle prejudice, and

   b. promote understanding.

6. Compliance with the duties in this section may involve treating some persons more favourably than others; but that is not to be taken as permitting conduct that would otherwise be prohibited by or under this Act.

7. The relevant protected characteristics are:

   age,
   disability,
   gender reassignment,
   pregnancy and maternity,
   race,
   religion or belief,
   sex and
   sexual orientation.

8. A reference to conduct that is prohibited by or under this Act includes a reference to:

   a. a breach of an equality clause or rule;

   b. a breach of a non-discrimination rule (*Equality Act*, 2010: Section 149).

It should be noted that a review of the public sector equality duty was announced in May 2012 (The Home Office, 2012), and any changes arising from this are only due to be announced after the text for this book was submitted in summer 2013.

Key contours of the legal landscape

The impulse behind new legislation in force, the coming together of the equality and human rights agendas and the establishment of the EHRC in 2007, may be traced to the government's desire to align its responses 'to the ECHR and EU directives on equal treatment and discrimination' (Riddell and Watson, 2011: 193). In summary, some of the legal frameworks which are applicable in relation to religion or belief in England and Wales therefore recognize the rights to:

- Have or hold (*ICCPR*, 1966: Article 18.1; *ECHR*, 1950: Article 9.1); and adopt or change (*ICCPR*, 1966: Article 18.1; *ECHR*, 1950: Article 9.1) religion or belief without coercion (*ICCPR*, 1966: Article 18.2).
- Manifest religion or belief (*ICCPR*, 1966: Article 18.1; *ECHR*, 1950: Article 9.1); individually or in community with others; in public or private; in worship, observance, practice and teaching (*ICCPR*, 1966: Article 18.1; *ECHR*, 1950: Article 9.1).
- Manifestation of religion or belief may be subject to limitations prescribed by law and necessary (*ICCPR*, 1966: Article 18.2) in a democratic society (*ECHR*, 1950:

Article 9.2) to *protect* public safety, order, health, *or* morals or the protection of the fundamental (*ICCPR*, 1966: Article 18.1) rights and freedoms of others (*ICCPR*, 1966: Article 18.1; *ECHR*, 1950: Article 9.2).

- To uphold the rights of parents or legal guardians to ensure the religion and moral education of their children in conformity with their convictions (*ICCPR*, 1966: Article 18.4).
- Protection against any stirring up of hatred against persons on religious grounds (*Racial and Religious Hatred Act*, Section 29).
- Protection against direct and indirect discrimination on the grounds of religion or belief in the exercise of the functions of a public authority and those who exercise public functions – hence in the provision of goods, facilities and services, when disposing of premises, when admitting pupils to educational establishments, when providing schools and transport as well as in the exercise of a function of a public nature by public authorities (*Equality Act*, 2010: Sections 13, 19 and 149).

Having reprised and summarized the key contours of the law, the following section outlines and discusses some key recent cases with regard to the having/holding/change of religion or belief and its manifestation.

Anti-discrimination/equality and holding/manifesting religion or belief: Recent case law

The recent nature of these legislative developments has acted as an access point attracting individual claimants and campaigning groups to this area of the law. Some of the cases which have emerged have had the perhaps unintended effect of 'setting up' protected characteristic grounds against one another as if they are necessarily opposed, and contributing to 'a widespread public perception that an increase in the protection of equality through human rights and discrimination law has led to an increase in "conflicts" between different social groups' (Malik, 2011: 22). The still recent nature of these legal developments has created a:

> reluctance to talk openly about distinctions between the different non-discrimination grounds . . . [instead reiterating] repeatedly the mantra that there was no 'hierarchy of grounds', i.e. that the different non-discrimination grounds were to be considered as being of similar weight and status when it came to applying anti-discrimination law. (O'Cinneide, 2011: 18)

Furthermore, many concerns have arisen in relation to the risk of competition between the equality grounds, the possible 'trumping' of equality over human rights in the new agenda and the overly dominant role given to the law to settle such questions (Malik, 2011: 22). Our research provides some insights into these developments, as we outline in the subsequent chapters of this book.

However, in reflecting on the decade of continuity and change in law pertaining to religion or belief, discrimination, equality and human rights, the first question to be addressed relates to whether the freedom of religion or belief has been as broadly upheld in England and Wales during the 2000-10 timeframe as it has been by the ECtHR? In connection with this, it should be recalled that ECtHR jurisprudence has interpreted Article 9's 'freedom of thought, conscience and religion' very broadly; an early case having accepted pacifism (*Arrowsmith v. UK*, 1978) within its ambit, that is, pacifism was accepted as a belief.

The case law in England and Wales has echoed this inclusivity, and arguably even stretched it further. *Grainger PLC v. Nicholson*, 2009, addressed the case of belief in man-made climate change, the environment and resulting moral imperatives, and accepted this philosophical belief as being of a similar cogency or status as religious belief, thus falling within the purview of the *Employment Equality (Religion or Belief) Regulations*, 2003. This can be contrasted with *Gnostic Centre*, 2009, where the Charity Commission did not grant charity status to the Gnostic Centre on grounds including the lack of evidence of shared morals or ethics among its followers, whereas in the Employment Tribunal case of *Greater Manchester Police Authority v. Power*, 2009, belief in spiritualism and the philosophical belief in life after death and psychic powers were deemed to fall within the *Employment Equality (Religion or Belief) Regulations*, 2003.

In reaching its conclusions, *Grainger v. Nicholson* cited other cases such as *Williamson v. Secretary of State for Education and Employment*, 2005, and *Eweida v. British Airways plc*, 2009. In *Williamson v. Secretary of State for Education and Employment*, 2005, note 34, para. 22), it was explained that:

> When the genuineness of a claimant's professed belief is an issue in the proceedings the court will inquire into and decide this issue as a question of fact. This is a limited inquiry. The court is concerned to ensure an assertion of religious belief is made in good faith [. . .] But, emphatically, it is not for the court to embark on an inquiry into the asserted belief and judge its 'validity' by some objective standard such as the source material upon which the claimant founds his belief or the orthodox teaching of the religion in question or the extent to which the claimant's belief conforms to or differs from the views of others professing the same religion. Freedom of religion protects the subjective belief of an individual. [. . .] [R]eligious belief is intensely personal and can easily vary from one individual to another. Each individual is at liberty to hold his own religious beliefs, however irrational or inconsistent they may seem to some, however surprising. [. . .] The relevance of objective factors such as source material is, at most, that they may throw light on whether the professed belief is genuinely held.

This broad inclusion of recognition for belief is evident in different areas of the law, including employment and within charity law. In considering whether the Druid Network (2010: para. 11) could be registered 'as a charity for the charitable purpose of the advancement of religion for public benefit and no other purpose', the Board Members of the Charity Commission noted that the 'test of public benefit, for both a charity established for the advancement of religion and one for the promotion of moral

or spiritual welfare or improvement for the benefit of the community, is the same'
(*The Druid Network*, 2010: para. 15) and the imperative that 'organisations seeking
registration as charities for the advancement of religion are not discriminated against
on the basis that they might be newly established or represent religious minorities'
(*The Druid Network*, 2010: para. 16). They then turned to the *Campbell and Cosans v.
UK*, 1982 (para: 38) test of what constitutes 'religion':

> [A] religion must be a sincere belief system of substance or significance, capable
> of benefiting society, having a certain level of cogency, coherence, seriousness and
> importance; as opposed to a self-promoting organisation set up to promote one or
> two persons, or a trivial system set up for, perhaps frivolous reasons.

The Board first satisfied itself that the Druid Network had the various characteristics
of a religion (*The Druid Network*, 2010: note 27, para. 54) as set out in *Campbell
v. Cosans* before considering various principles of the 'public benefit' requirement,
concluding that the Druid Network was established for exclusively charitable
purposes for the advancement of religion and for public benefit. 'Cogency' and
'coherence' do not imply measuring a belief against some kind of objective standard;
it may be personal and subjectively held. As argued in *Eweida v. BA*, 2009 (note 35,
para. 29),

> [I]t is not necessary for a belief to be shared by others in order for it to be a religious
> belief, nor need a specific belief be a mandatory requirement of an established
> religion for it to qualify as a religious belief. A person could, for example, be part of
> the mainstream Christian religion but hold additional beliefs which are not widely
> shared by other Christians, or indeed shared at all by anyone.

Freedom of belief *within* religion has also been upheld in the case law from England
and Wales. In the case of *R. (Ghai) v. Newcastle upon Tyne City Council*, 2010 (para.
19) for example, the judge draws attention to the possibility of a diversity of positions
among Hindus as to what Hinduism requires with regard to bodily cremation: 'What
we are concerned with in this case is, of course, what Mr Ghai's belief involves when it
comes to cremation, and it matters not for present purposes whether it is a universal,
orthodox or unusual belief for a Hindu.'

Overall, then, on the first question of whether religion or belief has been as broadly
upheld in England and Wales during the 2000-10 timeframe as it has been by the
ECtHR, it has arguably been stretched even further.

The second question relates to *manifestation* of religion or belief in the public
sphere and whether the case law in England and Wales suggests a stronger, similar or
weaker pattern of protection than does the ECtHR jurisprudence? The ECtHR's record
of protection of the public manifestation of religion or belief can be summed up as
chequered and inconsistent. So much so, that it is hard to predict where such public
manifestation is likely to be protected. This is because in some of its earlier jurisprudence,
the ECtHR seemed to suggest that public manifestation of religion or belief is a matter
'only' of 'choice', rather than – for example – of religious duty. In *Otto-Preminger-Institut*

v. Austria, 1995 (para. 47) the Court draws a spectrum of possible responses to such 'choice' of manifestation:

> Those who choose to exercise the freedom to manifest their religion, irrespective of whether they do so as members of a religious majority or a minority, cannot reasonably expect to be exempt from all criticism. They must tolerate and accept the denial by others of their religious beliefs and even the propagation by others of doctrines hostile to their faith. However, the manner in which religious beliefs and doctrines are opposed or denied is a matter which may engage the responsibility of the State, notably its responsibility to ensure the peaceful enjoyment of the right guaranteed under Article 9 (art. 9) to the holders of those beliefs and doctrines. Indeed, in extreme cases the effect of particular methods of opposing or denying religious beliefs can be such as to inhibit those who hold such beliefs from exercising their freedom to hold and express them.

Adhar and Leigh approach the question of manifestation from a religious perspective and identify the various legal approaches employed. To begin with, they argue, there needs to be clarification of 'whether proposed conduct or practices are *permitted, required or prohibited*, both by religion and the law' (Adhar and Leigh, 2005: 156). Of nine possible outcomes which they identify, the following three then give rise to questions:

> [m]ost acute is where the law *requires* what the religion *prohibits* and, conversely, where the law *prohibits* what religion *requires* [. . .] Equally, when a practice is *permitted* by a religion but legally *prohibited* [. . .] it may be argued that religious liberty is diminished, although this is perhaps contentious. (Adhar and Leigh, 2005: 156)

The explicit collapsing of the question of non-discrimination and equality on the basis of religion or belief into the broader equality spectrum through the *Equality Act* does not, however, allow for such nuances. As has already been noted, a wide range of religions and beliefs qualify, and are deemed by the courts to benefit from, freedom of religion or belief. However, most appeals for such protection are not being upheld on the basis of them being manifestations which can legitimately be limited. In most instances, and as will be seen in the following section's discussion of four key cases for the future development of law, policy and practice in relation to religion or belief, discrimination, equality and human rights, it is the precise facts of the case which is leading to such a determination rather than any emphasis on the general principle of freedom of manifestation, coupled with the need for the articulation of a strong rationale for any limitation.

The impact of legislation

It can certainly be observed that the legal picture has contained both continuity and change during the decade under review in the legal landscape of religion and belief. EU changes have been paramount and seem to have strongly overshadowed consideration of international standards and expert views and recommendations related to religion or belief. By far the most evident legal framework in cases related to religion or belief is the encompassing and ambitious innovation which is the *Equality Act*. Its traces are the most evident in the snapshot of the religion or belief landscape during this decade. Its impact on religion or belief has been somewhat challenging.

Taking the religion or belief 'protected characteristic' alone, there is little legal evidence to suggest that it has delivered more robust legal protection for the manifestation of religion or belief compared to the previous decade. However, it should not be forgotten that many religion or belief claimants may also be of an advanced age, with disability, female, racially diverse and/or of varied sexual orientation, and it is in relation to these protected characteristics that they could benefit most from the *Equality Act*. It is also arguable that many of the cases that have arisen over this decade have not represented effective or promising strategic cases for litigating the manifestation of religion or belief.

A possible line of analysis would be that, during this period, some campaigning groups have taken up the opportunity to assert their rights and have intentionally or by default drawn up 'red lines' on these charged and controversial questions. This might include sometimes overstretching the implications of a case and utilizing the media and politicians to get other messages across that have led to something of an imbalance. Broad claims concerning the 'banning of crosses' and of the idea that people of other than Christian religion (and especially Muslims) enjoy more protection than Christians may relate to the claims and concerns about unfair treatment against Christians and a sense of their growing marginalization as reflected in inquiries such as that by Christians in Parliament (2012), and reported in *Clearing the Ground: Preliminary Inquiry into the Freedom of Christians in the UK*.

Given the new opportunities for legal redress it is clear that having a new legal framework is having a complex impact in terms of people's identities and how individuals and groups are perceiving and articulating rights claims. In this context, Chapters 6-8 of this book present substantial reporting of unfair treatment, at least a proportion of which might, if tested through the legal process, be determined to be discrimination in a legal sense. At the same time, an exaggeration of specific legal cases has arguably been one of the strategies used to build up a dissatisfaction which, in some instances, may also have contributed to the development of a sense of victimhood.

It is arguable that aspects of this can be seen, for example, in the four cases that were taken to the ECtHR in 2010 and which the Court decided to consider at the same time, rulings related to which were made in January 2013. These four cases all concerned manifestation in the workplace and, specifically, Christians claiming discrimination in the workplace and violation of their Article 9 rights. They concerned wearing a cross in a customer-facing role at BA (Eweida) and as a NHS nurse (Chaplin), a Relate counsellor refusing to give sexual advice to homosexual couples (MacFarlane) and a Registrar refusing to carry out same-sex civil partnerships (Ladele).

The ECtHR heard all four cases together as *Eweida and others v. UK*, 2013. It is worth noting that the fact that the NHS State hospital had changed its uniform policy in 2007 (Chaplin having worked there since 1989), that BA changed its uniform policy in 2004 (Eweida having worked there since 1999) and the new *Civil Partnership Act* came into force in 2005 (Ladele having worked in Islington since 1992). In the case of MacFaralane, however, he had chosen to pursue Relate's post-graduate diploma in psycho-sexual therapy but was then unwilling to provide psycho-sexual therapy to same-sex couples.

The Court accepted that Eweida's wearing of the cross visibly was a manifestation of her religious belief and part of her desire to bear Christian witness. It is also important to note that British Airways amended its rules on uniforms in February 2007, so the case concerned her refusal to work between September 2006 and February 2007 and the fact that this had been without pay. Violation of Article 9 was found since 'where there is no evidence of any real encroachment on the interests of others, the domestic authorities failed sufficiently to protect the first applicant's [Eweida] right to manifest her religion, in breach of the positive obligation under Article 9' (*Eweida and others v. UK*, 2013: para. 95).

In Chaplin's case, again the Court recognized her reason for wearing the cross was a manifestation of her religious belief and the question was whether the interference with her wearing it was necessary. In this regard, the Court observed that 'the reason for asking her to remove the cross, namely the protection of health and safety on a hospital ward, was inherently of a greater magnitude than that which applied in respect of Ms. Eweida. Moreover, this is a field where the domestic authorities must be allowed a wide (what, in ECtHR jurisprudence is known as) 'margin of appreciation'. Furthermore, it was suggested that the hospital managers were better placed to make decisions about clinical safety than a court' (*Eweida and others v. UK*, 2013: para. 99).

In the case of Ladele, the Court expressed sympathy with the fact that 'it cannot be said that, when she entered into her contract of employment, the applicant specifically waived her right to manifest her religious belief by objecting to participating in the creation of civil partnerships, since this requirement was introduced by her employer at a later date' (*Eweida and others v. UK*, 2013: para. 106). They also acknowledged the strength of her religious conviction and the seriousness of the loss of her job. Nevertheless, the aim had been another of the Convention's objectives, that of securing the rights of others. A violation of Article 9 was not found either in this case or in that of MacFarlane. In the MacFarlane case, unlike in some earlier cases, the Court did not consider:

> an individual's decision to enter into a contract of employment and to undertake responsibilities which he knows will have an impact on his freedom to manifest his religious belief is determinative of the question whether or not there [had] been an interference with Article 9 rights. (*Eweida and others v. UK*, 2013: para. 109)

The question was whether a fair balance had been struck, and here the Court decided that 'the most important factor to be taken into account is that the employer's action was intended to secure the implementation of its policy of providing a service without discrimination' (*Eweida and others v. UK*, 2013: para. 109).

What much of the media coverage and hype around these cases – both prior to and after they had been referred to the ECtHR – failed to acknowledge were critical points such as the fact that BA had in fact changed its uniform policy; how the Christian applicants were not disadvantaged in comparison with colleagues of other religions; how the ECtHR had accepted that all four had been manifesting their religion and the care with which it examined the grounds for the interference with that manifestation. However, it should also be noted that the fact that appeal to Strasbourg reversed the decision in the Eweida case by finding a violation of Article 9, is also a comment on the fact that – at least in this case – UK judges had been overly restrictive regarding manifestation of religion in the workplace.

It would be unfortunate if these publicly fought cases result in more restricted judicial interpretations and a narrowed scope being offered manifestation of religion or belief in England and Wales, thus over-simplifying the complex variety of questions that may arise. In relation to this area of the law, a research report from Woodhead with Catto (2009: vi) had already warned of the risks lying ahead for the EHRC in assuming a mandate also for the protected characteristic of religion or belief, by alerting the Commission of the risks of:

- Clashes between equality strands (e.g. religion and sexual orientation).
- Discrimination by and within religious communities.
- Unfair treatment of secular and non-belief.
- Causing intra-religious resentment by favouring some minority religious groups over others.
- Alienating a majority Christian culture.
- Curtailing religious freedom in the quest for equality and good relations.

Putting aside the question of the Commission, it does seem that a number of these risks seem to have played out in the wider public sphere with regard to the public perception around questions of equality and discrimination in the area of religion or belief in England and Wales. Back in 2007, the then UN Special Rapporteur on Freedom of Religion or Belief (2008: para. 72) held, regarding the *Equality Act*, 2006, that:

> The approach taken by the pertinent anti-discrimination legislation seems to be quite balanced and there are specific exemptions or transitional provisions for organizations relating to religion and belief. Ultimately, balancing different competing rights can only be decided on a case-by-case basis taking into account the particular circumstances and implications of the case.

It would be too premature to conclude that the legal cases that have arisen in England and Wales over the decade in question are now failing to uphold such a careful balancing of competing rights on a case-by-case basis and with due consideration of the particular circumstances and implications of each case. The emphasis of the Special Rapporteur, however, offers a very timely reminder and articulates the public concerns that have arisen as a result of a number of high-profile legal cases that, in the eyes of the applicants, and many religious people more widely, appear to be stacked against them.

Certainly the domestic political scene and the media is a lot more polarized than before regarding the outcome of such cases. In the concluding Chapter 10, we will examine what the findings of the survey and fieldwork completed in 2011 show about how these issues might best be tackled, and offer our own recommendations about the most appropriate signposts for policy, law and practice in the future. We will also note the importance of trying to avoid those from either the media, religion or belief groups or the wider public who want to exaggerate the outcome of legal cases for their sectional benefit, from being successful in gaining undue attention or credibility among an unsuspecting political and public audience.

Religion or Belief Discrimination: Evidence and Methods

Focus of this chapter

As recently as only a few years ago, Woodhead with Catto (2009: 32) argued that 'the evidence base on religious discrimination needs to be improved'. This was indeed the case just over a decade ago when it was reviewed in the *Interim Report* (Weller and Purdam, 2000) of the Home Office commissioned research in 2000. Since then, although it remains incomplete, the evidence base has been growing and is now much stronger than it was.

In this chapter we briefly signpost some of the wider evidence base that now exists concerning discrimination and unfair treatment in relation to religion or belief in Britain before going on to summarize the methods used in our own research to contribute to that evidence base.

The wider evidence base on religion or belief discrimination

The richness and extent of the primary research data gathered by the 2011 research mean that, in order to do justice to this in a way that is also transparent (with regard to methods, as in this chapter) and accessible (through the presentation of sufficient examples, as in Chapters 6-8) to a diverse readership, this book must necessarily primarily focus on that data itself and its analysis. Therefore, while presenting key relevant aspects of the context for the research: historical (Chapter 2), religion and belief (Chapter 3) and legal (Chapter 4), there is no space in this book to review and discuss in detail other relevant research and associated literature.

However, what is possible to do here is to provide signposts to some of the key sources and to highlight some of the key challenges in researching and understanding this area. In this regard (as noted in Chapter 1), one of this book's co-authors was commissioned by the EHRC to undertake a further review of religious discrimination in Britain from 2000 to 2010. This can be accessed through Weller's (2011) *Religious Discrimination in Britain: A Review of Research Evidence, 2000–10* in a report that is available online for access at: www.equalityhumanrights.com/uploaded_files/research/research_report_73_religious_discrimination.pdf, and therefore, that report's discussion of other research will not be repeated here.

Issues in the creation of the evidence base

Modern research data on unfair treatment on the grounds of religion or belief has only been systematically collected and analysed in parallel with the re-emergence (as traced in Chapter 2) of the social and political recognition of religion or belief as a basis for discrimination, and as a distinctive variable in academic research. Until the early 1990s, the focus in both social policy and academic research was more on ethnicity, with religion being of only secondary concern, and often extrapolated on the basis of ethnic data.

However, in the mid-1990s, a shift began to take place in social policy, as signalled by the debates that emerged at that time concerning the possibility of including a religious affiliation question (see Chapter 3) in the decennial Census for England, Wales and Scotland (Weller and Andrews, 1998). Since then, not only both religion and belief themselves, but also religion and belief in relation to a variety of other factors (including that of discrimination) has increasingly been seen as something about which it is important to try to capture data. In particular, this has often been done (see Purdam et al., 2007) to inform both the implementation of equal opportunities policies and practices and in the context of the development and application of the new legal requirements (see Chapter 4).

However, one of the challenges in undertaking such research has been that while small-scale studies on religion have been able to achieve quite a high degree of detail, granularity and texture, their weakness has been that they are not very generalizable. At the same time, large-scale opinion polls and surveys face the challenge of capturing the perspectives and reported experience of relatively smaller parts of the general population, such as religious minorities.

In relation to qualitative data, the EHRC review highlighted that 'Much of the research that has been conducted in relation to "religious discrimination" has, more precisely, addressed the perception or reported experience of "religious discrimination". These meanings may be different to legal definitions of discrimination' (Weller, 2011: v). When examining equality statistics and evidence gaps in religion, Purdam et al. (2007), highlighted that while a number of key surveys conducted in the United Kingdom (such as the Census or the British Social Attitudes Survey) have asked about religious identity, they have not done so specifically about religious discrimination. Nevertheless, the British Crime Survey and the Citizenship Survey, as well as our 2001 project and the Poverty and Social Exclusion Survey, did include questions and data more directly concerned with religious discrimination, as did the (now abolished) Citizenship Survey. Such data can support exploration of the overlap and interaction between religion and other key aspects of people's identities including ethnicity and gender. For example, recent research by Heath and Martin (2012) using the Annual Population and Labour

Force Surveys has identified disadvantage, or what they term 'penalties' in employment in relation to Muslim women in particular but also Muslim men. Also relevant here is the work of Clark and Drinkwater (2009), and of Lindley (2002), who identified evidence of Muslim disadvantage in the labour market after controlling for other factors including ethnicity, which varied according to the different national and ethnic backgrounds within Muslim populations (see also Dale et al., 2006). Most recently, research by Donald et al (2012) has explored the responses of different groups to the law relating to religion or belief, including with reference to the workplace.

There are also three multi-country surveys that include questions and data of relevance to religious discrimination in the United Kingdom. These include the Eurobarometer Surveys, the European Social Survey (ESS) and European Values Survey (EVS) which is in turn linked with the broader, global, World Values Survey. These surveys both provide data of direct relevance to the United Kingdom (in the case of the Eurobarometer Survey in an undifferentiated way and, in the case of the EVS, with separate data for Great Britain and for Northern Ireland). However, they also allow that data to be contextualized within an understanding of these issues within the European Union (Eurobarometer) of which the United Kingdom is a member state, and the wider Europe (EVS) in which many countries are also States parties to the ECHR.

One of the difficulties involved in trying to locate our own research is that the evidence base that is directly applicable to England and Wales remains 'patchy' in the sense that what exists has been conducted with a range of geographical referents that make comparison difficult and has been conducted in a wide variety of ways. Thus, in relation to surveys, reviews and discussions in the United Kingdom, some have been specifically on Scotland (Nicholson, 2002; McAspurren, 2005; Bruce et al., 2005) and on Northern Ireland (O'Brien, 2010); there has been research (like our own) that has focused on England and Wales together; while there has been little that relates only to England or to Wales (see Chaney, 2009; Winckler, 2009). In itself this underlines the need for further research bearing in mind that the 'four nations state' of the United Kingdom is becoming increasingly distinctive not only in relation to national, cultural, linguistic and religious features, but now also in terms of substantial areas of governance and policy. Although Northern Ireland was beyond the scope of our research and the main focus of this book is on 'Britain' (rather than that of the United Kingdom), as Weller's (2011: ix) EHRC review notes:

> There is a relative lack of comparative research on religious discrimination and sectarianism across the parts of the United Kingdom. While Northern Ireland as such is beyond the scope of this review, given the much longer history there of legislation, policy and research relating to these matters, more comparative research could be helpful in better understanding unfair treatment on the basis of religion or belief and particularly in identifying 'good practice' to tackle it.

In relation to much of the larger-scale survey data that has been collected as part of wider European Union and/or European referenced research, it should be noted that it has been shaped by research questions and themes that may not always entirely match those which would fully reflect the specificities of Britain, the United Kingdom or its constituent countries.

Bearing all this in mind, the remainder of this chapter explains key aspects of how the survey, fieldwork and Knowledge Exchange Workshops, which generated the primary research data that is reported on in Chapters 6-8 and analysed in Chapter 9, were planned and implemented.

Research methods for survey, fieldwork and Knowledge Exchange data

The 2011 research

The heart of this book reports on and analyses the results of the 'Religious Discrimination in England and Wales Research Project: Theory, Policy and Practice (2000-10)' conducted in 2010-12. We explore the extensive, rich and textured primary survey and fieldwork evidence across key sectors of social experience. By comparison with similar research conducted in 2000, some unique longitudinal insight is possible. We consider experience in relation to education; employment and the media (see Chapter 6); criminal justice and immigration; housing; health care, social services, planning and other services; and funding and benefits (see Chapter 7); as well as in relation to other religious groups and in relation to religious groups from political, community and other pressure groups (Chapter 8). Because of this, the second section of this chapter now sets out the main approaches to and methods used in gathering the primary research data that are presented in each of the three chapters that follow.

The survey of religious organizations

Issues and approaches, sample and responses

During 2010-11, a postal and online questionnaire survey was undertaken of a stratified sample of 1,754 national and local religious organizations in England and Wales. A sample frame similar to that used in the survey completed in 2000 was constructed. It consisted of national, regional and local organizations, including small house-based groups and large 'umbrella' organizations to which other organizations are affiliated, together with places of worship of different religious groups, as well as inter-faith groups. As set out in Table 5.1 it was designed broadly to reflect the diversity of the religious population of England and Wales.

To enable longitudinal comparison of the results, the vast majority of the questions asked by the survey completed in 2000 were also asked in that completed in 2011. A number of new questions were also added (see below) in order to capture areas of change (especially in policy and in law) over the past decade. The hard copy and online questionnaires were piloted with a small number of organizations.

All of the 628 organizations that responded to the 2001 survey were included in the 2011 survey sample unless, after thorough searches, they were found no longer to exist. Where it was clear that this was so, they were replaced, as far as possible, by other

Table 5.1 Sample of organizations in 2000 and 2011, by religion

Religion	Sample in 2011	Organizations responding in 2011	Organizations responding in 2000 and included in the 2011 sample	Organizations responding in both 2000 and 2011
Bahá'í	50	36	20	16
Buddhist	100	39	28	14
Christian	645	187	237	82
Other Christian	67	21	41	16
Hindu	99	27	31	13
Inter-faith	108	26	20	2
Jain	43	7	7	2
Jewish	150	43	32	16
Muslim	300	69	65	23
Sikh	99	18	32	7
Zoroastrian	11	4	4	1
Pagan/NRM	65	20	20	8
Other	17	2	0	1
Total	1,754	499	537	201

Notes: 'NRM' is an abbreviation for 'New Religious Movement' – a terminology employed in the academic study of religion for groups that in popular discourse are sometimes labelled as 'sects' and/or 'cults'. 'Other Christian' is used in our research to differentiate groups that have an historic relationship with the Christian tradition but the nature of which is disputed by the majority and predominantly Trinitarian Christian tradition. 'Other' is used in our research for other groups that do not clearly fall into any other part of the project's taxonomy. Also included are 'inter-faith organizations' which are not composed of single religions. The project *Technical Report*, located on the project's website, provides further information on, and discussion about, the approach taken to sampling and the project's research methods in general. It can be accessed at: www.derby.ac.uk/religion-and-society.

similar organizations in terms of religious group and operation at a local or national level. Replacements were made using information from the database underlying the *Religions in the UK* directory (Weller, 2007a). However, where necessary (e.g. in particular in relation to Pagan and New Religious Movement organizations) searches in other directories and internet searches covering specific religious groups were conducted.

Four hundred and ninety-nine responses were received, giving an overall response rate of almost 29 per cent. The responses broadly reflect the pattern of different religious groups across England and Wales. The vast majority of those responding to the survey did so by paper copy, but a minority completed it in an online format. In terms of the longitudinal aspects of the survey, 537 (or almost 31 per cent) of the organizations that had been in the sample in 2000 and responded to that survey were also included in 2011. Of these, as again set out in Table 5.1 by religion, 201 organizations (almost 12% of the total sample) responded to both the surveys.

Limitations of the survey

Since the survey operates on the basis of self-reporting, its results inevitably reflect the particular perspectives of those responding to it. In addition, as with the survey of the 2000 project, and as critiqued by Macey and Carling (2011: 68-9), it is acknowledged that there are issues and limitations involved in surveying religious organizations rather than individuals. As was previously acknowledged (Weller et al., 2001: 5), this included the challenge for the person responding on behalf of the organization to be able to reflect the experience of the membership of their organizations or (in the case of some questions) of their religious group more generally. At the same time, not all of the questions sought an organizational response, since those concerned with policy and with measures to tackle discrimination specifically sought the personal views of the respondents.

In 2000, and as noted in its technical report (Weller et al., 2001: 147-70), one of the main reasons for surveying organizations rather than individuals was the absence, prior to the 2001 decennial Census, of other than (often quite widely differing) estimated data concerning the numbers of people associated with each religious group, thus making difficult the construction of an adequate sampling frame by reference to population. The *Technical Report* nevertheless articulated what could be achieved, noting (Weller, 2001: 5) that there was evidence that, before responding, at least a number of the respondents undertook wider consultation within their organizations.

To enable longitudinal comparison between the results of our survey completed in 2011 and that which took place in 2000, a very similar methodology was employed. As will be seen in Chapters 6-8, the results from organizations providing responses to both the 2000 and 2011 surveys therefore provide some additional evidence about how the reported experience of their members might have changed or been persistent over time for those particular organizations. Caution needs to be exercised in relation to the weight given to these results because it is unlikely the questionnaire was completed by the same person at each point in time, and the membership of the organization may have changed. This subset is also too small to allow detailed comparison by religious group or tradition. However, it does represent a unique data source for examining the changes in reported experience of unfair treatment over time for a specific group of organizations.

Survey analysis and results

In discussing the results from the survey in relation to each of the sectors of society covered in Chapters 6-8, at the start of each section within the chapter an overall picture is presented based on the total number of responses across all the organizations and religious groups. While, as previously explained, our sample was carefully constructed to reflect a range of factors, the overall picture that can be derived from the responses taken across all responding organizations is subject to limitations that could make such results misleading if read as offering more than indicative insight and/or if taken on their own. These overview indications are therefore complemented by more granulated and comparable data relating to the percentage/proportion of different responses derived from responding organizations *within* each individual religious group.

When considering the results from the project survey it is also important to note that, as with the results of the survey conducted in the previous project, *only those responses are reported where respondents indicated some experience of the specific area under discussion.* Thus, those respondents who indicated *no experience* of the specific area concerned are *excluded* from the analysis.

The presentation and discussion of the statistical data from the survey is followed by collations of selected brief comments contributed by survey respondents after each section in the questionnaire. These 'write-in' comments provide insight into some of the individual stories and experiences that are behind the statistical findings from the survey. They highlight not only specific instances of reported unfair treatment on the basis of religion, but also point to how the respondents perceive, and are affected by, such experiences. The comments have been selected to be illustrative of a range of the kind of issues identified by organizations across a range of religions.

The fieldwork

Fieldwork interview samples

Complementing the survey, semi-structured (individual and group) interviews were also conducted that involved 234 participants from the religion or belief, voluntary and community, public, private and legal sectors in five localities: Blackburn, Cardiff, Leicester, Norwich and the London Borough of Newham. With the exception of Norwich, fieldwork had also been conducted in these areas in the 2000 project.

The original areas were selected with a view to having a spread of different kinds of religion and belief demographics, including Wales (Cardiff) as well as England; locations with a large Muslim minority but only smaller numbers of other than Christian and Muslim religious groups (Blackburn); locations in which substantial other than Muslim minorities were present – as with Leicester, which could be said to be the Hindu and Jain 'capital' of England; and Newham as a cosmopolitan London Borough. The fact that four out of five of the fieldwork locations were also the focus of research in the fieldwork completed in 2000 enabled longitudinal comparison to be made also between the results of the qualitative research as well as the quantitative. However, our project also added Norwich as a fieldwork location – both as an urban area with a significant rural hinterland, and also as one that, during the decade under review, had seen some significant numbers of so-called new migrants from Eastern and Central Europe such as Poland, Bulgaria and Romania, following the accession of these countries to full EU membership.

Informed by aspects of an anthropological approach, the project's field researcher spent a total of approximately one month in each locality in order to try to gain a broad sense of the locality. Participants in each of the fieldwork interviews were identified with reference to local religious demographics through a combination of contacting religious groups on which the project held contact information; research into key organizations and contacts in the public, private and voluntary sectors; local media press releases and other media coverage; and finally, snowball sampling.

In total 234 people were involved in interviews. Table 5.2 shows the number of interviewees by category of interview and fieldwork location. Table 5.3 sets out a breakdown, by religion, of those who were interviewed and were aligned with a specific religious organization, while Table 5.4 sets out a breakdown, by religion, of interviews

Table 5.2 Interviews by location and category of interview

Location	People from religious organizations	Advice organizations	Services/ employers	Biographies	Total
Leicester	28	7	2	12	49
Cardiff	34	9	2	8	53
Blackburn	16	13	6	4	39
Newham	15	13	4	8	40
Norwich	26	8	10	9	53
Total	119	50	24	41	234

Note: The totals above include interviews with individuals on their own and those interviewed as part of a group.

Table 5.3 Interviews by religion of religious organization and location

Religion	Leicester	Cardiff	Blackburn	Newham	Norwich	Total
Bahá'í	6				2	8
Buddhist	4	2	1	3	2	12
Christian	4	13	9	4	6	36
Druid			1			1
Hindu	2	5	2	4		13
Inter-faith	1		2		1	4
Jain	5					5
Jewish	2	2			3	7
Muslim	2	2	1		1	6
Pagan	1	2			3	6
Sikh		7		2	8	17
Other	1					1
Sri Krishna Consciousness*		1		2		3
Total	28	34	16	15	26	119

Note: *Participants who identified themselves in relation to Sri Krishna Consciousness are noted separately here rather than under the category of Hindu because in this instance this is how they explained they wanted to be identified.

Table 5.4 Biographical interviews by religion and location

Religion	Leicester	Cardiff	Blackburn	Newham	Norwich	Total
Bahá'í		2				2
Buddhist	1					1
Christian	4	4	1	3	3	15
Hindu				1		1
Inter-faith				1		1
Muslims	3	2	2	2	1	10
Pagan	1				5	6
Sikh	3		1	1		5
Total	12	8	4	8	9	41

that were held specifically to explore the individual's own life experience rather that the experiences of organizations. Biographical interviewees involved a broad balance of males and females, and a spread of (estimated) ages between 20 and 80 years old.

Focus group samples

In addition to the fieldwork interviews, focus groups were held in each of the fieldwork locations involving, in all, 40 participants (5 in Leicester, 11 in Cardiff, 7 in Blackburn, 9 in Newham and 8 in Norwich) who understood themselves to be, in some sense, non-religious people. A key part of the 2011 project research design that went beyond what took place in 2000 was, in a more deliberate way, to try to capture the reported experience of those who do not see or understand themselves primarily by reference to the category of 'religion'.

One reason for this is that, in the decade since the 2000 research, the legal provisions brought in to address discrimination on the grounds of religion were framed in terms not of 'religion' only, but of 'religion or belief'. The intention of this has been for law and associated policy and practice also to cover those who live by other than religious ethical and/or philosophical systems and values. However, at least at present, the legal and policy terminology of 'belief' has not gained sufficient recognition to do full service in terms of the self-recognition of those whose participation in the project the focus groups were intended to secure.

Therefore, for practical purposes the project used the terminology of 'non-religious'. The limitations and difficulties involved in doing this are acknowledged. In particular, this is a 'negative' form of description. The terminology of 'secular' was not used by the project to frame its survey or fieldwork questions, and it should be noted that although this is frequently used in public debate as if there were a widespread shared understanding of its meaning, this is not the case (Weller, 2006). Similarly, as discussed in Chapter 1, the terminologies of 'religion' are also not without their own difficulties.

Partly because of the terminological issues noted above, the recruitment of focus group participants proved to be particularly challenging. Although there are relevant organized groups – such as humanist organizations, many of which are affiliated to the British Humanist Association, or secular/ist ones affiliated to the National Secular Society – these have a small active membership relative to the larger population that does not understand itself as religious as in the case of organized religious groups relative to those understanding themselves as religious. Thus, while national organizations and local groups of organized atheists, humanists and secularists were contacted, together with local individuals identified in the British Humanist Association's directory of humanist celebrants, it was important that participation should not be limited only to those affiliated to these organized expressions of the non-religious.

Instead, an attempt was made for participation in the focus groups to reflect the full and wide spectrum of those who might in some way recognize themselves as 'non-religious' or as simply being without any religious affiliation (see further Cheruvallil-Contractor et al., 2013). Because of the challenges involved in trying both to identify and engage such populations, the project fieldworker also used wider mechanisms to aid recruitment, including 'snowballing' (Atkinson and Flint, 2001; Noy, 2008) for three or four weeks prior to each focus group discussion.

Advertisements targeted at both general and more specifically non-religious audiences were placed online and a poster was widely disseminated both online and offline, asking readers if they were 'religious' and inviting those who did *not* see themselves as such to participate in the discussion. Finally, focus group venues were identified which it was thought would more likely be perceived to be neutral with regard to 'religion or belief', such as meeting rooms attached to libraries or community centres. Individuals who eventually participated in the focus groups were from different standpoints that may be considered 'non-religious', including those who were content to use the self-descriptions of 'humanist', 'atheist', 'secularist' but also those who did not consider themselves religious but who also did not subscribe to any other group or label.

Working with the fieldwork and focus group data

Each section of Chapters 6–8 includes direct quotations (which, it should be noted, are not edited for grammar) from the fieldwork interviews and focus groups which describe in more detail the different kinds of reported experience of unfair treatment. In the first instance, the selection was made of material which addressed the key aims and objectives of the research. Further selection took place that adds to the overall analysis, by way of either confirmation, further illumination, or contrast with and divergence from, what the quantitative results suggest. The experiences and stories told by people were organized and analysed through the use of NVivo software and discussed in relation to a number of themes (reflected in the titles of sub-headings of Chapters 6–8) that were identified from reflection on their stories.

It should be noted that participants in the fieldwork and the focus groups were assured of anonymity and confidentiality and so are not identified. However, in order to contextualize their comments and quotes, when these appear in Chapters 6–10 we have used 'labels' for participants. Depending on the context in which a comment or a quote is being used, this provides relevant information such as religion, ethnicity/'race', approximate age, gender, occupation and also, occasionally, location and other information that may help to contextualize the contributions of the participants. Nevertheless, because of our commitment to participants' anonymity, these labels often omit specific pieces or combinations of information that might have added to any risk of the participants being personally identified. The labels are therefore not always consistent across the text.

Local fieldwork area profiles

Introduction

Together with a brief overview of each area derived from the fieldwork conducted there, the religion or belief statistical profiles of these areas are included in Tables 5.5–5.9 as a contextualization for the project's fieldwork. These area profiles combine some key and directly relevant available quantitative data – statistics and 'facts' – about each of the areas. In each of these tables, the 2001 statistics for religion are derived from *Census 2001 Table KS07 Religion, local authorities in England and Wales*, while the 2011 figures are taken from *Census 2011: Table KS209EW: Religion, local authorities in England and Wales*. The figures for ethnicity are taken from *Census 2011: Table KS201EW ethnic group, local authorities in England; unitary authorities in Wales*. Data on unemployment is taken from a range of on-line sources associated with each of the local authorities concerned. But profiles also include qualitative data that quotes the opinions and experiences of research participants who lived and/or worked in each of these areas and are reflective, in a broad anthropological sense, of the key themes that emerged during the fieldwork and focus groups.

Blackburn

Blackburn is a town in the north-west of England with a total population of 147,489. In the results of the 2011 Census, among 348 local authorities in England and Wales, it ranks sixth for its Asian/Asian British: Pakistani population, and eleventh for its Asian/ Asian British: Indian population. It has relatively high levels of unemployment, at 9.9 per cent of the population. The 2001 Census indicated that Muslims constitute around 19 per cent of the population. During fieldwork discussions, participants estimated the Muslim population to be much higher, and this was broadly confirmed by the results of the 2011 Census as set out in Table 5.5, according to which Blackburn with Darwen has the third largest Muslim population in England.

Another indicator of the town's strong Muslim presence is that it has around 45 mosques. Just above 50 per cent of the population is, however, still reported as being Christian, while populations of other religious groups are much smaller. During fieldwork, participants commented that Blackburn may be understood as a town with

Table 5.5 Self-identification by religion in the 2001 and 2011 Censuses by numbers and proportions of the population of Blackburn with Darwen, and ranking by local authority

Religion	Numbers in 2001	Numbers in 2011	Percentage in 2001	Percentage in 2011	Ranking in 2011
Buddhist	159	306	0.1	0.2	283
Christian	87,001	77,599	63.3	52.6	308
Hindu	423	574	0.3	0.4	166
Jewish	53	54	0.0	0.0	304
Muslim	26,674	39,817	19.4	27.0	3
Sikh	138	161	0.1	0.1	186
Other religion	188	295	0.2	0.2	341
Total all religions	*114,636*	*118,806*	*83.4*	*80.5*	–
No religion	10,981	20,374	8.0	13.8	342
Not stated	11,853	8,309	8.6	5.6	341
No religion/not stated	*22,834*	*28,683*	*16.6*	*19.4*	–
Total	*137,470*	*147,489*			*N = 384*

Note: 'Ranking' is by numerical rank order of percentage of a particular religion population relative to 384 local authorities across England and Wales. Percentages may not total exactly 100% due to the cumulative effect of the decimal points.

two main and visible religious groups (Christian and Muslim) along with non-religious voices.

Socio-economically, Blackburn includes some of the most deprived areas in the country. This together with relatively high unemployment rates; a town centre that (according to Blackburn residents who were interviewed) is in dire need of an overhaul; and a general paucity of resources, means that there are tensions. In 2007, Blackburn was featured in a *BBC Panorama* (2007) programme documentary about divided cities and no-go areas, although as will be seen in the section on the media in Chapter 6, a large proportion of the fieldwork participants from Blackburn expressed anger about this depiction of their town. They recognized that there were some 'all-Asian' and 'all-white' areas in Blackburn, but they did not think this meant that people did not get on with each other.

However many interviewees felt that the 'Northern mill town' and *Panorama* stereotypes were unhelpful in these matters. By contrast, the following description of Blackburn in relation to matters of religion or belief in the town, and given by an elderly, white, inter-faith worker, reflects the overall anthropological sense of the town as gained from the fieldwork completed there in 2011:

> There are two dominant faiths in Blackburn, the Muslim and the Christian community. In terms of the interaction between the two faiths I think they are quite open and transparent, in terms of faith wise, we all seem to get on well together but there are going to be pockets of areas and individuals who will have a difference of opinion. How they then voice those opinions is a different matter itself. From a general note, we seem to have a good communication between all faiths.

Cardiff

Cardiff is the capital city of Wales and home to the Welsh Assembly Government, with a population of 346,090. According to results of the 2011 Census, from among our five fieldwork areas Cardiff has the second highest proportion (80%) of white (English/Welsh/Scottish/Northern Irish/British) people in its population. Norwich, another of our fieldwork locations, has the highest proportion. At the end of 2012, unemployment in Cardiff stood at around 4.3 per cent of the population. As Table 5.6 shows, its population includes a noticeable presence of all diverse religious groups.

As a port city Cardiff has a heritage of religious and ethnic diversity and one of the oldest Muslim populations in Britain, which may go back as far as the mid-1800s. Cardiff participants in the fieldwork seemed generally aware of the historical aspects of its diversity, including why some areas such as Bute Town are historically more diverse because of a history of seafarers living there. The vast majority of the participants in our fieldwork in Cardiff seemed to be relatively at ease with the extent of the city's diversity, as reflected in the census results. A white Christian woman voluntary services worker gave expression to what was, broadly speaking, also the research-informed sense of the city, as gained from the fieldwork completed there in 2011:

> I'm from Cardiff, born and bred, in Cardiff . . . old traditional area of Cardiff . . .
> Right on the edge of the docks area [. . .] So I'm just thinking about the 50 years

Table 5.6 Self-identification by religion in the 2001 and 2011 Censuses by numbers and proportions of the population of Cardiff, and ranking by local authority

Religion	Numbers in 2001	Numbers in 2011	Percentage in 2001	Percentage in 2011	Ranking in 2011
Buddhist	1,004	1,690	0.3	0.5	76
Christian	204,359	177,743	66.9	51.4	315
Hindu	2,392	4,736	0.8	1.4	68
Jewish	941	802	0.3	0.2	74
Muslim	11,261	23,656	3.7	6.8	54
Sikh	928	1,317	0.3	0.4	83
Other religion	760	1,406	0.2	0.4	142
Total all religions	*221,645*	*211,350*	*72.6*	*61.1*	—
No religion	57,440	109,960	18.8	31.8	37
Not stated	26,268	24,780	8.6	7.2	169
No religion/not stated	*83,708*	*134,740*	*27.4*	*39.0*	—
Total	*305,353*	*346,090*			*N = 384*

Note: 'Ranking' is by numerical rank order of percentage of a particular religion population relative to 384 local authorities across England and Wales. Percentages may not total exactly 100% due to the cumulative effect of the decimal points.

of my growing up. [Diversity and Cohesion has] always been part and parcel of the Cardiff I've known. I have lived in other cities [. . .] and I've always thought about Cardiff as somewhere where maybe it's cos there's a lot of longstanding communities. [. . .] I'd be fascinated to know about places like Norwich, where maybe for the first time some communities are experiencing different groups moving into the area. Think they're going to go through tensions that maybe happened here a 100 years ago I don't know.

Reflective of this woman's contribution, fieldwork participants in Cardiff seemed generally at ease with the city's various religious and non-religious groups. However, in comparison with the fieldwork city of Leicester, there seemed to be comparatively little overt or organized inter-faith and inter-community dialogue activity in Cardiff. Furthermore, participants reported that where this exists, dialogue initiatives seem to be driven and funded by community bodies rather than being funded by the government. Many participants in the fieldwork and in the Knowledge Exchange Workshop held in Cardiff made a distinction between Cardiff city and 'the Valleys', which were seen as less diverse and perhaps less accepting of diversity.

This was also an aspect of the location's 'Welshness', in relation to which it is important to note that Wales has no established church, the Church in Wales having been disestablished in 1920. A majority of the visible religious minority interviewees also mentioned being happier to live in Wales than in England, commenting that they felt the indigenous population of Wales was perhaps more hospitable and friendly than in England. Reflecting this, a number of black and minority ethnic communities had begun the process of identifying themselves as 'Welsh'. In this context self-descriptions also of 'Welsh Muslim' and 'Welsh Hindu' were heard, while within this a small minority expressed a commitment to learning the Welsh language.

There was a perception that the commitment and sensitivity to faith issues on the part of the Welsh Government was better than in England, which was also reinforced by the general perspective of participants in the project's Knowledge Exchange Workshop held in Cardiff. This was on the grounds that, since devolution, they had a sense that government had in general become closer and more accountable. Comments were also made about discrimination related to being Welsh.

Leicester

Leicester is a city in the English East Midlands, with a population of 329,839. In the 2011 Census, 28 per cent of its population is categorized as Asian/Asian British: Indian which is the highest out of all (348) local authority areas in England and Wales. As illustrated in Table 5.7, Leicester is also a religiously diverse city with large Christian, Hindu, Muslim and Sikh populations and significant Jewish, Buddhist and Bahá'í populations. It also has one of the largest Jain populations in England. In 2012, it had an unemployment rate of around 6.2 per cent.

In the course of the fieldwork, Leicester also came across as a city that seemed to be very aware of its religious and ethnic diversity. There are a number of publicly funded and voluntary bodies involved in inter-faith dialogue and other initiatives for religion and belief groups, although there were some criticisms that such interventions do not always connect with the wider public. Nevertheless, the research participants in Leicester were generally of the opinion that, because of these activities, Leicester is more cohesive, having better inter-faith and inter-community relations than other British cities. In this connection, reference was made to 'the Leicester way of life'. Reflective of an overall sense of the city gained

Table 5.7 Self-identification by religion in the 2001 and 2011 Censuses by numbers and proportions of the population of Leicester, and ranking by local authority

Religion	Numbers in 2001	Numbers in 2011	Percentage in 2001	Percentage in 2011	Ranking in 2011
Buddhist	638	1,224	0.2	0.4	121
Christian	125,187	106,872	44.7	32.4	347
Hindu	41,248	50,087	14.7	15.2	3
Jewish	417	295	0.1	0.1	183
Muslim	30,885	61,440	11.0	18.6	11
Sikh	11,796	14,457	4.2	4.4	12
Other religion	1,179	1,839	0.4	0.6	45
Total all religions	*211,350*	*236,214*	*75.5*	*71.6*	—
No religion	48,789	75,280	17.4	22.8	255
Not stated	19,782	18,345	7.1	5.6	343
No religion not stated	*68,571*	*93,625*	*24.5*	*28.4*	—
Total	*279,921*	*329,839*			*N = 384*

Note: 'Ranking' is by numerical rank order of percentage of a particular religion population relative to 384 local authorities across England and Wales. Percentages may not total exactly 100% due to the cumulative effect of the decimal points.

from the fieldwork completed in 2011, a male Brahmakumari research participant observed that:

> I think on one level Leicester is a very tolerant society and it's probably about exception to a lot of other cities [. . .] or certainly up north where it's very much an us and them type of attitude. Here I think the reason why it works is people are willing to educate others. People are willing to open their doors to show them what their religion, what their faith, what their philosophy is about and when people see that basically, the underlying theme is the same as what they believe in. They want happiness, they want peace, they want contentment but it's just that they perhaps go in a different way and when you break down these barriers that's when you remove prejudice, that's when you remove fear. So that's the unique thing about Leicester.

Secular perspectives are also a very visible part of this in Leicester because of it being the home to the historic Leicester Secular Society and its Secular Hall which was first opened in 1881.

A number of fieldwork participants mentioned a march organized by the English Defence League (EDL) in Leicester in October 2010. Interestingly, rather than focusing on the march as such, the narratives that were shared focused on Leicester's reaction to the march – which was embodied in a 'One Leicester' event which was a celebration of diversity and community cohesion and was organized by the city council, community leaders and religion or belief groups on the day after the march.

Newham

The London Borough of Newham has a population of 307,984. It has the smallest proportion (17%) of white (English/Welsh/Scottish/Northern Irish/British) population out of all (348) local authority areas in England and Wales. Newham is also one of the most ethnically and religiously diverse of all the cities. In addition, it is one of the most socially and economically deprived areas in London and in England. It has the highest unemployment rate of all London Boroughs at 15 per cent of the population.

As can be seen from Table 5.8, according to the 2011 Census, its diversity has increased since 2001. Similar to Blackburn, Newham has large Christian and Muslim populations (second largest in England). However, unlike Blackburn it also has large Hindu and Sikh populations. Historically Newham had a large Jewish presence but over the last century this community has almost entirely moved out.

Participants often said that discrimination in Newham is frequently based not on religion or race but on economic considerations. Many research participants, and in particular those who had lived in Newham for the last twenty years or more, commented that they had lived through and observed previous demographic changes as new populations moved in and some older ones moved out. This overall sense of the

Table 5.8 Self-identification by religion in the 2001 and 2011 Censuses by numbers and proportions of the population of the London Borough of Newham, and ranking by local authority

Religion	Numbers in 2001	Numbers in 2011	Percentage in 2001	Percentage in 2011	Ranking in 2011
Buddhist	1,592	2,446	0.7	0.8	32
Christian	114,247	123,119	46.8	40.0	342
Hindu	16,901	26,962	6.9	8.8	7
Jewish	481	342	0.2	0.1	153
Muslim	59,293	98,456	24.3	32.0	2
Sikh	6,897	6,421	2.8	2.1	19
Other religion	664	1,090	0.3	0.4	213
Total all religions	*200,075*	*258,836*	*82.00*	*84.0*	—
No religion	21,978	29,373	9.0	9.5	348
Not stated	21,838	19,775	9.0	6.4	283
No religion/not stated	*43,816*	*49,148*	*18.00*	*15.9*	—
Total	*243,891*	*307,984*			*N = 384*

Note: 'Ranking' is by numerical rank order of percentage of a particular religion population relative to 384 local authorities across England and Wales. Percentages may not total exactly 100% due to the cumulative effect of the decimal points.

Borough, gained from the fieldwork completed in 2011, is reflected in the following observation from a voluntary sector employee in the Borough:

> As immigration has continued and as our Newham borough has become more cultured and diverse a lot of these people with their prejudice views have either changed their views, I would like to think, and acclimatised to diversity either grudgingly or have embraced, which is what it should be.

Linked with this were a number of comments about Newham's legacy of religious and ethnic diversity. For example, it was noted that as new faith communities moved in they needed places where they could worship but that they did not always have the spaces or resources. An innovative response to this was by using space in community centres that, reportedly, could be hired at reasonable rates. Participants described community centres that in the 1980s and 1990s simultaneously hosted Muslim, Hindu, Sikh and Pagan worship as well as minority Christian groups, such as Lithuanian and black majority churches. Some of these groups – particularly South Asian Muslim, Sikh and Hindu communities – have since become more established and have found the resources to establish their own places of worship, while other groups that have moved to Newham continue to use shared community spaces.

Norwich

Norwich is a city in the east of England but with a significant rural hinterland. It has a population of 132,564. The population has the highest proportion (87%) of white (English/Welsh/Scottish/Northern Irish/British) from among the five fieldwork areas in this project. It has an unemployment rate of 4.7 per cent.

Table 5.9 Self-identification by religion in the 2001 and 2011 Censuses by numbers and proportions of the population of Norwich, and ranking by local authority

Religion	Numbers in 2001	Numbers in 2011	Percentage in 2001	Percentage in 2011	Ranking in 2011
Buddhist	485	978	0.4	0.7	35
Christian	73,428	59,515	60.4	44.9	331
Hindu	348	1,017	0.3	0.8	113
Jewish	239	241	0.2	0.2	101
Muslim	887	2,612	0.7	2.0	116
Sikh	102	168	0.1	0.1	169
Other religion	619	886	0.5	0.7	17
Total all religions	*76,108*	*65,417*	*62.6*	*49.4*	—
No religion	33,766	56,268	27.8	42.5	1
Not stated	11,676	10,827	9.6	8.2	39
No religion/not stated	*45,442*	*67,095*	*37.4*	*50.7*	—
Total	*121,550*	*132,512*			*N = 384*

Note: 'Ranking' is by numerical rank order of percentage of a particular religion population relative to 384 local authorities across England and Wales. Percentages may not total exactly 100% due to the cumulative effect of the decimal points.

Norwich was the fieldwork location that was added to the project as compared with the research completed in 2000. It is very different from the other fieldwork locations in that, as can be seen from Table 5.9, it has significantly less religious and ethnic diversity. Research participants in Norwich recognized its difference and spoke about having a sense of being disconnected and 'tucked' away from the rest of the country.

Historically, Norwich was a rich medieval Christian city and has a large number of historic church buildings. Like Liverpool it has two Christian cathedrals – Anglican and Catholic. Many participants described it as until recently having been almost 'mono-cultural'. However over the last decade there has been an observable increase in its religious and racial diversity, as is also evident in a comparison of census figures from 2001 and 2011. Reflecting the overall sense of the city gained from the fieldwork completed there in 2011, as two Buddhist women in Norwich put it, making intersecting comments:

> Well there's been a big change in Norwich I think. And that is being that the living here has changed dramatically. [. . .] Norwich, because its never had like, a motorway up to it, and so on, it's been a little enclave on its own. And it was, I found it, very old fashioned. [. . .] Totally un-politically correct. [. . .] So I think, I think although I've got no evidence of it, I think it's probably changed quite a lot, in terms of prejudice, in all sorts of ways. [. . .] It's like, wow people actually have, you know, different, just different appearances, and there's a bit more diversity I think, than there used to be, and that, with that brings tolerance.

As part of this, a number of Norwich residents spoke about an observable increase in Eastern European migrant populations, albeit that these have been concentrated mostly in rural areas of Norfolk surrounding Norwich – such as in the Great Yarmouth/ Thetford/King's Lynn 'triangle' – with Norwich being at the centre of the 'triangle'.

According to the 2011 Census Norwich also has the distinguishing feature of now having the highest population of 'no religion' respondents to the Census question on religious affiliation (in the 2001 Census, it was Brighton and Hove). As yet, it does not seem that there is any consensus around understanding the specific local factors that might have led to this change.

Knowledge Exchange Workshops

During Autumn 2012 (see Chapter 1 for dates and locations), a series of five Knowledge Exchange Workshops were held in Cardiff, Derby, London, Manchester and Oxford. They were not organized as traditional dissemination events to communicate and discuss finalized research results. Rather, they were an integral part of the research process. In total, 211 practitioners took part, enrolling in the workshops under a primary or related category for their work or identity. The attendees included 40 from the public sector; 8 from the private sector; 106 from the religion or belief sector; 45 from the voluntary and community sector; and 12 from the legal sector.

In each workshop, following a plenary session, participants were split into breakout groups, as far as possible according to sector. In these groups, attendees were asked to address whether and how far the project's interim findings resonated with the experience of their organization or group; how far that experience diverged from the interim findings; and whether they identified any additional issues.

Evidence from these workshops has been incorporated into the development of our project findings. In particular it contributed to the identification and discussion, in Chapter 10, of policy, legal and other options for tackling discrimination and unfair treatment on the basis of religion or belief including the project's *Policy Brief* document, a copy of which can be accessed from the project website at: www.derby.ac.uk/religion-and-society.

Engaging with the research findings

Having outlined the rationale, planning and methods used for the survey and fieldwork completed in 2011 and the Knowledge Exchange Workshops completed in 2012, in Chapters 6-8 we focus on the key findings from our research.

6

Experience of Unfair Treatment in Education, Employment and Media

Introduction

In the 2000 research, education together with employment and the media were the areas in which reported experience of unfair treatment was most often highlighted, with the media being identified as 'the most frequent source of unfairness by people from all religious traditions' (Weller et al., 2001: 8). This has remained the case in the 2011 research. We consider these three spheres below.

Unfair treatment in education

I think I shouldn't be bullied just because I go to church. (Interview with a white, female, Christian secondary school pupil)

Education in social and religious context

Schools, colleges and universities are contexts in which identities are first articulated and negotiated not only by pupils and students, but also by their parents and guardians. Such institutions are also often one of the first sustained points of contact between young people and the state. The education sector across the United Kingdom has been subject to considerable policy and legal change in the last decade, both in terms of curriculum content and the impact upon education of equalities legislation.

Experience of unfair treatment in education: survey findings

Survey findings: The overall picture

The surveys completed in 2000 and in 2011 collected the reported experience of unfair treatment among members of religious organizations in relation to: the attitudes and behaviour of school teachers, college and university staff, education officers, school pupils and college/university students, as well as the content of RE and Citizenship

Studies, the practice of collective worship, together with organizational policies and practices in education. Responses to the questions provide a valuable insight into how members of religious organizations experience unfair treatment in relation to this area. As is the case across a number of other policy areas since the survey completed in 2000, the level of reported unfair treatment on the basis of religion in the area of education has on the whole declined.

In the survey completed in 2000, 41 per cent of responses indicated experience of unfair treatment, of which 10 per cent indicated that the unfair treatment was frequent and 31 per cent that it was occasional. In the survey completed in 2011 (where on average the questions were answered by 440 respondents), overall 35 per cent of responses highlighted frequent or occasional experience of unfair treatment, of which 6 per cent indicated that the unfair treatment was frequent and 29 per cent that it was occasional. Despite the overall reported decline, the level of reported unfair treatment is still substantial, thus indicating the scale of the impact on people's lives. However, again for most religious organizations that reported unfair treatment on the basis of religion in the sphere of education, this was occasional rather than frequent.

The reported incidence of unfair treatment did vary considerably across different religious traditions. For example, in the survey completed in 2011, only 12 per cent of Buddhist responses reported experiencing unfair treatment compared with 69 per cent of Sikh responses.

Within the sphere of education, the area in which reported experience of unfair treatment was most common concerned the attitudes and behaviour of school pupils at 54 per cent of (334) organizations. But levels of reported unfair treatment were considerably lower in relation to school policies, with 32 per cent of (332) organizations reporting this. These findings broadly reflect the patterns found in the survey completed in 2000. In that survey, 65 per cent of religious organizations reported unfair treatment of their members in relation to the attitudes and behaviour of school pupils (Weller et al., 2001: 173, 178). However, since 2000, the evidence indicates a decline in the overall incidence of the reported experience of such unfair treatment.

With regard to the content of teaching in schools, unfair treatment was reported in relation to Citizenship Studies by 17 per cent of (279) organizations, the RE curriculum by 36 per cent of (332) organizations and RE teaching by 37 per cent of (326) organizations. This compares to 2000 where the overall incidence of unfair treatment was higher across the key areas of Citizenship Studies (20% of organizations), the RE curriculum (42% of organizations) and RE teaching (45% of organizations).

In terms of the type of educational institution, in 2011 higher levels of unfair treatment were reported in relation to schools compared with colleges/universities. Higher levels of unfair treatment were also reported concerning the behaviour of teachers: 42 per cent of (328) organizations compared with college and university staff at 32 per cent of (279) organizations. Also higher levels of unfair treatment were reported in relation to the policies and practices of schools compared with the policies and practices of colleges/universities.

It is also important to look further at the differences between reported experience of unfair treatment in relation to the policies and practices of organizations in order to inform discussions regarding the development and implementation of the law, policies and good practice. For example, 32 per cent of (332) organizations reported unfair treatment of their members in relation to school policies compared to 37 per cent of (332) organizations in relation to school practices.

Overall a pattern can be identified in which higher rates of unfair treatment were reported in relation to organization practices as opposed to policies. Moreover, when looking across a ten-year period, it is in relation to the practices of organizations rather than their policies that higher levels of unfair treatment are reported. We now consider differences by religion in the sphere of education.

Unfair treatment in education: Survey findings by religion

Given the relatively smaller numbers of organizations responding to the survey from within some religious groups, some of this data needs to be treated with caution. What follows focuses on the religions with larger numbers of responding organizations: namely, Christian, Hindu, Jewish, Sikh, Muslim and NRM/Pagan organizations, but other religions are included in the analysis where practical.

Table 6.1 provides a summary of organization responses by religion to all the questions in the sphere of education. In this and other similar tables that follow, the results are sorted by religious group in ascending order by the combined rate of reported frequent and occasional unfair treatment. As indicated above and as was the case in the survey completed in 2000, there is evidence of considerable differences between religions in terms of their reported experience of unfair treatment. Sikh, NRM/Pagan and Muslim organizations were the most likely to report any kind of experience of unfair treatment on the basis of religion in the education sector (Weller et al., 2001: 173–9). In the survey completed in 2011, Sikh and NRM/Pagan organizations were the most likely to report frequent unfair treatment. Christian

Table 6.1 Reported experience of unfair treatment across the sphere of education as a whole, by religion

Religion	Frequent unfair treatment	Percentage	Occasional unfair treatment	Percentage	Combined percentage	No unfair treatment	Percentage	Total responses
Buddhist	12	4	24	8	12	273	88	309
Zoroastrian	0	0	8	13	13	52	87	60
Bahá'í	19	4	56	13	18	352	82	427
Christian	51	3	413	26	29	1153	71	1617
Jain	3	4	23	27	31	58	69	84
Hindu	20	7	77	28	36	175	64	272
Other	0	0	9	36	36	16	64	25
Other Christian	0	0	88	40	40	135	61	223
Jewish	10	3	142	38	41	219	59	371
Inter-faith	15	8	59	33	42	104	58	178
Muslim	58	9	251	38	47	352	53	661
NRM/Pagan	33	21	64	40	60	64	40	161
Sikh	42	20	105	49	69	67	31	214
Total	**263**		**1,319**			**3,020**		**4,602**

Note: All education question section responses combined. The mean number of organizations responding to each of the questions in the education section is 440.

Table 6.2 Unfair treatment: Attitudes and behaviour of school pupils, by religion

Religion	Frequent unfair treatment	Percentage	Occasional unfair treatment	Percentage	Combined percentage	No unfair treatment	Percentage	N
Hindu	0	0	9	47	47	10	53	19
Christian	8	7	56	46	53	58	48	122
NRM/Pagan	2	18	5	46	64	4	36	11
Jewish	0	0	19	66	66	10	35	29
Muslim	6	12	27	55	67	16	33	49
Inter-faith	1	8	8	62	69	4	31	13
Other Christian	0	0	13	77	77	4	24	17
Sikh	2	13	11	73	87	2	13	15

Note: Where response numbers are low religions have been excluded from the table. Caution should be exercised where individual cell counts are low.

organizations also reported considerable unfair treatment, but it was much more likely to be occasional.

Overall and across most religions, since 2000 there seemed to be a decline in the reported experience of unfair treatment in the sphere of education, though a small increase was reported from the relatively low number of responding Sikh organizations. In Table 6.2 we look in more detail at reported experience of unfair treatment in schools and the attitudes and behaviour of pupils. Again, considerable differences in the levels of unfair treatment reported by organizations from different religions are identified.

As Table 6.2 highlights, Sikh and 'Other Christian' organizations were the most likely to report that their members had experienced unfair treatment due to the attitudes and behaviours of school pupils, while Hindu, Christian and NRM/Pagan organizations were the least likely to state this. Even so, nearly half or more of the organizations in each of these traditions reported some experience of unfair treatment, which highlights the impact on people's lives in this area. At the same time, unfair treatment is, on the whole, occasional for all organizations.

These findings are underlined by the results from the organizations that responded to both the surveys that were completed in 2000 and 2011, where there was evidence of a decline (from 54% to 48%) in the reported experience of unfair treatment of their members in relation to the attitudes and behaviours of school pupils. However, such unfair treatment as was being reported had become almost entirely occasional. In addition, of those organizations that reported their members experiencing unfair treatment in 2001, 67 per cent of (74) organizations continued to report experiencing unfair treatment in 2011.

Understanding unfair treatment in education

The survey also collected detailed information on specific experience of unfair treatment. Examples given included: pupils' attitudes and behaviour; teachers' attitudes and behaviour; curriculum content; dress restrictions; school admissions; timetables and holidays. In general, the kinds of issues raised were very similar to those in 2000. In Box 6.1, a selection is presented that highlights some of the everyday impact and/or complexity in people's lives, which we go onto explore in more detail in the fieldwork.

Box 6.1 Unfair treatment in education: Survey comments

Bahá'í comments:

> *The release of children from school on all Bahá'í holy days – generally, schools only allow absence on 2 days.*

Christian comments:

> *A local college funded displays for Ramadan and Divali, but wouldn't fund anything for Easter.*

> *My wife is a 'Bible Explorer' presenter for Walk Through the Bible. One head teacher objected that if he let her into the school the children might want to start attending church!*

> *Pupils are taught the theory of evolution as fact and scorned for believing in God.*

> *Insistence on giving same sex relationships the same status as male/female relationships. Sex before marriage and abortion.*

Jain comments:

> *Jainism is not treated equally with other major religions.*

Muslim comments:

> *Islam as a subject is treated as secondary not fair amount devoted . . . The ratio of ethnic minority staff, especially Muslims is very low.*

> *The RE curriculum on Islam is based on Sunni Islam beliefs and fails to differentiate some fundamental differences between schools of thought.*

NRM/Pagan comments:

> *We are consistently given no acknowledgement or recognition.*

Sikh comments:

> *Primary school teacher did not know what a Sikh head covering was on boy pupil and embarrassed boy in front of school friends.*

Unfair treatment in education: Fieldwork findings

Participants in fieldwork on education

Fieldwork was conducted in five localities – Leicester, Cardiff, Blackburn, Newham and Norwich. Interviews and focus group meetings were conducted with education specialists, local authority, education staff and individuals from among a range of religious communities with experience of education as staff, students or parents of school children.

Experience of unfair treatment from schools and teachers

During the fieldwork, the general perception voiced by a number of participants across all five fieldwork locations and from different religion or belief backgrounds was that schools and teachers had, over the past decade, become more aware of religious diversity in their classrooms. This was attributed partly to equality laws as well as to equality and diversity policies adopted within schools, and which require teachers to be more aware of religious and other diversities and how to deal equitably with students from different religious and non-religious backgrounds. Parents and older siblings of students cited this as being quite different from when they were in schools a decade or so ago. For example, a white Orthodox Jewish man highlighted that:

> [Previously] in the school system [they] didn't really care whether you were Jewish or Muslim or anything like that [. . .] it was no use coming to say we've got a particular Muslim holiday and they would say 'So what, it's got nothing to do with us' you know and that's it. So they were very unsympathetic, times have changed [. . .] everybody's being very careful about what they do now.

From the 2000 research it was reported that, 'some teachers are very negative towards, and apparently sometimes also seek actively to undermine, the religious beliefs and practices of Muslim pupils and parents' (Weller et al., 2001: 27). However, the general feeling reported among the 2011 research participants was that the situation since then has somewhat improved.

Nevertheless, Muslim students and parents in all five fieldwork locations still reported negative experiences, particularly in relation to the approaches taken by schools and teachers to issues around clothing as is discussed further below. More general issues around the signalling of religious identity were not limited to Muslims. For example, a young, white Pagan woman interviewee told us about the negative attitudes her teachers had towards both her and her faith when, at school, she had filled out a form on her religion or belief identity:

> . . . I was walking back with a set of my teachers [. . .], cos I'd been busted for something I shouldn't have been doing and I heard the phrase, 'Did you hear what those little pricks did?', 'Oh yeah, one even put down Pagan on her form.' And I sort of looked and said, 'That would be me', of course they were hugely apologetic.

Non-religious parents also reported concerns about the attitudes of teachers to the extent that some parents preferred to home-school their children. Their concerns included religious assemblies (discussed below in more detail in the section titled 'School collective worship, visits and celebrations').

Attitudes of school pupils

As noted above, in both the 2001 and 2011 surveys, the attitudes and behaviour of school pupils were cited as being among the most frequently reported examples of unfair treatment. At the same time, the evidence suggests a reduction in the reporting of such unfair treatment. This was attributed to more inclusive RE syllabi, better-informed teachers and generally more diverse classrooms. Classrooms were generally reported to be more diverse in all the fieldwork locations areas and particularly in Leicester, Cardiff and Newham. While this was generally the case, there are exceptions. For example in Blackburn it was reported that some schools are almost entirely Asian-Muslim and others are white. However some schools are still trying to bridge this gap by pairing such schools and encouraging shared events so that students can meet each other. In Norwich, diversity was reported to be a more recent phenomena with schools not having as much diversity as in the other cities visited, although a school that was in close proximity to the university reported an increase in Middle Eastern children due to their parents studying at the university.

Nevertheless the negative attitudes of some students towards particular groups were reported to be as much of a concern as were the attitudes of staff. For example, two white (one male and one female) Christian teenagers reported being bullied at school because they were recognized as being religious.

> Definitely, I mean I get bullied quite a lot just because I know my Bible stories I get bullied a lot just for that.
>
> Yeah, if we pray in assembly or we are told this story from the Bible or we talk about bible quotes and stuff for exams and I know them and people just laugh at me and call names and stuff.
>
> Religion is on a downer in our school.

Similarly a male Muslim private sector worker of Middle Eastern origin described the unfair treatment that his two elder sisters faced a few years ago in school when wearing headscarves. As he summarized it: 'So I mean things like you know name calling, ninja, is a typical one, you know I mean at more than one point trying to pull off the scarf.'

This man was also of the opinion that such discrimination tended to vary based on the area in which a school was located and was also informed by the demographics within particular schools. When his two younger sisters went to a different school in another area, they did not experience any unfair treatment. However, reflecting a pattern of unfair treatment that continues particularly to bear upon Muslims, a female Muslim police advisor in Cardiff concluded that, 'Education-wise in terms of youngsters from different faiths I think definitely Muslims get a lot of stick in school.'

At the same time, sometimes instances of unfair treatment were reported from within a specific religious community. One Muslim woman who lives in Newham and who does not wear a headscarf stated that her daughter was bullied by her Muslim co-students who told her that her mother would 'go to hell because she did not wear a headscarf'.

Clothing requirements, services and facilities in schools

As reported in the 2000 research, and as is also apparent from the issues identified in the research completed in 2011, visible markers of religious identity continue to be contentious. Among these, the *niqabs* or face-veils worn by some Muslim women seem to be the most contentious. As one South Asian male Muslim interviewee stated:

> Unfortunately there is as we speak in college or maybe a few of the education institutions in Blackburn that actually have a policy that if you walk in with a *niqab* you're actually asked to remove your *niqab* otherwise you cannot access their building or you cannot go through their school. So I feel that these are the sort of issues that unfortunately we need to sort of remove and make a clear distinction that it's each individual's choice and if their interpretation of their religious teachings are that this is how they should dress in particular, each human being should respect that human being's choice to follow their own interpretation of their religion.

A Muslim woman who is also from Blackburn explained that a small number of schools in her local area (that has a large Muslim community) had policies against the wearing of face-veils or *niqabs*. She stated that she could understand that the school did not want students to wear *niqabs*. However, in some instances the policy had been extended to parents too, with the consequence that mothers who wore *niqabs* could not attend meetings in school or attend school events. She considered this to be an extremely unfair and demeaning experience for these mothers. It is also significant to note that given the large proportion of Muslims in Blackburn, there is possibly more discussion about the face-veil in narrative of participants from that location, although this was a subject that came up for discussion in other areas too.

A number of Muslim participants across the different fieldwork locations, however, also acknowledged that debates around the *niqab* or face-veil worn by some Muslim women are complicated and multifaceted and, among other things, include issues to do with health and safety and the religious necessity of the practice. One teacher in Blackburn stated that she asked a young primary age female student to remove her headscarf on the grounds that because the scarf was fastened with a safety pin, she felt this was a health and safety hazard in the playground. She was also aware that since the student was very young, wearing a headscarf was not a religious requirement for her. The student's parents, however, felt that this was unfair treatment and removed the student from the school.

Other issues that were reported from the research completed in 2000 included participants' discomfort around sport, mixed showers and arts activities. A decade on, these issues were not raised during the fieldwork except for mention of an example (reported by a Hindu teacher) in which a male Muslim pupil felt unable to participate in swimming lessons and his parents moved him to another school, although it was then explained that when his academic progress suffered he was brought back to his original school.

In relation to dietary matters, fieldwork participants in all five areas reported that religious restrictions were generally catered for by schools and that a considerable amount of good practice had developed in this regard. As a white Christian female public sector employee in education stated:

> You'll find that a lot of schools who run their own kitchens ensure that for the students that they've got from the Muslim community that there are Halal foods [. . .] their meats provided by an HMC approved Halal supplier and have their kitchens inspected [. . .] through the [. . .] Council of Mosques.

Religious festivals and attendance at school

In the fieldwork completed in 2000, participants reported difficulties with religious festivals clashing with important education events. In the fieldwork completed in 2011 there is evidence of positive change with both the parents of students and school authorities citing a greater awareness about important dates and the importance of advance planning to ensure that, as far as possible, dates do not clash. A middle-aged white male member of the group who understand themselves to be 'Messianic Jews' stated:

> I mean, no one in our community has a problem taking time off for the high holy days. [As] a high school teacher, and I was given unpaid leave for the high holy days. [. . .] Some of them will just take it as holiday, others will take it off unpaid, but again, there's no discrimination shown there.

This was evident in areas which have a smaller proportion of religious minorities. A white Christian female head teacher in Norwich stated that:

> If there is a festival, Ramadan, Eid, they would have to have that time off school, and in some communities, I know particularly if they have a large number of Muslim families will work it out so that the teachers can have training days on those days, so school is closed. So if you know far enough in advance you can do that but our days are obviously set by our local authority, so we are not as flexible as some communities where they have more significant numbers of Muslim families.

A number of participants across fieldwork location areas stated that schools are usually well-networked within their local communities and have access to local religious leaders who can offer advice in difficult situations. One such Muslim 'advisor' described where a school concerned had given Muslim students the day off for Eid. However one particularly committed Muslim GCSE student turned up at school in 'very bright clothes'.

> A head teacher phoned me at about 2 o'clock [. . .] one of the girls had come to school wearing very bright clothes because it was Eid. He asked whether she should be sent home. My suggestion is that you just tell her next time to wear uniform or

take a day off. We have agreed with the local authorities that they will take day off on Eid you know but they will not be marked as absent.

This narrative highlights the strong links that the school had with its local community and also the good practice of the local authorities in recognizing the needs of diverse religious groups.

School collective worship, visits and celebrations

A number of fieldwork participants cited increased recognition and understanding in relation to the observance of religious festivals. However, concerns were expressed about aspects of school visits to places of worship, talks by religious and non-religious representatives and celebrations of religious festivals. The matters raised included how talks and events were explained to students as well as the students' participation or otherwise in them. In most instances such visits are part of the RE curricula of schools and are aimed at broadening students' worldviews and their understanding of different religious and non-religious groups in their local communities. Many participants said that such visits/talks/events were usually fit for purpose and, in a number of instances students, staff and parents reported good experiences. These included events that were organized as part of an international week. As a Christian female employee in public sector education observed:

> The schools as a community came together for international week. The communities around the school have got together, contributed gifts and ideas and expertise and resources to help the schools celebrate. They had weddings from different cultures, they had culturally diverse foods, alternative therapies and they were raising money for charitable projects around the world.

However some participants said that events of this kind did not have the social impacts that were intended and that both religious and non-religious participants expressed concerns about the intentions and execution of such events. For example, some non-religious parents felt that visits and celebrations of this kind could become part of a process of 'indoctrination' into a particular form of Christianity which they wanted their children to avoid. A white, male atheist participant who spoke in schools about humanism told us that after one particularly successful event he felt that the school concerned dissuaded him from further visits. He stated: 'I think that the big battleground is education because religions think that if you can get at children in schools you can in someway influence them.'

Non-religious parents had similar concerns about collective worship and religious assemblies in schools. Although parents in England and Wales have the option of allowing their children to opt out of religious assemblies they felt that this could lead to their children being perceived as different and perhaps also to experience unfair treatment on this account. During the fieldwork interviews, it was reported that some Muslim students avoided such visits and events. This in turn was said to have become a problem for teachers and for those of other than

Muslim religion who were seeking to make a contribution. A white male Christian Evangelical pastor stated:

> I wouldn't call it segregation, I wouldn't call it discrimination but it was an unfortunate thing in that before I gave my talk, that wasn't even a Bible story, it was a story I had written all the Muslim kids had to leave.

These stories underline some of the difficult challenges facing education when arguing that it is an important means for tackling unfair treatment on the basis of religion or belief which is done in Chapter 10.

RE and RE teachers in schools

As expressed by research participants in each of the fieldwork cities there is considerable diversity of opinion about RE curricula and teachers. What follows is an indication of the varied and often divergent views and experiences that were discussed. A large number of participants were of the opinion that RE syllabi had widened considerably and now included aspects of all major religions. This was seen as different practice and as a positive change in comparison with ten years ago. A South Asian male Hindu stated:

> . . . well when I was bought up, it was just Christianity, there wasn't anything other than a Christian who was considered, it was like frowned upon. I go into schools, schools come in and visit the ashram so I guess from an early age children being taught a bit more religious tolerance you know, discrimination, yeah I'm sure they have a better understanding of different religions.

However, other participants felt that RE syllabi still focused too much on Christianity and not enough on certain religions. A South Asian male stated:

> . . . there is definitely a lack of exposure for Sikhs in terms of awareness of what the faith is. I mean you question the extent to which each faith gets in terms of their exposure to schools, and I think there is definitely a need for a bit more.

In the Knowledge Exchange Workshops interim findings from the research completed in 2011 were shared with practitioners from the public, private, voluntary and community, religion or belief and legal sectors. In a number of these workshops, concerns were expressed that Academies and Free Schools would not be giving an integral place to RE. Other (mostly Christian) participants felt that the widening of the syllabi for RE meant that they no longer included enough about Christianity. As a white female Christian secondary school student stated:

> . . . we used to go to the cathedral like once a month, but then they got less and less because people started complaining what was the point of going to the cathedral and stuff. [. . .] but if they were taught more about Christianity then they would at

least learn to keep their opinions to themselves and if they didn't believe in it they
don't have to blurt it out and make fun of other people who do [. . .] and I think I
shouldn't be bullied just because I go to church.

One non-religious young man felt that this 'erosion' of Christian culture was also
problematic for him. Although he was non-religious, he felt that Christian contexts
including religious celebrations were an essential and integral aspect of what he
perceived to be British culture. However, across the fieldwork areas, non-religious
participants often expressed concerns around both the content and the pedagogy of
RE curricula. Many non-religious participants stated that, in RE, religion was often
presented to students as being based on 'truths' rather than 'contestable beliefs that
religious people adhered to'. RE and also religious celebrations in schools were often
seen as part of a process of indoctrination. These participants mentioned the need for
RE to be more objective and to give students the opportunity to question and challenge
religious belief. A non-religious, white man stated:

I think education is a major problem [. . .] how we all start from the standpoint that
you're Christian when really you should be starting from the perspective of a blank
slate you know [. . .] so that you can learn about each religion from the beginning
and make your own decisions about such things.

A young white woman atheist said: 'it frightens me to death that children would be
brought up in that kind of environment at school whether their parents believed or
not that they would be teaching that evolution wasn't fact, so that concerns me'. Non-
religious participants agreed that it was important to give children some form of ethical
and moral education. However they did not think that RE was necessarily the best way
to do this.

A number of participants also shared views and concerns about who should teach
RE. Religious participants from Christian and Muslim backgrounds said that they did
not feel that it was appropriate for RE to be taught by non-religious teachers. As a white
male Christian secondary school student put it:

When we are studying stuff like religion and science and stuff because it is part of
the syllabus I get made fun of just because I stick up for my beliefs in debate, even
some of my teachers [. . .] was saying that she didn't believe in God and stuff and
I'm like she's an RS [Religious Studies] teacher and it just gets a bit weird. 'Cos like
even when the RS teacher isn't like backing you up and she doesn't exactly stop
them from saying stuff.

From another perspective on the same issue, a non-religious white female participant
discussed the experiences of her friend who was an RS teacher but was more interested
in philosophical approaches and thought that a philosophical or ethical approach
would be more appropriate:

I have a really close friend who is training as a Religious Studies teacher but she is not religious at all. She is interested in the philosophical frameworks, that religions create for people to explore wider issues. She'd much rather be a philosophy teacher but they don't do that at schools. I think that would be a better framing, if you learnt philosophy or ethics at school you'd have a wider view of the world and would be able to integrate science into your beliefs.

Again, these contested views around RE, its teachers and what is taught underline the challenges faced by the formal school education system if it is to play a major role in tackling unfair treatment on the basis of religion or belief.

Standing Advisory Councils on Religious Education (SACREs)

SACREs are bodies which oversee and also consider provisions of RE in a local authority area. They were created following the 1988 *Education Reform Act*, under which they were empowered in relation to a range of matters to do with RE and also collective worship in schools. For example, schools can apply to their local SACRE for a so-called determination to deal with collective worship outside the general norms and expectations laid down in the *Education Reform Act*.

The report on the fieldwork completed in 2000 did not specifically highlight or comment on SACREs. However, the fieldwork completed in 2011 included a range of different participants with different levels of involvement in SACREs. The religion or belief component of the SACRE membership (which is also composed of teacher and local authority representatives) usually seeks to reflect the religion or belief composition of local communities.

Participants from larger religious groups often viewed and described as 'mainstream' generally felt that their religions had adequate and proportional representation within SACREs. However smaller groups, including NRMs, Pagans and non-religious groups, felt unfairly treated with regard to their membership status and voting rights. It was usually a struggle for these groups to secure SACRE representation and then they stated that were usually only given 'co-opted' membership which did not give them any voting rights. These participants welcomed the opportunity to participate in SACRE meetings and influence RE curricula. However, they also felt that their influence was limited. As expressed by a white male humanist:

> . . . we waited how many years about 20 years was it for the [. . .] humanists to be represented on the council's SACRE [. . .] they continually ignored our requests or turned down our requests to have a member on there and when we did, got two actually [. . .]. We've got no voting rights so we're on the local council, the overseers of religious educations meant to be improving religious education, there's an option there to have a speaker in who'll talk about non-religious belief, non religious perspective on religion, but we've got no voting rights, we're powerless.

'Faith-based schools'

In the fieldwork completed in 2000 a number of interviewees raised the issue of what are often referred to as 'faith-based schools', including for Muslim and Jewish children. Opinion was divided between whether Muslim or Islamic schools could offer a conducive and appropriate environment or whether such schools could be divisive. In the fieldwork completed in 2011, these divergent opinions remained. However, the focus of public debate had since shifted from a previously almost exclusive focus on Muslim or Islamic schools in particular to issues around 'faith schools' in general. Those (mainly religious) participants who were supportive of such schools cited, among other arguments, the general pastoral support that they felt their children received. As a white female Christian put it:

> . . . my children went mostly to a Christian school but it wasn't necessarily because of the Christian side of it it's just that I liked the pastoral care the way the children were treated and the work ethic in a secular school sometimes that isn't there. You do find that faith schools are sort of patronised by people who want their children to learn and want their children to learn in a certain atmosphere, [. . .]. I think you can guarantee that if you send your child to any faith school that they will probably get along better than at a secular school.

Other participants, including some who were religious, felt that 'faith schools' limit the interactions that students have with the wider society. For example, a South Asian Progressive Jewish man argued that: 'Personally I like the idea of children mixing. I think part of what makes Britain is that we do mix.' Many non-religious participants felt that 'faith schools' continued the process of 'indoctrinating' children into religious beliefs. As expressed by a white non-religious man:

> I do feel undue weight is given to religion particularly in the context of faith schools [. . .] being a non-believer is a position relative to religion. So there aren't hordes of humanists out there in organized social groups going to start schools. And I feel that it's just facile to think that a Jewish or Muslim faith school isn't going to continue the indoctrination.

Unfair treatment was also reported in many of the fieldwork locations, particularly by non-religious participants, in relation to the admission procedures of 'faith schools', especially since many of these required parents to demonstrate some form of religious affiliation. Thus non-religious focus group participants stated that, if their local school happened to be a 'faith school', then they were faced with two options: either they had to pretend that they were religious in order to secure a place for their child, or they had to find alternative educational options. One non-religious mother (who had also been concerned about collective worship in schools) reported that she had become involved in developing home schooling, while another non-religious father told us that he and his wife took their children to the school in the next village which meant a much longer commute for them.

Another reported concern of unfair admissions came from a Christian Pentecostal mother who felt that local Church of England schools were unfair towards applicants from her community, even though she said they offered places to applicants from other than Anglican backgrounds. Such issues were, though, not limited to Christian-based schools. A local authority staff member recounted a case in which a Muslim school was reportedly unfair towards an applicant from a background different to its own and initially refused to offer a place to this student (it was not clear whether this student was from a different Muslim denomination or from an other than Muslim faith). It was stated that when the council informally intervened, by having 'strong words' with a representative of the school, a place was offered to this student.

Further and higher education, lecturers/tutors and students

The fieldwork completed in 2000 did not specifically highlight matters to do with further and higher education. In the fieldwork completed in 2011, as with school education, comments from fieldwork participants broadly echoed what was said about change and improvement in attitudes. Nevertheless, a number of examples of unfair treatment arising from hostile attitudes were reported. Often unfair treatment or comments seemed to stem from a dichotomy between religious and non-religious perspectives. Further and higher education institutions were generally seen as providing a space for the pursuit of 'rational' knowledge and, for some, religion was perceived as 'illogical' and 'irrational'. As a middle-aged Christian woman of South East Asian origin, and who is mature learner, put it:

> I won't use the word discriminated but I've been treated sometimes unfairly. One, because of . . . I don't know whether it's because of my race or my religion. I remember one time because I voiced my opinion. That time I was going to college in Blackburn and training to be an accountant and I remember this time my business math teacher, he started on religion and was calling it a load of rubbish and for sure I was the only person in that class [who was religious]. I could say that I was treated unfairly because it wasn't right for him to bring up religion in a class of business mathematics.

'Race', ethnicity, religion and education

Experiences of unfair attitudes were sometimes perceived to be related to 'race' as well as to religion. Overlaps and interconnections between 'race' and religion were also reported from the fieldwork completed in 2000. In the 2011 fieldwork, a male South Asian Hindu who is employed in a voluntary organization that offered legal support to individuals who experienced discrimination mentioned an instance in which a Nigerian Muslim student experienced what some might identify as Islamophobic attitudes and comments from his teachers. In an incident that occurred quite soon after the events of 11 September 2001, he explained:

> Immediately as he arrived the lecturers made comments about Muslims and their religious beliefs and obviously categorising extremist views with the moderate

Muslim views and automatically identified our client as being in that category because of his appearance [in Muslim attire].

Conversely, a South Asian female Muslim university student reported that although she was unaware of any legal frameworks or equality codes to which her university adhered, she was generally positive about her experiences of being a Muslim on campus.

There is a lot that we get to do [. . .] So I think as a Muslim on campus it is really really good. I actually have no idea about any discriminatory laws, or what applies on campus, whether the university has a special code, because I haven't come across it myself but I am assuming that they would have something.

We turn now to examine the issue of employment.

Unfair treatment in employment

Beliefs are respected, but the practice of the conduct consistent with those beliefs is not allowed for. (Survey comment from a Christian respondent)

Employment in social and religious context

Employment is a sphere of central importance in people's lives, not only in relation to their personal economic circumstances and life chances and that of their families, but also in relation to matters of identity and well-being. As noted in Chapter 4, over the past decade, the employment sector has been an area of increased legal protection for religion or belief alongside other aspects of identity, having been the first sector in which religion or belief equalities were introduced, in compliance with EU Directives on Employment Equality. Such developments included the *Religion and Belief (Employment) Regulations*, 2003, later strengthened by the provisions of the *Equality Acts*, 2006 and 2010.

Experience of unfair treatment in employment: Survey findings

Survey findings: The overall picture

The surveys completed in 2000 and in 2011 collected the reported experience of unfair treatment of members of religious organizations in relation to employment across the public, private and voluntary sectors including in relation to the Employment Service. Respondents were asked about the reported experience of their members in relation to unfair treatment from the attitudes and behaviour of colleagues and managers, as well as in relation to the policies and practices of these organizations.

The level of reported unfair treatment in employment on the basis of religion has, on the whole, either stayed the same or declined. In 2000, 37 per cent of organization responses indicated experience of unfair treatment in employment, of which 9 per cent indicated that the unfair treatment was frequent and 28 per cent that it was occasional.

In the survey completed in 2011 (where, on average, these questions were answered by 438 respondents) overall 30 per cent of organization responses indicated experience of unfair treatment, of which 4 per cent indicated that unfair treatment was frequent and 26 per cent that it was occasional. Despite the overall reported decline, the level of reported unfair treatment is still substantial, indicating the scale and impact on people's lives.

The reported incidence of unfair treatment on the basis of religion or belief in the sphere of employment varied considerably across different religions. For example in 2011, 4 per cent of (405) Buddhist responses as compared with 54 per cent of (770) Muslim responses and 62 per cent of (222) Sikh responses indicated unfair treatment. The most common reported experience of unfair treatment in employment concerned the attitudes and behaviour of private sector colleagues, with 46 per cent of (324) organizations and the attitudes and behaviour of private sector managers with 44 per cent of (327) organizations indicating unfair treatment. This compares with reported experience of unfair treatment from colleagues in the public sector in 40 per cent of (327) organizations and from public sector managers in 39 per cent of (326) organizations.

These findings broadly reflect the patterns found in the survey completed in 2000, where 54 per cent of the organizations reported incidences of unfair treatment experienced by their members from the attitudes and behaviour of private sector colleagues, which was again the most frequent commonly reported area of unfair treatment in employment. However, it is also notable that since 2000 there has been a reduction in the reported incidence of unfair treatment in this area.

Given the recent policy focus on employment and equality, it is important to compare the reported incidence of unfair treatment in relation to the policies and practices of employers. In the survey completed in 2011, overall 33 per cent of (311) organizations indicated experience of unfair treatment on the basis of religion in relation to private sector employer policies compared to 36 per cent of (313) organizations in relation to private sector employer practices. This compares with 29 per cent of (318) of organizations indicating unfair treatment in relation to public sector policies and 34 per cent of (316) organizations in relation to public sector practices. Overall, the percentage differences are small but the patterns suggest some consistent evidence concerning the implementation of policies and their impact on people's working lives.

These findings broadly reflect the patterns found in the survey completed in 2000. Forty per cent of organizations indicated experience of unfair treatment on the basis of religion in relation to private sector employer policies compared with 44 per cent in relation to private sector employer practices. This compared with 35 per cent of organizations indicating unfair treatment in relation to public sector policies and 42 per cent in relation to public sector practices.

The evidence provides a useful insight into how regulations and good practice are impacting on the ground in people's daily working lives. As in other spheres of people's lives, it seems that organization practices are some way behind stated polices. It could be argued that, after almost a full decade of legislation and good practice initiatives in the sphere of employment in particular, that a greater fall in reported unfair treatment might have been expected since the survey completed in 2000.

Unfair treatment in employment: Survey findings by religion

It is important to consider in detail, and by religion, the differences concerning reported experience of unfair treatment from responding organizations. Given the relatively smaller numbers of organizations responding to the survey from within some religious groups, some of this data needs to be treated with caution. What follows focuses on the religions with larger numbers of responding organizations, namely: Christian, Hindu, Jewish, Sikh, Muslim and NRM/Pagan organizations, but other religions are included in the analysis where practical. Table 6.3 provides a summary of the responses by religion to all the questions in the sphere of employment.

As indicated above, and as was also the case in the 2000 research, there is evidence of considerable differences between religions in terms of their reported experience of unfair treatment on the grounds of religion or belief in the sphere of employment. In the survey completed in 2011, Sikh, NRM/Pagan and Muslim organizations were the most likely to indicate unfair treatment on the basis of religion, with Muslim and Sikh organizations being the most likely to report frequent unfair treatment in this sphere.

There are some parallels with the results of the survey completed in 2000 when Muslim, Sikh and Hindu organizations were the most likely to report experience of unfair treatment (Weller, 2001: vii–viii). In that survey, while Christian organizations reported their members as experiencing considerable incidence of unfair treatment, it was more often occasional.

Looking specifically at reported experience of unfair treatment in the attitudes and behaviour of work colleagues in the private sector, considerable differences by religion can again be identified.

Table 6.3 Reported experience of unfair treatment across the sphere of employment as a whole, by religion

Religion	Frequent unfair treatment	Percentage	Occasional unfair treatment	Percentage	Combined percentage	No unfair treatment	Percentage	Total responses
Zoroastrian	0	0	0	0	0	54	100	54
Buddhist	2	0	16	4	4	387	96	405
Other	0	0	3	8	8	34	92	37
Jain	0	0	11	10	10	104	90	115
Bahá'í	0	0	51	10	10	452	90	503
Other Christian	0	0	48	20	20	198	80	246
Christian	44	2	426	24	26	1,307	74	1,777
Hindu	3	1	97	31	32	213	68	313
Jewish	3	1	117	37	38	196	62	316
Inter-faith	7	4	66	38	41	103	59	176
NRM/Pagan	12	6	76	39	45	106	55	194
Muslim	126	16	288	37	54	356	46	770
Sikh	27	12	123	55	68	72	32	222
Total	**224**		**1,322**			**3,582**	**70**	**5,128**

Note: All employment question section responses combined. The mean number of organizations responding to each of the questions in the employment section is 438.

Table 6.4 Unfair treatment: Attitudes and behaviour of private sector colleagues, by religion

Religion	Frequent unfair treatment	Percentage	Occasional unfair treatment	Percentage	Combined percentage	No unfair treatment	Percentage	N
Buddhist	0	0	1	4	4	23	96	24
Baháʾí	0	0	6	18	18	27	82	33
Christian	3	3	46	41	44	63	56	112
Hindu	0	0	9	50	50	9	50	18
Jewish	0	0	12	57	57	9	43	21
Other Christian	0	0	11	58	58	8	42	19
Inter-faith	2	18	5	45	63	4	36	11
Muslim	10	21	21	44	65	17	35	48
NRM/Pagan	2	17	8	67	84	2	17	12
Sikh	2	14	10	71	85	2	14	14

Note: Where response numbers are low religions have been excluded from the table. Caution should be exercised where cell counts are low.

As Table 6.4 highlights, Sikh and NRM/Pagan organizations were the most likely to report that their members experienced unfair treatment due to the attitudes and behaviour of work colleagues in private sector employment. Unfair treatment was, on the whole, occasional rather than frequent, though Muslim organizations were the most likely to report frequent unfair treatment in this specific area of employment. From among the organizations that responded to both the surveys that were completed in 2000 and 2011, there is evidence of very little change in the reported experience of their members' in relation to the attitudes and behaviours of private sector colleagues. However, of those organizations that reported their members experiencing unfair treatment in 2001, 57 per cent of (53) organizations continued to report experiencing unfair treatment in 2011.

Understanding unfair treatment in employment

Respondents to the surveys completed in both 2000 and 2011 were asked to provide details of specific examples of unfair treatment in relation to employment. Examples given included: attitudes and behaviour of managers and staff, rights to religious holidays and flexible working, dress restrictions, unfair treatment in relation to recruitment and promotion and lack of recognition for religious customs. In general, the kinds of issues raised were very similar to those in 2000. In Box 6.2, a selection is presented that highlights some of the everyday impact and/or complexity of unfair treatment on the grounds of religion or belief and what this means in people's lives.

Box 6.2 Unfair treatment in employment: Survey comments

Bahá'í comments:

Employer not allowing Bahá'í to take Bahá'í holiday. Bahá'í calendar was not reflected in work calendar whereas Islam, Hindu holy days were.

Christian comments:

Occasionally employers force staff to work on Sundays even though it is not necessary. It is understood that some people have to work on Sundays for example police, firemen or nurses but this is sometimes not necessary for shops.

Discrimination against those with a traditional Christian position on gender and sexuality issues.

Discrimination in the workplace is normal, but it is more in attitudes than outright action.

Hindu comments:

As practising Hindus, many of our members do not drink alcohol, which is often seen in the workplace as a social barrier.

Jain comments:

Spreading malicious rumours that vegetarians get ill by malnutrition so they are not worth employing.

Jewish comments:

Attitude of job centres to signing on Jewish holidays.

Muslim comments:

Many teachers and youth workers were not allowed to present Muslim perspectives – they left employment.

Not comfortable with Muslim dress.

NRM/Pagan comments:

British Army, Royal Air Force and Royal Navy. We can be 'other' but not 'Odinist'. We can have died for country, but you can't be Odinist!

Sikh comments:

Some private organizations during interview stage recommend we remove turban to fit in and cut our hair.

Unfair treatment in employment: Fieldwork findings

The following section is based on interviews and focus group discussions that were conducted with participants in five cities in England and Wales. The sample included individuals and groups from among employers, including human resource managers, equality and diversity officers in public institutions, policy-makers and local authority regulators; representatives of business development organizations; and individual employees who subscribed to a range of religious and non-religious standpoints in relation to the workplace.

Applying for jobs

A number of individuals who were interviewed in different fieldwork locations stated that discrimination began with the application process. As explained by a white woman working in the private sector in Cardiff:

> I was doing some recruitment with a client, we were reviewing CVs, there was an application from an individual who had all the right transferable skills and background that was being looked for and there was a comment about oh, I'm not sure about his name though. Would our customers engage with this person if they saw his name? And immediately I turned round and said that's not justification, so I do believe there is some stereotyping out there.

Although, as in the sphere of education, visible religious symbols and clothing can be associated with unfair treatment, interviewees also cited instances where unfair treatment had taken place even before a personal interview had taken place. For example, soon after sending off an application, a young Muslim explained that he received a rejection letter that criticized the quality of his application. He had heard that applications with 'Muslim sounding names' are sometimes discriminated against and therefore he re-sent his application form after changing his name and a few details on the application, but making sure that the qualifications and experience levels remained the same. He was surprised that he received an invitation for interview. He realized that he had been discriminated against and took this case of unfair treatment to an employment tribunal and stated he received an out-of-court settlement.

Such discrimination is not limited to the visible religious minorities but also affects Christian groups whose religiosity is more evident in what might be seen as increasingly non-religious environments. A white Catholic woman working in the third sector described a similar case, except that she was at the opposite side of the employer–employee dichotomy. She was part of a selection panel who were reviewing applications to create a shortlist of people to invite for interview:

> We were sorting hundreds of applications and I can clearly remember somebody reading through an application form and saying, 'Oh she sounds really good' [and then a few seconds later] 'oh hang on she's a religious nutter, we wouldn't want her', because the person had chosen to put on their application form that she were a practising Christian and very active in her local parish . . . It was like, 'Oh ha ha, that's funny, you know', but I was like, 'Actually that's not funny, that's offensive' and then it was all, 'Oh we didn't mean it, it was a joke, of course we wouldn't discriminate on those grounds,' but it was said and I heard it. I don't

think [discrimination occurred in this case] because there were enough people there to challenge it, but [discrimination] could have [occurred] in a different situation.

As was reported from the 2001 fieldwork, experiences of unfair treatment can also occur further on in the application process. In the 2011 fieldwork a young Sikh man told us about his experience of unfair treatment linked with his wearing of a turban:

> Where my sister works, I went there for a kind of job interview and they just said straight away that they wouldn't want me to work there just in case people say stuff to me. The job was being a waiter in a bar. They just said they didn't want punters to be rude to me because I wore a turban and she was scared that they would so she wouldn't even consider employing or interviewing me.

This participant felt he was discriminated against because he wore a turban. A number of Sikh men who were interviewed in all five fieldwork locations reported an increase in occurrences of unfair treatment after the events of 11 September 2001 and the war in Afghanistan. Media imagery of Taliban and Al-Qaeda members usually showed them wearing turbans and since Sikh men also wear turbans, many respondents reported that they were mistakenly being perceived as being associated with such groups and often bear the brunt of Islamophobia. The young Sikh man's experience described above appears to be indicative of a wider reported trend of the 'proxy' or 'misplaced' unfair treatment experienced by turban-wearing Sikh men. When asked if he sought any form of legal action or whether he reported the case, that young man said that he had not: 'I just left it really. I was angry about it so I left it. I didn't want to work for them anyway after they said that.'

Many non-religious participants reported feeling that their employment chances could be negatively impacted by the 'exemptions' given under equality laws to religiously based institutions as touched upon in Chapter 4 and as will be discussed again in Chapter 10. A woman whose husband was a teacher made the point that since she lived in an area with a higher density of faith schools she believed that her currently unemployed husband's opportunities of finding a job would be vastly reduced.

Offensive and insensitive behaviour at work

As in the fieldwork completed in 2000, in the fieldwork completed in 2011 participants continue to identify offensive behaviour at work as a problem. A Pagan woman reported offensive comments in the workplace that were directly addressed to her, or were made in her presence, and which made direct or indirect reference to stereotypical views about her beliefs: 'Can you fly? Do I look like I have wings? Could you make someone fall in love with me? Do you dance naked in the woods?' Quite a number of Pagan (mostly, but not always) women interviewed in Leicester, Cardiff and Norwich, spoke of experiencing offensive language and prejudice once their religion became known in the workplace. But offensive behaviour in the workplace was also reported by interviewees from a variety of religious and non-religious backgrounds.

For example, a South Asian Muslim councillor perceived that she was not treated as a 'proper' councillor due to her ethnic and religious background and that her position was almost tokenistic. Many Bahá'í and Muslim participants in different fieldwork locations stated that their avoidance of alcohol sometimes caused misunderstandings during socializing events at work. An Anglican parish priest in Norwich whose congregation was 'quite evangelical' explained that a number of parishioners who worked in the medical profession had mentioned to him that when they were at work, certain conversations, particularly around issues such as abortion and euthanasia, would abruptly stop when they entered the room.

People in 'religious' professions

People working in religious settings or in religious roles may be considered as a distinctive category in terms of evidence and discussion around discrimination, equality and employment. This is a 'category' that was not explicitly discussed in the report of the 1999–2001 research. However in the 2011 fieldwork, considerable evidence emerged in terms of individuals working in religious contexts reporting unfair treatment. By virtue of their profession – either because of official designations, the clothes they wear, or the work that they do, these interviewees or their beliefs were often highly visible in their work contexts. Furthermore they often worked in religiously plural contexts which could, on occasion, lead to unfair treatment. A middle-aged white woman Pagan prison chaplain told us about her experiences at work:

> Some will just assume that I am a Christian minister unless they say, 'oh are you a Pagan minister?' I do some general duties and I have been around and had some quite interesting conversations with some of the inmates. One of them basically said I should be damned; I shouldn't be alive because I am a witch, because he is Roman Catholic. He said that in the Bible it says 'suffer a witch not to live' and so he said I shouldn't be alive.

Other examples were also cited. A Buddhist chaplain felt that he was not given the same access to facilities that had been given to other chaplains. A number of Anglican vicars told us that they experienced rude and occasionally offensive language because they were recognized as vicars due to wearing their 'dog collars'. A Christian priest was welcomed into the new community in which he had recently moved. His style of preaching attracted a number of different church groups who invited him to participate in their events. However, when it became known that he was homosexual, these same groups shunned him and turned him away. A humanist celebrant also encountered issues and explained that: 'People ask what do you do and I say I am a humanist celebrant at funerals and they know I am not religious. I have literally had people turn and walk away. And then I have discovered that they were devout Catholic.'

In one complicated case that highlights the issue of competing rights and perspectives, a Muslim chaplain identified that he felt he had been discriminated against when he was not allowed to display posters/leaflets about Muslim concepts of modesty and avoidance of alcohol. In a separate interview this matter was brought up again with a Christian interviewee who worked in the same place, stating that the posters were removed because it was felt that team members and service users who were not Muslim would find them offensive.

Dress codes at work

The findings on education highlighted how adherence to religious dress codes has continued to be a contentious issue in educational contexts. In the workplace, while some instances of unfair treatment that appear to be directly connected with dress codes remain, the 2011 field evidence suggests (like the results of the survey) that these are more infrequent than frequent. It also suggests that such instances are linked more with the attitudes of individuals and problems with the implementation of policies by individuals rather than the policies as such, which were generally recognized as being well-developed and sensitive to the needs of different religious and non-religious groups. As explained by a white, female and non-religious public sector employer in Leicester: 'We had an incident where there was a conflict between a teaching assistant who wanted to wear a full veil and the school that felt it was inappropriate, but they are incidents rather than apparently widespread.'

A relevant example to cite at this point is the experience of the young Sikh man mentioned earlier who stated that he was not interviewed because he wore a turban. Similarly, a number of different interviewees in one of the fieldwork locations mentioned the case of a female police officer who converted to Islam and started wearing a headscarf to work – following which she experienced prejudice and unfair treatment from her colleagues. A white, female Pagan participant also discussed the unfair treatment experienced by her mother: 'My mother was asked to take her pentagram off at work. They said it was against the rules for her to wear an occult symbol while at school while Christians were allowed to wear [their religious symbols].'

Holidays and days off from work

Interviewees had different experiences of how their requests for leave were dealt with. A Christian man told us that his son was told during interview that he would not be offered the job, because, when asked, he refused to work on Sundays. This is consistent with quite a number of the write-ins to the survey that highlighted this issue in a way that was not so present in either the survey or the fieldwork in the research completed in 2000.

In 2011, and in some contrast to the findings of the survey about continuing, albeit reduced, levels of unfair treatment in employment, among fieldwork participants the general consensus was that employers and legal frameworks in the United Kingdom were more sensitive to the needs of diverse communities than in some other European countries. For example, a Jewish woman of German descent said: 'Well I, I think we've always felt very protected by the law here [as opposed to in Germany]. I mean, no one in our community has a problem taking time off for the high holy days; everyone is allowed to take time off.'

Self-censorship?

In the fieldwork completed in 2000 there was quite a strong sense of many Pagans feeling that they needed to keep their religious identities secret in workplace contexts, especially where these were in education or social care. In the fieldwork completed in 2011, a number of Pagan participants (e.g. in the previously noted case of the prison chaplain, and in other instances) mentioned having an initial reticence about disclosing their religion in particular in religious contexts as they felt this would lead to prejudice and discrimination. However many Pagans reported that, in the end, they did now feel comfortable to talk with work colleagues about their religion. For example, a white, female Pagan explained the following about this change in way in which she and members of her community are perceived:

> Yeah, I think that people are more aware of what a person who calls themselves a Pagan is. So we are not considered as weird as we used to be. [. . .] That's really what a Pagan is, somebody who follows traditional beliefs of the countryside. [. . .] More sort of awareness of, they're not sort of devil worshipers, they're not weird, whereas before people had all sorts of ideas about somebody who considered themselves Pagan, perhaps coloured by their own religion, but also coloured by society as a whole.

Issues of reasonable accommodation at work

The participants in the fieldwork completed in 2000 commented on the difficulties they that faced and/or perceived in relation to discussing their religious needs with employers. In the fieldwork completed in 2011, the following comment by a Druid participant echoes a general perception in the fieldwork about employers who are often flexible and who try their best to provide for diverse employees' needs:

> I've heard of people having problems within the work environment and getting leave, not just within the Druid Network but with any religion really apart from the Christian holidays which tend to be public holidays. I suppose we've got to look at it from the employer's perspective as well. If you're a small employer you may be expected to give an employee time off when others are working. You can call it discrimination if you wanted to but I don't think it is. I think it's a matter of – if you aren't Christian or you've a different faith or religion, you've got to accept that we do live within a Christian culture and that predominates. I find that most employers now are very flexible.

However, a number of non-religious participants complained that their religious colleagues had the option of also taking extra holidays on festivals and other religiously significant days and that this was a privilege that the non-religious did not have. In another narrative an interviewee who was a teacher was given access to prayer space that was too far from the main school building. When she and other colleagues complained, matters were not resolved and instead took a turn for the worse, and many of the colleagues who pursued this issue in support of her faced disciplinary action.

Unfair treatment in employment: Changes over the decade

In narrating the situation in relation to unfair treatment and employment over the past decade the majority of fieldwork participants affirmed that there had been improvements in organizational policy and practice around discrimination and employment related to religion or belief. One South Asian male councillor who was also formerly the head of a Christian organization even went so far as to state: 'I do not believe that there is discrimination in the work place.'

Participants stated that legal frameworks have created at least an awareness among employers and in their policies, concerning the needs of an increasingly more diverse workforce. It was noted by participants that implementation of the legal frameworks outlined in Chapter 4 has led to employers drafting their own diversity and inclusivity policies which are disseminated via training programmes and policy documents. As a female, Hindu, medical doctor explained: 'I will tell you, frankly, I work in a hospital for the past 10 years, in our organization we have that policy statement where it says all are considered equivalent with regard to the law and people must be treated fairly.' But while policies were noted as being usually inclusive, it was also noted that problems remain with the implementation of the policies as well as around the attitudes of individuals. Our fieldwork evidence suggests that instances of unfair treatment continue, albeit some more hidden and subtle than others.

Thus, while what was reported by interviewees suggests that there have been improvements over the last decade (just as the survey suggests a reduction in the reported incidence of unfair treatment in employment) issues still remain to be resolved. As a white female Human Resources staff member from the private sector put it:

> I think nowadays because of the changes, I think there [is an] increase in awareness of employers even if, I don't know if it would still change their opinions, [. . .] they would be far more conscious that there'd be consequences for not accommodating. [. . .] so I do think that the legislation and changes over the years have identified to people there are things they need to consider and they cannot justify discrimination because they don't believe in a religion themselves and they have to accommodate individual needs and differences. [. . .] I do think they're [legal frameworks to prevent discrimination on the basis of religion or belief] helpful. I think that there are small employers [. . .] and if not small employers, large employers with poor attitudes of line managers as individuals that can and will still discriminate.

Overall, the general feeling among participants in the field research completed in 2011 across all five fieldwork locations was that discussions around discrimination in the workplace with regard to religion and belief need to continue. As noted in the beginning of this section, employment was the first area within which equalities laws in relation to religion or belief came into force in England, Wales and Scotland, with the

Employment (Religion or Belief) Regulations, 2003. Therefore, if law can and does make a difference to matters of unfair treatment, then employment might therefore, on the face of it, be expected to show some of the results indicated above. Even here, however, awareness and use of the law as evidenced in the number of religion or belief cases taken to employment tribunals has taken time to build up (see Weller, 2011: 31).

As noted in the field research evidence above and in Chapter 4 on legal developments, employment in particular can be an area where different rights and responsibilities and protected characteristics can come into some tension and conflict with each other. This is also the case in terms of the interface with employment and contract law which, generally speaking, has been seen in both the United Kingdom and European Courts to take precedence over other relevant matters in the employment setting unless there is a clear case of direct or indirect discrimination.

There are also new developments that have come about partly as a consequence of the equalities laws and their approach to exceptions in employment-related matters for religion or belief organizations on 'genuine occupational grounds'. High-profile controversies and legal cases reflect this. We now turn to examine reported experience of unfair treatment in the media.

Unfair treatment in the media

It seems that if a crime is committed by a Muslim, their religion is always mentioned. This is not the case for other religious groups. (Survey comment from a Muslim respondent)

The media in social and religious context

While education has a powerful role in shaping knowledge and understanding, the role of the media is even more ubiquitous in both shaping and reflecting people's attitudes and perceptions including how people view themselves and the communities in which they live. This includes newspapers and the mass media of radio and television and new media including social media such as the internet, Facebook, Twitter and the like.

Survey findings on unfair treatment in the media

Reported experience of unfair treatment in the media

The surveys completed in 2000 and in 2011 collected the reported experience of unfair treatment of members of religious organizations in relation to a wide range of media, including: national and local television, radio and newspapers; and the attitudes and behaviour of journalists; as well as coverage of religious organizations and religions.

The questions covered the key areas of the media and, as such, provide a valuable insight into how members of religious organizations experience unfair treatment in relation to this area. The level of reported unfair treatment on the basis of religion or belief in the sphere of the media has, on the whole, declined. In the survey completed in 2000, 57 per cent of all responses indicated experiences of unfair treatment, of which 20 per cent indicated it was frequent and 37 per cent that it was occasional.

In the survey completed in 2011 (where on average the questions were answered by 446 organizations) overall 51 per cent of responses highlighted unfair treatment, of which 17 per cent indicated that it was frequent and 34 per cent that it was occasional. This also appears to be a consistent pattern that can be identified in the qualitative evidence and across the different areas of the media. Despite the overall reported decline, the level of reported unfair treatment is still substantial. As with other spheres, the reported incidence of unfair treatment on the basis of religion or belief also varied considerably across different religions with 14 per cent of Buddhist responses and 79 per cent of Muslim responses indicating experiences of unfair treatment.

In terms of areas within the overall sphere of the media, the most commonly reported experience of unfair treatment concerned the attitudes and behaviour of journalists from national newspapers/magazines, at 65 per cent of (357) organizations; the attitudes and behaviour of television journalists/presenters, at 62 per cent of (316) organizations; coverage of organizations' religion in national newspapers/magazines, at 69 per cent of (367) organizations; and coverage of organizations' religion on television, at 65 per cent of (336) organizations. It is clear that unfair treatment in relation to the media is a key concern for many religious organizations. Lower levels of reported unfair treatment were reported in relation to local media in general but the levels were still substantial with, on average, 40 per cent of (320) organizations indicating experience of unfair treatment. Other media highlighted as sources of unfair treatment included: films, advertising, the internet, social networking websites and blogs.

These findings broadly reflect the patterns found in the 2000 research where 70 per cent of religious organizations report unfair treatment in relation to the attitudes and behaviour of journalists from national newspapers/magazines; 67 per cent in relation to the attitudes and behaviour of television presenters; 72 per cent in relation to the coverage of their religion in national newspapers/magazines; and 71 per cent in relation to coverage of their religion on national television.

Unfair treatment in the media by religion

It is important to consider, in more detail and by religion, the differences concerning reported experience of unfair treatment from responding organizations of different religions. Given the relatively smaller numbers of organizations responding to the survey from within some religious groups, some of this data needs to be treated with caution. Table 6.5 provides a summary of the responses by religion to all the questions in relation to the media

As Table 6.5 highlights, taken as a whole, Muslim, Other Christian, NRM/Pagan and Jain organizations were the most likely to indicate unfair treatment on the basis of religion in relation to the media, with Muslim, NRM/Pagan and Sikh organization responses being the most likely to report frequent unfair treatment. In this, again, there are some parallels with the findings of the survey completed in 2000.

As noted, there has been an overall decline in the reported experience of unfair treatment since 2000, and there are some examples where reported experience of

Table 6.5 Reported experience of unfair treatment across the sphere of the media as a whole, by religion

Religion	Frequent unfair treatment	Percentage	Occasional unfair treatment	Percentage	Combined percentage	No unfair treatment	Percentage	Total responses
Buddhist	11	3	40	11	14	319	86	370
Bahá'í	20	5	70	19	24	286	76	376
Zoroastrian	0	0	12	25	25	36	75	48
Hindu	58	17	74	22	39	202	60	334
Inter-faith	25	12	61	29	41	128	60	214
Christian	211	12	632	35	47	945	53	1,788
Other	1	3	22	55	58	17	43	40
Sikh	36	20	74	41	61	70	39	180
Jewish	58	13	229	50	63	167	37	454
Jain	13	18	40	54	72	21	28	74
NRM/Pagan	53	30	79	45	75	44	25	176
Other Christian	34	14	161	64	78	55	22	250
Muslim	329	47	221	32	79	151	22	701
Total	**849**		**1,715**			**2,441**		**5,005**

Note: All media question section responses combined. The mean number of organizations responding to each of the questions in the media section is 446.

unfair treatment has declined considerably. These include for the combined rates of reported occasional and frequent unfair treatment for Christian (from 57% to 47%), Hindu (from 66% to 39%) and Bahá'í (from 35% to 24%) organizations.

At the same time, overall, organizations from some religions reported similar or increased combined frequent and occasional experience of unfair treatment since 2000. These include NRM/Pagan, Jain and Jewish organizations. The media is therefore different from the other two main areas of reported unfair treatment covered in this chapter in that the picture of change is less consistent and more mixed.

Looking specifically at unfair treatment in relation to the coverage of religion in national newspapers/magazines (one of the areas with the highest levels of reported unfair treatment) considerable differences by religion can again be identified.

As Table 6.6 highlights, in relation to the coverage of respondents' religion in national newspapers/magazines 'Other Christian', Muslim, NRM/Pagan, Sikh and Jewish organizations are the most likely to report that their members experienced unfair treatment in the coverage of their religion. While for most religions, the unfair treatment reported is more likely to be occasional, it is striking that the exception to this is where nearly two-thirds of Muslim organizations report frequent unfair treatment. From among the organizations that responded to both the surveys that were completed in 2000 and 2011, there is very little decline in the reported experience of unfair treatment of their members in relation to the attitudes and behaviours of journalists from national newspapers and magazines. However, of those organizations that reported their members experiencing unfair treatment in 2001, 71 per cent of (62) organizations continued to report experiencing unfair treatment in 2011.

Table 6.6 Unfair treatment: Coverage of respondents' religion in national newspapers/magazines, by religion

Religion	Frequent unfair treatment	Percentage	Occasional unfair treatment	Percentage	Combined percentage	No unfair treatment	Percentage	N
Bahá'í	1	4	10	37	41	16	59	27
Buddhist	1	4	11	39	43	16	57	28
Hindu	6	26	6	26	52	11	48	23
Christian	27	20	61	46	66	46	34	134
Inter-faith	4	31	5	38	69	4	31	13
Jewish	9	26	18	53	79	7	21	34
Sikh	3	23	8	62	85	2	15	13
NRM/Pagan	5	36	7	50	86	2	14	14
Muslim	32	63	13	26	89	6	12	51
Other Christian	3	17	13	72	89	2	11	18

Note: Where response numbers are low religions have been excluded from the table. Caution should be exercised where cell counts are low.

Understanding unfair treatment in the media

Respondents to the surveys completed in 2000 and in 2011 were asked to give details of any specific examples of unfair treatment. Examples given included: lack of coverage; publishing negative aspects of religion; referring to a person's religion when it was not relevant; excluding religion; misrepresentation; offensive material/coverage; ridicule; ignorance and lack of knowledge; biased views and racial and religious stereotyping. In general, the kinds of issues raised in 2011 were very similar to those in 2000. In Box 6.3, a selection is presented that highlights some of the everyday impact and/ or complexity of unfair treatment on the grounds of religion or belief and what this means in people's lives.

Box 6.3 Unfair treatment in the media: Survey comments

Buddhist comments:

Buddhism is portrayed sometimes as a very new-age religion with little depth, meditation not infrequently is ridiculed as something ostentatious (in the national press only, primarily).

Christian comments:

The Evangelical/Pentecostal wing of the church in the UK is growing well, yet the media concentrates on the shrinking liberal or traditional wings of the church. This is unbalanced, unfair and either ignorant or prejudiced.

Lack of respect for what will cause offense. Christianity treated as 'fair game'.

Generally Christian ministers are caricatured by the media as ineffective do-gooders.

Jain comments:

> *Coverage of 'Jain' religion is very poor. Lots of people are not aware of this most ancient religion.*

Jewish comments:

> *The more local the media is, the more fair it tends to be, and the less likely to marginalize.*

Muslim comments:

> *Everyday instances of Muslim-bashing that affects the mental health of Muslims – thank goodness British people in general don't trust the media.*
>
> *Frequent combination of 'Islamic' and 'Muslim' with 'terrorist' or 'extremist' Local press.*

'Other' religion comments:

> *Contemporary spirituality does not fit their tick boxes.*

Pagan/NRM comments:

> *The recent granting of a charity number to Druids was attacked by the papers.*

'Other Christian' comments:

> *Coverage about polygamous groups in USA tends to be incorrectly linked to our church.*

Unfair treatment in the media: Fieldwork findings

Introduction

Participants in the fieldwork completed in 2011 were asked about their perspectives on the media and about any experience unfair treatment on the basis of religion or belief.

In general, participants from all religious and non-religious groups and across all five fieldwork locations mentioned misrepresentation and unfair portrayals of religion. As in the previous research, participants frequently made reference to the 'pervasive role of the media and to its power to contribute to a negative perception of their religious traditions and communities' (Weller et al., 2001: 89–90).

Marginalization of religion in the media

Many participants from across most religious groups and in all five fieldwork locations felt that negative or inaccurate media coverage played a part in what a white Christian Pentecostal pastor in Blackburn called the 'marginalization of religion', and which he felt permeated media representations of all religions. A white middle-aged Anglican Christian chaplain from Leicester positioned this disconnection between the media and portrayals of religious belief as a result of a religious and non-religious dichotomy that he identified as being prevalent in British society:

> Well, I think secularism or humanism anyway is part of the national arena and there is no doubt about that. In science and religion there is a lot more media space given to humanism . . . I get sometimes quite cross that religion in the media is not taken seriously and if there is a debate with secularists or humanists the latter seem to be given the higher ground and I don't think that is fair. There is an academic reality to religion which is often underplayed.

In addition to such comments about the media misrepresentation of all religions, many representatives of religious groups also reported more specifically about negative portrayals in relation to their own specific religion and/or tradition or movement within it. An Anglican Christian vicar identified the sense of disempowerment that was felt among members of his parish who recognized the Christian foundation of England but who increasingly felt a sidelining of the Christian faith. He reported that other faiths were becoming more visible and that more recently concerns were also voiced within his parish when plans were announced to include humanist and secularist viewpoints on the local BBC 'Thought for the Day' programme. This was perceived as an erosion of Christian values from the BBC which was part of their establishment and therefore 'theirs'. He summed up the feeling within his parish with the comment that: 'It's almost like losing the empire all over again, it's just that it's the empire of your own country.' In the poignancy of this one can see complex aspects of the relationship between religion, belonging, loss and nostalgia in the context of a changing religion and belief landscape.

Other concerns voiced by a number of Christians reflect notions of a religious and non-religious dichotomy that was described earlier. A male Christian Salvation Army voluntary sector worker spoke of how Christian beliefs and values are being portrayed as 'illogical' and 'irrational' by 'some sections of the media who have sort of latched onto the very aggressive atheism that there is at the moment'. Another concern was raised about the use of the name of Jesus Christ in inappropriate contexts. As explained by a white male Evangelical Christian pastor:

> Well actually to be honest if you're talking now specifically about the Christian faith, I think there's a lot of discrimination in the broadcast media – where the name of Jesus Christ is used quite freely as a swear word, as an expletive. It's not bleeped out, it's not . . . the F word will be bleeped out but they can say Jesus, Jesus Christ, you know that sort of thing.

Many Roman Catholic Christian participants reported about the negative press coverage of the media which was often, although not always, linked by them to perceptions of the media as secular and atheistic. As a white Catholic Christian woman put it:

> Coming back to the Catholic community have you know these issues because you keep hearing about it in the media, when the Pope came [. . .] there was so much

commentary in the media about you know the spending on the Pope's visit and religion and the police.

Most Muslim interviewees in all five fieldwork locations reported being concerned about the disproportionate media attention devoted to Islam and Muslims, which particularly focused on acts of terrorism and on Islamism, and which were seen as leading to the perpetuation of stereotypical views of Islam and Muslims. The South Asian male chair of a Muslim umbrella organization summarized such views by talking about 'two religions, one is the media Islam and one is the real Islam and that is why it is important that we reflect the true picture to the general public, and for that we need to educate them'.

A number of Jewish participants interviewed in three of our fieldwork locations – Leicester, Cardiff and Norwich, spoke about what they saw as bias and antisemitism in the media particularly in coverage of the Middle-Eastern conflict. As a Jewish woman from Cardiff expressed it: 'The media is quite anti-religion and also anti-Jewish and anti-Israel which was unfortunate.' Some religious groups (including those with larger populations such as the Sikhs and the Hindus) and other smaller groups such as the Bahá'ís and Jains felt that they are not heard at all in the media. This is, they believed, partly because too much attention is given to certain other religious groups and in other instances because their particular groups – as well as some others – are not perceived as especially newsworthy. Therefore, as a young Sikh man from Leicester put it, there is, 'definitely a limited amount of exposure that Sikhs have had in terms of the media. I mean because of 9/11 there has been a lot more talk about Islam, but there has never been anything about any other faith.' From a Bahá'í perspective, as articulated by a Bahá'í woman of South Asian heritage living in Norwich: 'They say oh Bahá'ís you know no news there, forget it, almost as if they put it in the pending tray.'

Many non-religious participants also reported a religious and non-religious dichotomy that was prevalent in the media. However, in their perception they felt that this had led to stereotypes of non-religious stances and people as militant, dogmatic and anti-religion which were inaccurate. They also felt that the media was biased towards religion and gave more coverage to religious groups, and that the non-religious do not have a voice in the media. As a white humanist male from Cardiff succinctly argued, 'There's a distortion in the media because humanists don't have a powerful legal body,' or, as expressed at more length by a non-religious woman in Leicester:

> . . . there are a lot of issues around religion that are in the media and they will ask people who have a faith to talk about it but they don't necessarily get somebody on [who is non-religious] [. . .] So I think as non-believers you don't get a voice or you don't hear your voice heard [. . .] The only people that are allowed to talk about religion and the effect of religion are people with faith.

Negative images and sensationalism

As noted in Chapter 5, in 2007 *BBC Panorama* ran a programme about Blackburn (one of the fieldwork locations in the 2011 research). The programme explored the theme of 'separated communities' in Blackburn, including what was sometimes argued, in effect, to be segregation between predominantly Muslim Asian communities and white communities that were perceived as Christian. A number of the research participants from Blackburn (including from both Christian and Muslim backgrounds, as well as among employees in the public and private sectors) felt that the programme was an unfair representation and presented a negative image of Blackburn.

They agreed that Blackburn had some issues around community cohesion that the local government, voluntary and community groups were collectively addressing. They also felt that there was also considerable good practice, including inter-faith dialogue and community cohesion activities, that this particular programme did not cover. As a Muslim male employee of South Asian origin working in the public sector explained it, 'some of the issues around separation we're aware of, I think the way the media portrays an issue, it sensationalises a story. You have to accept that, and it is for those reasons there was a lot of disappointment towards *Panorama*'.

Similar comments about media sensationalism were made by participants from across most religious groups and in all local contexts. In particular, many participants felt that the reporting within the media of legal cases relating to discrimination on grounds of religion or belief was inaccurate and exaggerated and had the potential to alienate people and communities, as well as to create perceptions of legal frameworks as inaccessible and perhaps unfair. As a white male Druid participant stated, 'I think 90% of the time it is the media that's just hyping it up anyway.'

The media's lack of coverage of positive news

As in the fieldwork completed in 2000, a large proportion of participants from across different religious groups reported that good news is often ignored by the media. A young male Sikh participant from Leicester spoke of a lack of understanding of different religions that he believed was, in part, being perpetuated by a lack of reporting about these faiths. For example, because of his distinctive turban and South Asian ethnic origin, he was often mistaken to be a Hindu, Persian or a Muslim. Only rarely was he recognized as a Sikh and he attributed this to the lack of exposure within the media of Sikh contributions to British society:

> I think if we look at the Sikh contributions, for example we have the Langar which is an open kitchen for all, [. . .] has fed thousands of people who are not of the Sikh community, from homeless people just to people who come in for a free meal. And the idea behind that is that it is contributing back to society and having an impact and sharing what we have with others and that does mean money, time and expertise and what we have so it is a wider thing.

A non-religious South Asian equality and diversity specialist in local government similarly commented about how the media tended to ignore the positive work that councils and other public sector organizations were undertaking to promote inter-faith dialogue and community cohesion. According to a retired Anglican chaplain, the media have a great responsibility and role to play because, 'unfortunately they sensationalise the extreme and the normal every day cheek by jowl relationships that one faith has with another within a culture like Leicester is actually very often passed over. Unfortunately the positives are so often ignored'.

Local media: More positive reporting

The 2011 survey results highlighted more reporting of unfair treatment from the national media as compared with the local. This was mirrored in the fieldwork by participants from across religious groups and also by local government representatives who reported that there is more positive reporting of religion or belief in the local media, than in the national media. As a young Muslim male of Arab origin from Cardiff put it:

> The local media is pretty well balanced [. . .]. It doesn't take a specific stance not like the tabloid papers, the national tabloid papers probably will report on things from a slightly different angle. All the local stuff I've seen hasn't been like that. [. . .] Local media I think has been supportive.

Local journalists were said to be often helpful and remained in contact with religious organizations, inter-faith organizations and local government. Media reports were usually helpful in garnering publicity for events and positive work. As an example of this, a Jewish woman interviewee in Leicester provided clippings from the local newspaper that had run a series of articles on Mitzvah day celebrations in her city, which had been organized by the Jewish community and which involved a strong element of inter-faith activities. The white male chair of a Christian Evangelical organization reported about the positive coverage of church activities in his local media including food banks, which he said would be 'another very good example that gets a lot of positive media coverage at the moment. Street Pastors and food banks are covered regularly in the local newspaper and the stories about them so people have heard about them'.

Positive media impacts

During the fieldwork, some positive impact from the media was also reported. For example a large number of Pagan group participants felt that they were more acceptable within society because of the ways in which paranormal abilities were portrayed in the media particularly in fiction and films. As one white male Pagan explained:

> But it's not just that, it's anybody with paranormal abilities as well [. . .], instead of considering to be abnormal and their things to be paranoid, it's become more acceptable for the portrayal of them within the media, not strictly Pagan but a lot of Pagans know that they're related talents, like human talents, like telepathy etc and to see them if you like portrayed in the media or certainly in fiction like [my friend] was talking about has become more acceptable. It's less, less on the outside.

A Muslim participant stated that he felt his own awareness of legislation had improved due to media coverage of cases around discrimination with regard to religion or belief. A flip-side to media coverage of legal cases was, however, also noted. As a private sector employer noted media coverage can lead to equality and diversity law being perceived as 'Black and Minority Ethnic (BME) laws':

> [The media] highlights as we said earlier BME religions as opposed to all other religions and sometimes the publication in the media is usually on the cases that extreme cases and unfortunately doesn't promote the positive steps and the positive outcomes of the legalisation.

Negative media impacts

A Muslim voluntary organization employee of Middle Eastern origin and living in Cardiff stated that he perceived the media to be problematic. As an example he discussed the experiences of his wife who chose to wear a face-veil or a *niqab*. He felt that recent media coverage of France and Belgium banning the face-veil always portrayed the *niqab* as discriminatory towards women or 'that there was something wrong about it'. He believed that such media reporting affected perceptions among people and had created stereotypes of Muslims which indirectly led to unfair treatment of Muslims including the name-calling, abuse and (occasionally) violence that his wife and other Muslims he knew had experienced.

International events impact upon incidents of unfair treatment and discrimination on the basis of religion or belief in Britain. A large proportion of Muslims reported that they experienced increased levels of Islamophobia after acts of terrorism and subsequent media coverage; the Iraq and Afghanistan wars (and related events/protests); as well as other events such as the Danish cartoon controversy. A male Muslim public sector employee in Blackburn argued that damage is done to community relations by media coverage of specific types of incidents: 'Something could have happened where an individual does something and rather than naming the individual which we wouldn't mind, to use his religion as an identity.'

The new media

Access to and use of new media by community organizations was commented upon by a number of participants. On the one hand they noted that the internet provided an unprecedented opportunity effectively to increase the reach of these organizations. This was not something that was highlighted in the 2000 fieldwork, but was perceived by participants as one of the significant changes over the last decade. As a Hindu participant from Leicester put it, 'What other changes? The internet purely because you can access information so quickly, young people are able to . . . I think there's other things like the impact of Facebook shouldn't be underestimated.'

Social media such as Twitter and blogs have opened up participation to the general public, giving them a means through which they may challenge stereotypes and misrepresentation that they may perceive. A young Muslim male fieldwork participant of South Asian ethnic origin described 'fantastic online blogs' that have 'scrutinised the British tabloid press and they found that certain stories are actually conjured up by the right wing press'. Similarly the local chair (a white middle aged female) of a Pagan organization discussed how the internet and digital media allowed Pagans to challenge an unfair article about Paganism that appeared in a national newspaper, giving the following example:

> And she wrote absolute damning reports . . . because factually some of the facts were so off the wall, they were not true facts, or they were true facts but they were taken so far out of context they were not true facts . . . if you see what I mean. And you know this report went up and all of the Pagan forums went into meltdown basically because there are a lot of online Pagan forums and things like that. And some of them actually went to get a retraction or at least an apology from the [newspaper].

However not all participants reported positive experiences of the 'new media'. Some stated that the internet offered opportunities and freedoms for different types of voices to be aired, including the expression of unfair and offensive views. For example, a Christian from an ecumenical group in Cardiff summarized:

> it has given courage to fascists to talk more openly about their prejudices and particularly with the rise of the internet where anonymous sort of online nastiness is sort of made easier. You know I browse through quite a lot of sort of online forums and discussion boards and things and the nastiness that is there is something that's quite new to me, relatively new to me and quite new to society I think, but then online discussion groups are nasty about everything I think.

Conclusion

This chapter began by noting the continuity in the results of the research completed in both 2000 and 2011, in that the social spheres of education, employment and the media were the areas in which unfair treatment was most often highlighted, with the media being identified as 'the most frequent source of unfairness by people from all religious traditions' (Weller et al., 2001: 8). At the same time there have also been important aspects of change. Not least this has included a general overall reduction across all these spheres in the reporting of unfair treatment in the survey, although in relation to the media this was less marked.

The fieldwork identified that education had, broadly speaking, become more inclusive (and especially in RE) and that there were signs that the introduction of equalities and human rights laws were associated with some discernable change towards more inclusivity, especially in public sector employment. In relation to the media, the fieldwork continued to identify very strong concerns. This also applied to aspects of the development, over the past decade, of the so-called new media. At the same time, these developments were identified as having brought benefit in terms of the ability of a religion or belief group to present information directly about itself to a wider public rather than being dependent on the mediation of publicly owned or private sector media corporations.

Having presented the survey and fieldwork findings for these three continuing areas of relatively high incidence of reported unfair treatment, the next chapter goes on to explore unfair treatment on the grounds of religion or belief in other key sectors of social life, including: criminal justice and immigration; housing; health care; social services; planning and other services; and funding.

7

Experience of Unfair Treatment in Criminal Justice and Immigration; Housing; Health Care; Social Services, Planning and Other Services; and Funding

Introduction

In this chapter, the nature and extent of unfair treatment on the basis of religion or belief is explored in the context of a range of other important sectors, including criminal justice and immigration; housing; health care; social services; planning and other services; and funding. In some of these areas, not all organizations may have direct experience such as, for example, in relation to criminal justice.

Unfair treatment in criminal justice and immigration services

We do now have a Pagan oath but some courts still do not allow this or accept it or make it easy for people to use. (Survey comment from a Pagan)

Criminal justice and immigration services in context

This section examines people's reported experience of unfair treatment in relation to the areas of criminal justice and immigration. Specifically this includes experience as reported by religious organizations in the survey, and as narrated by individual and group participants in field research interviews and focus groups, with particular reference to the police, legal services, the prison service, the probation service and the immigration service.

Only limited coverage is given in this section to legislation that is specifically focused on religion or belief equality, discrimination and human rights. Such issues have been addressed in Chapter 4 and are also considered in the concluding chapter (Chapter 10) of this book.

Survey findings on criminal justice and immigration services

Reported experience of unfair treatment in criminal justice and immigration

The surveys completed in 2000 and 2011 collected the reported experience of unfair treatment of members of religious organizations in relation to criminal justice and immigration. Respondents were asked about: the reported experience of their members in relation to unfair treatment from the attitudes and behaviour of staff in the police, legal services and the prison, probation and immigration services, as well as in the policies and practices of such organizations. As previously explained, in reporting on the survey findings we focus on the responding organizations that indicated that they had experience of the particular sphere.

In 2011 (where, on average, these questions were answered by 435 respondents), overall 23 per cent of responses highlighted experience of unfair treatment, of which 6 per cent indicated that the unfair treatment was frequent and 17 per cent that it was occasional. This compares to 2000 when overall 31 per cent of responses indicated experiences of unfair treatment. Of these 10 per cent indicated frequent unfair treatment and 21 per cent of responses indicated occasional unfair treatment (Weller et al., 2001: 175–6 and 181–2).

The reported incidence of unfair treatment on the basis of religion or belief in the sphere of criminal justice and immigration in 2011 also varied considerably across different religions with 3 per cent of Bahá'í responses, 53 per cent of Muslim responses and 65 per cent of Sikh responses indicating experiences of unfair treatment.

In terms of particular areas within the sphere of criminal justice and immigration, in the survey completed in 2011 the most commonly reported experience of unfair treatment concerned the attitudes and behaviour of immigration staff, at 36 per cent of (240) organizations; of police staff attitudes and behaviour, at 30 per cent of (338) organizations; and of prison inmate attitudes and behaviour, at 28 per cent of (175) organizations. Much lower levels of unfair treatment were reported in relation to the attitudes and behaviour of lawyers, at 15 per cent of (285) organizations.

In relation to the policies and practices of the organizations involved in implementing law and criminal justice, the results of the survey completed in 2011 suggest a substantial decline in reported experience of unfair treatment as compared with the results from the survey completed in 2000. In 2000, 23 per cent of the organizations identified experience of unfair treatment on the basis of religion in relation to the policies of the police compared to 33 per cent in relation to their practices. In 2011 in relation to police policies, 16 per cent of (322) organizations indicated experience of unfair treatment on the basis of religion as compared with 27 per cent of (324) organizations in relation to police practices. Although this represents a decline as compared with a decade ago, across the different sectors, together with prisons and the immigration service also within the overall sphere of criminal justice, this is also one of the largest gaps between reported experience of policies and practices.

In relation to prison services, in 2011, 21 per cent of (185) organizations indicated experience of unfair treatment on the basis of religion in relation to prison policies compared with 25 per cent of (181) organizations in relation to prison practices. This compares with 2000 in which 31 per cent of organizations indicated experience of unfair treatment on the basis of religion in relation to the policies of the prisons compared to 38 per cent of organizations in relation to the practices of the prison service.

With regard to the immigration service in 2011, 30 per cent of (233) organizations indicated experience of unfair treatment on the basis of religion in relation to the policies of immigration services compared to 33 per cent of (234) organizations in relation to immigration services practices. This compares with the survey completed in 2000 in which 40 per cent of organizations indicated experience of unfair treatment on the basis of religion in relation to the policies of immigration services compared to 43 per cent in relation to the practices of immigration services. Again, although the differences are not large, the overall and consistent pattern of the evidence suggests that, in criminal justice and in immigration, as in other sectors, the practices of organizations are more likely to be the source of reported unfair treatment on the basis of religion as compared with an organization's policies.

Unfair treatment in criminal justice and immigration by religion

It is important to consider in more detail, by religion, the differences concerning reported experience of unfair treatment. Given the relatively smaller numbers of organizations responding to the survey from within some religions, some of this data needs to be treated with caution.

As Table 7.1 highlights, overall Sikh and Muslim organizations were the most likely to indicate unfair treatment on the basis of religion in relation to the spheres of criminal justice and immigration, with Muslim, Sikh and inter-faith organization responses being the most likely to report frequent unfair treatment. There are some

Table 7.1 Reported experience of unfair treatment across the sphere of criminal justice and immigration as a whole, by religion

Religion	Frequent unfair treatment	Percentage	Occasional unfair treatment	Percentage	Combined percentage	No unfair treatment	Percentage	Total responses
Bahá'í	0	0	9	3	3	302	97	311
Buddhist	9	3	12	4	7	270	93	291
Other Christian	2	1	12	6	7	183	93	197
Jewish	1	1	14	7	8	185	93	200
Christian	17	1	136	10	11	1146	88	1,299
Zoroastrian	0	0	3	16	16	16	84	19
Other	2	6	6	19	25	24	75	32
Jain	0	0	22	26	26	62	74	84
Inter-faith	16	13	20	16	29	87	71	123
Hindu	24	10	60	25	35	152	64	236
NRM/Pagan	6	5	37	31	36	78	64	121
Muslim	107	17	233	36	53	307	47	647
Sikh	18	13	73	52	65	49	35	140
Total	**202**		**637**			**2,861**		**3,700**

Note: All criminal justice and immigration question section responses are combined. The mean number of organizations responding to each of the questions in the criminal justice and immigration section is 435.

Table 7.2 Unfair treatment: Attitudes and behaviour of police staff, by religion

Religion	Frequent unfair treatment	Percentage	Occasional unfair treatment	Percentage	Combined percentage	No unfair treatment	Percentage	N
Baháʼí	0	0	2	7	7	27	93	29
Buddhist	0	0	2	8	8	23	92	25
Jewish	0	0	2	9	9	21	91	23
Other Christian	0	0	2	12	12	15	88	17
Christian	2	2	14	12	14	101	86	117
NRM/Pagan	0	0	6	46	46	7	54	13
Inter-faith	2	17	4	33	50	6	50	12
Hindu	1	5	10	46	51	11	50	22
Muslim	12	22	23	42	64	20	37	55
Sikh	3	21	10	71	92	1	7	14

Note: Where response numbers are low religions have been excluded from the table. Caution should be exercised where cell counts are low.

parallels here with the results of the survey completed in 2000 when Muslim, Sikh and NRM/Pagan organizations were the most likely to report experience of unfair treatment of their members. In 2011, while Christian organizations reported that their members experienced a considerable incidence of unfair treatment, it was more often occasional than frequent.

Looking specifically at the reported experience of unfair treatment and the attitudes and behaviour of police staff (one of the areas within the overall sphere of criminal justice and immigration with the highest levels of reported unfair treatment) we can again see considerable differences by religion. Although higher levels of unfair treatment are reported in relation to immigration staff, the focus here is on police staff because of the more general role that the police play in people's daily lives.

As Table 7.2 highlights, in relation to the attitudes and behaviour of police staff Sikh, Muslim and Hindu organizations are the most likely to report that their members experienced unfair treatment. For all responding organizations, unfair treatment is on the whole occasional. From among organizations that responded to both the surveys that were completed in 2000 and 2011, there is a relative decline (from 32% to 25%) both in the overall reported experience of unfair treatment in relation to the attitudes and behaviour of police staff, and also in its frequency. However, of those organizations that reported their members as experiencing unfair treatment in 2000, 54 per cent of (37) organizations continued to report experiencing unfair treatment in 2011.

Understanding unfair treatment in criminal justice and immigration

Respondents were asked to provide details of specific examples of unfair treatment in the sphere of criminal justice and immigration that their members reported having experienced. These examples include: visa and entry into United Kingdom, dress restrictions, verbal abuse, police responses, ignorance of religious customs, oath and allegiance compliance and prison chaplaincy services. In general, the kind of issues raised were very similar to those in 2000. In Box 7.1, a selection is presented that highlights the everyday impact of unfair treatment on the grounds of religion or belief and what this means in people's lives.

Box 7.1 Unfair treatment in criminal justice and immigration: Survey comments

Buddhist comments:

> *During 11 years as Buddhist chaplain I experienced discrimination and obstruction from co-ordinating chaplains in prisons. Prison service rules and policies were frequently ignored.*

Christian comments:

> *Refusal to believe that young people or refugees are Christians. This refers to both police and immigration staff.*

'Other Christian' comments:

> *Christian Science chaplains are not allowed to conduct services in prisons.*

Jewish comments:

> *Most rabbis etc. come from outside EU and therefore need permission. It is even worse for their wives to be allowed in and to work.*

Muslim comments:

> *Coroner's Office. Policies and systematic delays in establishing cause of death and allowing burial.*

> *Many Muslims who have experience with the immigration/border agency have told us that they are branded as terrorists/extremists without having the right to put their views across.*

Pagan/NRM comments:

> *Prisons: do not treat [. . .] ministers as ministers of religion formally but do provide access. Immigration: do not accept [. . .] ministers as ministers of religion.*

Sikh comments:

> *Been asked to remove turban in full public view/Refusal of court entry due to kirpan. This is on the increase since 9/11. For someone else's doings Sikhs are paying the price.*

Zoroastrian comments:

> *Zoroastrians are a persecuted minority in Iran and many immigration employees have never heard of them.*

Unfair treatment in criminal justice and immigration: Fieldwork findings

Introduction

Approximately a third of interviewees across the five field research locations chose to speak about their experience of the criminal justice system and immigration. Interviewees sometimes spoke out of their own experience but also commented on issues that were experienced by friends and acquaintances and also news reports that they had heard or seen in the media.

Interviews and meetings were held with people who worked in the criminal justice system (including police and legal representatives), in immigration (including charities who worked with asylum seekers) and in related areas.

The police

This section is informed both by interviews with police representatives and also with members of the public who had experience with the police. As in the field research completed in 2000, interviews with police representatives explored police–community relations and multi-agency initiatives. In the field research completed in 2011, it was also possible to explore the responses of the police to laws around preventing discrimination including police and local authority initiatives to make it easier for members of the public to report instances of religion or belief discrimination and hate crimes on the grounds of religion or belief.

Among the interviewees in the field research completed in 2011 and again across all five field research locations (including both police employees and members of the wider community) there was a general sense of improvement in the services offered by the police. As a white middle-aged Anglican Christian, interviewed in Blackburn, put it: 'I mean the laws that are in place now, they seem for the last ten years to have actually had a very positive impact.'

As a police officer in Leicester said, 'So you know I think that things have improved in general, but there's always room for improvement and we can get better, but from sort of ten years to now, yes definitely.' However, because the field research completed in 2011 began only around a few years after the *Equality Act*, 2006 came into force, it was noted that current procedures to report discrimination tended to focus on other equality strands such as race and disability, with only limited coverage of discrimination with regard to religion or belief. Indeed, police representatives in all field research locations, and especially those working in areas of significant religious diversity, spoke about increasing coverage of religion or belief in equality frameworks as being a focus of their immediate strategy over the next year or so. As a female representative of the police explained:

> I can't think of any cases [discrimination with regard to religion or belief] that have come through and that's something that we need to look into and obviously promote it, because it might be that people are not reporting it. So this is what the second part of the project is about awareness within the community. I've only started doing this second phase of the project about four months ago so it will

be about reaching out into the community, going out to places of worship and making sure that the message gets across to the people in those areas, that they can report.

Not all good practice?

However not all participants from all the religion or belief groups reported such good practice. Prejudices and/or misinformation remained about smaller religious populations. For some groups, such as Pagans, the misinformation echoed historical prejudices which were often considered offensive and potentially damaging to the community. As a white Pagan woman active in a regional Pagan group explained:

> I noticed that a few months back the police produced a document about dealing with different religions when they had to question people and arrest them for things and I was quite intrigued by some of the ideas they put in that about Pagans – that Pagans are probably going to have knives and swords.

Such comments about the misinformation about Pagans were reported in all three field research locations where Pagan participants were interviewed – Leicester, Cardiff and Norwich – and are mirrored in the comments from this group of white male and female Pagans:

> And there's a handbook as well where Pagan . . .
>
> If you find people being tied up, naked and whipped in the woods then don't automatically arrest them because they might be Pagans doing a ritual.
>
> And if they're carrying a couple of knives ask them what they use them for! That sort of thing.

A number of participants in all five areas reported the unfair treatment of Muslims mostly in the wake of terrorist attacks or as part of preventing violent extremism measures. Such issues were reported by Muslim groups and also by people who worked with Muslims or had Muslim friends. Muslims were reportedly often stopped and searched. The white female director of a race equality community organization told us about police raids that she felt were sometimes unnecessary and often insensitive particularly with regard to Muslim women. This organization offered support and signposting to legal aid to individuals who felt that they had been discriminated against and stated that such cases of discrimination by the police towards Muslims were frequently brought to them:

> On top of that, the kind of discrimination we see from the state, from the police, for instance around, we've dealt with quite a few cases of people where they have been raided and anti-terrorism laws or basically any interaction between community and anti-terrorism laws where houses have been raided, the treatment of whole families during those raids, the kind of comments that have been made particularly where it is gendered response towards women, particularly, police raids tend to

occur early hours of the morning that's their policy. Muslim women who have not had chance to cover their hair, the police making comments about that as soon as they come in, very common response seems to be 'oh we've seen your hair already, no point trying to cover it up'.

One young man in Newham told us about being stopped while on the way to his law exams. This was soon after the 7/7 London bombings. He was carrying a rucksack full of his books and sported a large beard, which he felt was partly why the police stopped him. He was not, in fact, a Muslim but a Hindu, although he felt that he had been perceived as a Muslim. The police officer tried to send him away without a receipt acknowledging that he had been stopped. However, the young man insisted he wanted one and was given a receipt 15 minutes later.

Nevertheless, according to a prominent middle-aged male Muslim community leader of South Asian ethnic origin, the situation of Muslims in the United Kingdom is much better than in the rest of Europe:

> I have done a talk in Budapest with the national policing agency, who have looked at Spain, France and some of European countries, where individuals speak about three and four times a day nearly every day of their working life being stopped by police. No data is collected and hence there is a discrimination element there. Whereas in the UK there is at least some safeguard in relation to that. So everything is not bad, there is a good part to it.

Occasionally police reactions to the rights of competing equality strands can lead to perceptions of unfair treatment. A white Christian Presbyterian minister explained that he had felt unfairly treated by the police when he tried to read from the Bible on issues around homosexuality:

> Those of us who are heterosexual in our beliefs and faith beliefs, we're viewed to be the odd ones. We're not the ones who are out of order but that's how it's perceived. Quite often the police would come to us and make statements. One man said you can't be saying this in public. I said I'm only reading from the Bible and he said it's illegal. I said no it's not illegal. I said I have a son who is a barrister and therefore I know what's legal.

Community consultation, involvement and training

In the research completed in 2011, interviewees from most religious groups and in all field research locations reported that they generally had good contacts and supportive relationships with the police. They reported that the police consulted with local religious leaders, visited places of worship and, in consultation with community groups, often took preventive measures if there were any community tensions.

The quotations below highlight examples of good practice of this kind across different field research locations. As a middle-aged male Sikh community leader of South Asian origin put it: 'I know the local community police officer and she has approached me and said how do we get this message out? Do they want [us] to come to the temple, the mosques, how can we take it to the people?' Or, as noted by a middle-aged male Hindu community leader of South Asian ethnic origin: 'The police always rings us. There are some Hindu families, and Muslim families are a lot so the police always have a [presence] . . . patrolling there [outside the temple] so it makes you feel safe.. . .' As a white middle-aged male ecumenical Christian pastor said:

> At least we have a good relationship with the police here and I work with them. They come here, have tea and coffee and we just work together [. . .] I did speak to a police community support officer and he did say that he would contact a colleague just to walk those two streets at special times of the day just to make sure that there was peace and harmony. I thought that was very kind of him just to do that.

As a Muslim community leader explained:

> There's a major contribution made by the police, the local council and I think one of the successes is consultation with all members of different communities. So they will speak to community leaders, they will speak to Imams, they will speak to people at a grass roots level as well so they involve people. [. . .] they will sit people down from different faiths.

The participants quoted above, and who were representatives of local and regional religious organizations, indicated appropriate levels of support and engagement with the police. This included patrolling outside places of worship if there was the likelihood of any trouble. Thus, the level of police engagement, as reported by interviewees and particularly with regard to the protection of places of worship, seems to have improved as compared to the findings from the field research completed in 2000 when religious organizations raised concerns, such as the need for more 'police coverage of places of worship', to which the response was often that there were insufficient resources' (Weller et al., 2001: 54).

As in the previous research a number of examples were identified of police working with community groups in order to enhance their equality and diversity training. In all the field research locations, we met a number of community leaders from all religious backgrounds who had trained police officers about their religion. Sessions offered included information about basic religious belief and cultural sensitivities.

Religion, race and ethnicity in the criminal justice system

As was also evident in the field research completed in 2000, there continued to be significant areas of overlap between unfair treatment in relation to religion, race and ethnicity. For example, a female Muslim Race Equality Officer in the public sector, and of Somali origin, recalled being shouted at by a police officer who, without realizing that she was an educated public sector employee, shouted 'If you can't read then you shouldn't be driving' and 'Get out of this country'. She was not sure whether he said this to her because of her race or ethnicity, or because she was identifiable as a Muslim woman because of the headscarf/*hijab* that she wears.

At the same time, as discussed above, many Muslim participants reported being stopped and searched by the police because they were visible as Muslims. Approximately two-thirds of the Muslim population in Britain are of South Asian origin, and Hindu and Sikh groups who are also of South Asian origin, reported being similarly stopped and searched, which they felt was unfair treatment and discriminatory. Sikhs being mistaken for Muslims was also reported in the survey write-ins. Since these groups shared the same racial or ethnic background as Muslims, they also felt targeted by unfair treatment. A female Hindu doctor of South Asian ethnic origin gave another example she had heard:

> A young man from an Asian [Hindu] community was coming in the underground and swiping his oyster card, there were a few policemen there with dogs, he just glanced at him and all of a sudden . . . they took him . . . they took this lad, taking him into a police station and questioned him and put his name on the register so that was discrimination.

Similarly, many participants from among black Christian groups felt that young men within the community were often harassed by the police. In these instances the religious background of the 'victim' was not always evident but his racial or ethnic background was. The problems involved in identifying the racial/ethnic and/or religious dimensions of an incident were discussed with the police and with support workers. A black female Christian race equality specialist who works in the voluntary sector expressed the view that, particularly in African Caribbean communities, it is often difficult to judge whether someone has been discriminated against because of his or her race or religion:

> I mean something that springs to mind straight away is around Afro-Caribbean community and . . . the number of stop and searches but that is where there is a combination of a visual identity which is around race but also around the association with Rastas, yeah it is a racial discrimination and yes that gets reported to us, it's constant, constant sense of surveillance not being able to escape the police.

A female Muslim police advisor gave an example about young Somali men being targeted by stop and search activities. She stated that this unfair profiling of all Somali youth was perhaps also influenced by suspicions of gang culture among these young people. According to her, such instances were often complicated and it was difficult to separate race, religion and other sociopolitical contexts. By contrast as another (white Christian female) police officer in Leicester told us, there are issues around the reporting of hate crime and victims often themselves being unsure of the basis on which they have experienced unfair treatment:

> So you know, they are reporting that they are being victims of hate incidents or hate crime but they are saying it is because of their race but it might be because

of their beliefs and that may be simply that and really to answer that question I suppose, it's on there, it's on the forms but you know they just need to respond really, so not sure.

A similar phenomenon was reported from the field research completed in 2000, in which police and support workers argued that 'a bully or perpetrator of harassment will ultimately use whatever vulnerabilities they attribute to their victim in order to inflict harm' (Weller et al., 2001: 54). Sometimes the perpetrators of such harassment are themselves aware of legal frameworks and also of loopholes within these frameworks which they then use to their benefit, which is what appeared to have happened in one complicated case narrated by a male Hindu race equality support worker of South Asian ethnic origin:

> . . . a client of ours is from a Hindu background and was living next to a white working class guy who very openly said that he was part of the BNP [. . .] and for years this person used to racially abuse them because of their Hindu faith and because of their Asian Indian Hindu background [. . .] so he wasn't just blatant racism but just general antagonism and that's the face of racism now that you don't have to say things to be racist it's your whole demeanour that make you a racist. [. . .] sometimes it wasn't specifically attacking the Hindu religion but it was attacking Asians as a whole, so for example he was throwing burnt toast over the wall implying that we're black [. . .] He threw white paint over their garden to imply that it was a white country [. . .] and he actually said it as he did it – forgive me for being very explicit, he threw contraceptives over the garden saying 'all of you lot should start using these'.

Bad policy or insensitive individuals in criminal justice and immigration

During the field research completed in 2011 a small number of participants reported inconsistent treatment by different members of the police force or in different situations. They felt that this was indicative of overall policies and legal frameworks that were robust, but that there were individuals who had prejudices and who therefore treated people unfairly. As a middle-aged Sikh man of South Asian ethnic origin put it, 'I know there is an Equality Act but at the end of the day it depends upon individual people.'

A young, male Muslim community worker of Middle Eastern ethnic origin stated that his wife (who wears a face veil) was repeatedly abused and on one occasion attacked by miscreants in the city centre who he felt were possibly motivated by her religious practice. However, although he made many complaints to the police, he felt that the issue was not dealt with seriously. On the other hand, when the police visited his local mosque to investigate complains about a bomb being stored in the mosque premises, he said they were extremely courteous and understanding and took care not to disturb worshippers in the mosque. When the suspected 'bomb' was ultimately discovered to be a gas cylinder (for a barbecue), they apologized appropriately. Overall, given the situation, our interviewee felt that this was a reasonably positive experience thanks to the sensitivity of the police officers involved in the search.

Another elderly Sikh man of South Asian origin in Newham told us what happened to his nephew when he reported an incident of road rage, which became a religiously motivated hate crime when his turban was taken off by the perpetrator:

> . . . so my nephew went to the police, gave them the registration number of the motorbike, the person, and there was a black person on the counter and she said, we know who that person is. Two weeks later he went back for interview, asked what had happened and the white sergeant who was there totally denied that that number existed. So within groups, there is still doubt, with the police, if you know who the police are, you'll find things will get done.

According to a small number of participants from various religious backgrounds and also those working in the voluntary sector to support victims of crime, some police staff (and including Hate Crime officers) make excuses such as 'Well there's counter allegations, there's not much we can do.' Participants felt that such excuses can potentially lead to delays in legal processes and frustration for victims, and also that offenders can sometimes be let off easily. A voluntary support worker who works with victims of hate crime summarizes this issue well:

> Our concern is when you give a person with prejudice power to do things that is how things would change so for example a police officer has power to do things and if that person has prejudice already built in them over time.

Accommodating religious needs in criminal justice and immigration

While the notion of accommodation for religious needs was not specifically cited, there is evidence that through interactions with different community leaders and groups the police are aware of the needs of these groups and where reasonably possible, try to accommodate them. For example, a Hindu community leader in Cardiff told us about the police being understanding during Diwali celebrations which went on till quite late in the night and which ended with a fireworks display. It was also reported that faith advisors were also available to most police departments to advise on cultural and religious sensitivities in specific instances and prayer rooms and prayer facilities are often available in police stations. According to a Sikh man of South Asian ethnic origin who was also a community leader both within the Sikh community and in wider inter-faith contexts:

> Even in the police headquarters we have got the prayer room established. So I think that things have moved on but if you think that 100% we have achieved this goal, no it can never be achieved even by any strict rules or regulations or any legislation.

The Prison Service

The field research interviews did not generally touch upon the prison service which, clearly, only directly affects a minority of the population. However, interviews with prison chaplains provided some insights about religion and belief in the prison service. A white middle-aged male Buddhist prison chaplain told us how despite the prison he worked at having had an expensive refurbishment, the prison still did not have a multi-faith room. He also felt that as a Buddhist chaplain he was not allowed the same facilities to which Christian chaplains had access. At the same time, he recognized that, over the past decade, positive change had taken place in prison chaplaincies in that they had become more inclusive towards all the different religious groups:

> When I first became a prison chaplain in 1999, it was a Christian chaplaincy. They would call in other people to visit. If a prisoner specifically wanted to see a Buddhist or a Muslim or a Hindu, then they had people they could call in but that all began to change shortly after I joined . . . within a year of joining. About a year later they appointed a new chaplain general who [. . .] decided that we were all chaplains because previously they wouldn't accept people of other religions as being called chaplains.

This sense of greater inclusivity was echoed by many other chaplains in describing their own work with prisoners from their respective religious communities. Even less widely known groups with small prison populations felt that their religious needs were met. A white Baháʼí chaplain who stated he had only spoken to two Baháʼí prisoners during his career as a chaplain, reported that, although initially prison officials did not know much about the Baháʼí faith, once they had the appropriate information, they made special provisions for these prisoners including keeping food aside for them during fasting periods when they only ate at dawn and after sunset. As a retired elderly white Anglican Christian female chaplain explained, in her opinion this positive change was due to the education of prison staff and also to the development of more diverse chaplaincy teams:

> There was a lovely poster that we used to have up with I think four babies, a white one, an Asian and a couple of black ones, and they were all little babies of only a couple of weeks old and the caption is no-one is born racist and prejudiced, and you know the culture you live in and what you are taught. And I think teaching people is as valuable for all. . . . those are the two things in the prison service that made the real difference: [education and training] and recruitment of a wider variety of officers because it used to be just sort of ex-service men came out of army or somewhere and went straight into the prison service.

Within the field research one instance of reported unfair treatment was narrated by a white voluntary sector support worker who worked with victims of hate crime and discrimination. It was about the treatment of Muslim women who visited their relatives in prison: 'Muslim women in particular I know going into prisons and being searched and the issues around searches and where the search is being conducted by men or women and in view.'

Lawyers and the courts

The field research interviews completed in 2011 did not give rise to much exploration of issues related to lawyers and the courts. In the report of the 2000 research, interviewees commented on the availability of prayer facilities and also on the occasional inappropriateness of the training for solicitors and barristers (Weller et al., 2001: 57). In the field research completed in 2011, nothing similar was reported. However, a white female legal support worker argued that the time taken to complete some legal proceedings made some victims of discrimination-related crimes feel let down.

> Yeah, I had a case recently a lady was assaulted, her and her brother were assaulted by a neighbour and it went through the court procedure [. . .], it's a very difficult process for her, it took six months from when it happened for it actually to go to court. And she felt very much let down at the end of it by the court system, given the sentence that this person received.

Some participants from a variety of religious backgrounds reported being able to take an oath in courts using their own religious scripture or beliefs. As reported by some Pagan participants this included the option to take a Pagan oath. Non-religious participants had the option to 'affirm' rather than take a religious oath while giving evidence in court. However, not all non-religious participants were aware of that option and a number expressed concern that not taking an oath would have a negative impact on their credibility. For example, as it was articulated by a non-religious white man in Cardiff:

> And that may colour people's attitudes to you, if they think you are some sort of troublemaker or eccentric as I say, that may colour the attitude of the jury or a magistrate takes towards you, and I know a number of people who have given expert witness testimony in court who are non-believers but they actually do swear on the Bible because they feel that if they don't it will undermine their credibility at some point.

During the field research, the *niqab* or face-veil worn by some Muslim women was discussed in many contexts, including that of the courts, and with views being expressed by people from many different backgrounds. For example, a middle-aged white Mormon woman wondered if it was appropriate to wear it in court; about what reasonable accommodation may be undertaken to facilitate freedom of expression; and what the wider implications of any rulings might be on people's freedoms more generally:

> I think there are perhaps times where the full veil perhaps in an interview situation, in a court situation I can understand where that might be a barrier but surely that could be accommodated by privacy arrangements, these things can all be accommodated I'm sure without impinging on somebody's right to express their religious or ethnic preferences and again there's the argument.

The Mormon woman went on to express her argument that 'So it's such a loaded and complicated field but I feel we should be free to express our religious practices as we wish. If that should impinge upon the freedom of other people then perhaps that needs to be addressed but more often than not it's simply a personal preference and doesn't impinge upon other people's rights or freedoms.'

Immigration

During the field research, the topic of immigration was frequently spoken about, although often in very general terms. Participants spoke about immigration and media coverage of issues around immigration and migrants. As mentioned in the report of the 2000 research, 'because of ancestral origins outside of the United Kingdom, some religious minorities have much more experience of the immigration system than the population at large. Those who have not been immigrants or asylum seekers themselves may still have come into contact with the system through the experiences of family members or others in the community' (Weller et al., 2001: 58). In the same report it was stated that unfair treatment often occurred during entry clearance procedures for people entering the country for arranged marriages, in relation to which immigration staff lacked in cultural sensitivity. Though in the field research completed in 2011, this was not mentioned by any participant.

However religion did not always form part of these discussions. Although the recent increase in Eastern European migrants was often mentioned by participants from all religious and ethnic backgrounds and in all the field research locations, this was not usually linked to discrimination on the basis of religion or belief as such because the religious identity of these groups was not always evident. At the same time, people of Eastern European origins were often recognizable by their accents and inability or limited ability to speak English and it was noted that, coupled with perceptions around competition for resources this, on occasion, led to discrimination. At the same time in relation to religion or belief groups, the small number of fieldwork participants who were of Eastern European origin themselves explained that they had felt welcomed into local church communities, while a fieldwork participant who worked with these communities in Newham commented that 'they were quite easily integrated or welcomed by the Catholic Church here because they share a common liturgy'.

Nevertheless, as in the previous research, some participants from Buddhist, Hindu and Muslim religious groups, in particular, mentioned recurring problems in securing visas for religious ministers. Also, in one case, a white non-religious participant stated that while applying for a visa to travel to India, he had to 'choose' a religion for himself and his partner as this was a compulsory question on the electronic visa form. He said it made him reflect on the progress that has been made in the United Kingdom in the census and other forms which allow for a non-religious option: 'I mean we went to India at the beginning of the year and on their visa form you have to tick a religion and I think I put us down as Buddhists or something just because you had to tick something!'

Asylum seekers

A number of issues were reported in relation to asylum seekers, some of which were more general, such as those set out by this non-religious youth support worker in Norwich:

> Well because you know the law itself is already set in a way that asylum seekers are already discriminated against already, they don't have access, they cannot work, they cannot have access to higher education, they cannot, all this they cannot access except [. . .] support, they cannot access other benefits you know so they are already discriminated against so it is very difficult now to say because the law is already there so it is difficult.

A small number of participants also reported incidents of unfair treatment that were more specific to religion or belief. A Methodist Christian of Pakistani background recounted his own experiences while seeking asylum in the United Kingdom. He spoke Urdu as his first language and since his Urdu translators were of Pakistani origin and also Muslim, he felt that the translator did not correctly translate what he said. This participant was ultimately successful in his asylum application and now supports other asylum seekers. He feels that current asylum seekers also continue to face the problems that he faced. Many Christian asylum seekers who come from countries with small Christian populations and whose practices are culturally quite different from Christian practice in the United Kingdom, face the added challenge of having to prove their Christian faith. In this process, the questions that asylum seekers are asked in order to prove their religion are often culturally inappropriate as Christian practice varies according to cultural contexts. According to a white male Anglican priest in Blackburn:

> In the questionnaires that the asylum seekers get for Christians, strange things like what does the colour red and white mean, and what fruit did Adam eat, and it [the bible] doesn't mention [a specific fruit or] colours and so the Christians, even if they're sincere, they have a very difficult time proving that they're actually committed because they've never seen that written anywhere, its not in the Bible and its more religion than it is from the Christian faith.

Examples like this suggest a lack of religious literacy. In the field research completed in 2011, the problem of having to 'prove their faith' was reported only in relation to Christian asylum seekers. However, some other individuals and organizations working with asylum seekers reported positive experiences of the immigration system and of being successfully able to make the case for asylum seekers who were Christian. As with police practice there seem to be appropriate legal frameworks as indicated by the positive experiences of some asylum seekers, however there also seem to be inconsistencies in how these frameworks are implemented.

The sphere of criminal justice is an area in which – as can be seen in the reports of the field research completed in 2011, the complex and contested relationship between religion, race and ethnicity comes particularly to the fore in the way in which individuals are treated as part of the perceptions of the religious, racial and ethnic groups to which they are perceived to belong. We now move on to consider the area of housing.

Unfair treatment in housing

Member's acquaintance moved north and when staff at estate agent saw her and husband walk in looking for house, were negative and claimed none of the houses advertised were available. Only changed attitude when discovered her husband was a doctor who'd be working in the local hospital. (Survey comment from a Muslim respondent)

Introduction

Housing is a key aspect of people's lives and a basic human need. Religion and culture can affect housing needs and preferences and people's views about what facilities should or should not be provided in the neighbourhood. A home is often a centre for wider family life and also brings people into contact with neighbours, communities and a wider shared space and belonging.

Reported experience of unfair treatment in housing

The surveys completed in 2000 and 2011 collected the reported experience of unfair treatment of members of religious organizations in relation to: the attitudes and behaviour of estate agents, letting agents, landlords, council staff and neighbours and other tenants. In addition, reported experience of unfair treatment in relation to housing organizations' policies and practices in the public and private sectors were collected.

The questions covered the key areas of housing and, as such, provide a valuable insight into how the members of religious organizations experience unfair treatment in relation to the area. As is the case across a number of policy areas since the survey completed in 2000, the level of reported unfair treatment on the basis of religion in the area of housing has on the whole declined.

In 2000, 24 per cent of organization responses indicated experience of unfair treatment, of which 6 per cent indicated that unfair treatment was frequent and 18 per cent that it was occasional. In the survey completed in 2011 overall 16 per cent of responses highlighted frequent or occasional experience of unfair treatment, of which 2 per cent indicated that unfair treatment was frequent and 14 per cent that it was occasional. This also appeared to be a consistent pattern that can be identified in the qualitative evidence and across the different areas of housing. But despite this and the overall reported decline, the level of reported unfair treatment is still substantial, indicating the scale of the impact on people's lives.

The reported incidence of unfair treatment on the basis of religion or belief in the sphere of housing varied considerably across different religions. For example, there were no reported experiences of unfair treatment from Zoroastrian organization responses compared to 47 per cent of Muslim responses.

In the survey completed in 2011, the most commonly reported experience of unfair treatment in housing concerned the attitudes and behaviour of neighbours in areas where people owned or were buying their own home, and the attitudes and behaviour of other council and private tenants and private sector landlords. In total 27 per cent of (304) organizations reported unfair treatment from their neighbours (where people owned or were buying their own home). This compares to 37 per cent in 2000.

Comparing between housing sector providers, the highest levels of reported unfair treatment were in relation to the attitudes and behaviour of private sector landlords. In this, 21 per cent of (287) organizations reported unfair treatment, while the levels of reported unfair treatment were lower in relation to the attitudes and behaviour of council staff, estate agents and housing trust staff. In terms of policies and practices of council housing services, levels of reported unfair treatment were a little lower in relation to the policies of housing organizations than in relation to their practices. Although the difference is small, the pattern is still consistent with the other sectors covered by the research.

Unfair treatment in housing: Survey findings by religion

It is important to consider in more detail, and by religion, the differences in relation to reported experience of unfair treatment from responding organizations of different religions. Given the relatively smaller numbers of organizations responding to the survey from within some religious groups, some of this data needs to be treated with caution.

As Table 7.3 highlights, overall Sikh and Muslim organizations were the most likely to report that their members had experienced unfair treatment on the basis of religion

Table 7.3 Reported experience of unfair treatment across the sphere of housing as a whole, by religion

Religion	Frequent unfair treatment	Percentage	Occasional unfair treatment	Percentage	Combined percentage	No unfair treatment	Percentage	N
Zoroastrian	0	0	0	0	0	54	100	54
Other	0	0	0	0	0	36	100	36
Buddhist	0	0	6	2	2	345	98	351
Christian	5	0	78	4	3	1654	95	1737
Bahá'í	0	0	14	3	3	410	97	424
Other Christian	2	1	16	6	7	240	93	258
Jewish	0	0	26	14	14	162	86	188
Jain	0	0	16	15	15	88	85	104
NRM/Pagan	0	0	34	22	22	119	78	153
Hindu	5	2	72	25	27	210	73	287
Inter-faith	4	3	37	30	33	84	67	125
Sikh	8	5	48	31	36	101	64	157
Muslim	77	10	272	37	47	389	53	738
Total	**101**		**619**			**3,892**		**4,612**

Note: All housing question section responses are combined. The mean number of organizations responding to each of the questions in the housing section is 434.

Table 7.4 Unfair treatment: from neighbours when owning or buying a home, by religion

Religion	Frequent unfair treatment	Percentage	Occasional unfair treatment	Percentage	Combined percentage	No unfair treatment	Percentage	N
Buddhist	0	0	2	9	9	20	91	22
Christian	0	0	13	12	12	96	88	109
Other Christian	0	0	2	13	13	14	88	16
Baháʼí	0	0	4	14	14	25	86	29
Jewish	0	0	6	33	33	12	67	18
Sikh	1	8	3	25	33	8	67	12
Hindu	1	6	9	50	56	8	44	18
Muslim	7	14	23	47	61	19	39	49

Note: Where response numbers are low religions have been excluded from the table. Caution should be exercised where cell counts are low.

or belief in relation to housing. There are some parallels here with the 2000 survey, where Muslim, Sikh and Hindu organizations were the most likely to report experience of unfair treatment. However, again, overall and across most religions there would seem to be a decline in the reported experience of unfair treatment since 2000.

In the surveys completed in 2000 and 2011, the attitudes and behaviour of neighbours when owning or buying a house is the most frequently reported source of unfair treatment in relation to housing and, once again, there are considerable differences by religion.

As Table 7.4 highlights, Hindu and Muslim organizations are the most likely to report that their members experienced unfair treatment from neighbours when owning or buying a home. Buddhist and Christian organizations were the least likely to state their members experienced unfair treatment. Unfair treatment is, on the whole, occasional for all organizations, though Muslim organizations are the most likely to report frequent unfair treatment from neighbours when owning or buying a house. From among organizations that responded to both the surveys that were completed in 2000 and 2011, there is evidence of a limited decline (from 31% to 27% of organizations) in the reported experiences of unfair treatment from neighbours. However, of those organizations that reported their members experiencing unfair treatment in 2001, 44% of (27) organizations continued to report experiencing unfair treatment in 2011.

Understanding unfair treatment in housing

Respondents were asked to provide details of specific examples of unfair treatment in relation to housing. These examples include: the attitudes and behaviour of neighbours, tenants and landlords. In general, the kinds of issues raised in 2011 were very similar to those in 2000. In Box 7.2, a selection is presented that highlights the everyday impact and/or complexity of unfair treatment on the grounds of religion or belief and what this means in people's lives.

Box 7.2 Unfair treatment in housing: Survey comments

Christian comments:

> *A neighbour shouting and swearing abuse because they go to church.*
>
> *Councils will not rent property to Christian Church organizations such as this one.*

Hindu comments:

> *For vegetarian Hindus living with non-vegetarians is a problem.*

Muslim comments:

> *Asian people find it difficult to get housed in areas which they want, i.e. in areas of established Asian areas.*
>
> *Estate agents discourage ethnic people moving into certain areas and do not pass offer to vendors.*
>
> *Once they see a Muslim covered they automatically assume we don't understand English.*
>
> *Muslim members within the community have reported that invariably they are the recipients of some of the poorest standard of housing available within the area as there is a perception that they will take up whatever is on offer.*

Sikh comments:

> *The Sikh aged get accommodation away from our temple.*

Inter-faith comments:

> *Neighbour with mental health problems v. abusive and very noisy to neighbouring Muslim family so that family scared to go outside and children couldn't sleep at bed-time. Council failed to attend to matter.*

Unfair treatment in housing: Fieldwork findings

Generally improved but . . .

In relation to unfair treatment on the basis of religion or belief, discussions with participants seemed to indicate a general improvement in facilities and provision for housing. Repeatedly during interviews in each of the five field research locations, participants from different religious and ethnic backgrounds asserted that housing was one of the sectors that had seen considerable improvement.

However, the concerns expressed by individuals in the field research completed in 2011 are similar to those expressed in that completed in 2000. These include tensions due to 'turf wars'; disputes between neighbours; changing religious landscapes in towns and cities; inconsistencies in planning permission; and the issue of vandalism. It was, however, noticeable that in most instances the discriminatory attitudes/

occurrences seem to have been directed towards religious organizations more than towards individuals and so are reported on within the section on 'Services'. It is notable that the non-religious participants who were consulted did not describe any issues or experience of unfair treatment in relation to housing.

Individuals, unfair treatment and 'ghettos'

In the field research interviews, very few individuals mentioned experiencing discrimination in housing. However, in two separate incidents participants who were undertaking work in the voluntary sector mentioned examples of individuals who they believed were treated unfairly by their local authority with regard to their housing needs. The first example was narrated by a white Anglican parish priest working with a family of Pakistani Christian asylum seekers. The family was housed in an area where they were facing what they felt was unfair treatment from the local, predominantly Pakistani Muslim, population. The council offered to move the family to a 'safer' place. However these plans were cancelled at the last minute leading to considerable sustained stress for the family. In the second example, a white female participant who worked with a race and equality voluntary organization described how a Muslim woman was offered accommodation in an area that was dominated by far-right politics:

> The day that she was shown her house, she got comments shouted at her, [. . .] she said 'I'm not going to be able to take this', she was told that, [. . .] this is the housing officer who said this to her, this is the environment we are in now, you have to, you have to get used to it, in terms of that kind of discrimination, it's acceptable because of the implication was what you've done, what your community has done, this was after the 2005 bombings, and then she continued to be called 'Bin Laden's Bitch' in the street, she was walking with her child, and comments about being a ninja, things like that. We did manage to get her moved, but it was a struggle . . .

In another case a South Asian female voluntary sector employee described how her Asian Hindu client was verbally abused by his neighbour who was a white far-right activist. According to this participant, 'it wasn't specifically attacking the Hindu religion but it was attacking Asians as a whole'. Often, as in other instances of unfair treatment, it can be difficult to separate race/ethnicity and religion and of these examples raise concerns about the perceived ghettoization of cities and towns in British cities. Participants sometimes commented about the 'Muslim', 'White', 'Hindu', 'Posh' and/or 'Rough' side of town. This was not always in the context of unfair treatment, discrimination or 'divided British societies', nevertheless they remained a feature of narratives around diversity. However, in contrast to these narratives about segregation, as has been mentioned in the section on the media in the previous chapter, a number of participants in Blackburn expressed strong criticism of the *BBC Panorama* programme, which they thought portrayed Blackburn as a segregated city.

Indeed, a female inter-faith activist reported that the programme had been what inspired her to participate in inter-faith activities.

> I think despite the *Panorama* programme a few years ago which was a very bad view of Blackburn I thought. It was wrong in what it concluded, that we were a very segregated town. That's what made me go to an inter faith forum because I wanted to do some work on that.

Unfair treatment was also reported in relation to properties rented from religion or belief organizations. A white middle-aged Christian woman felt that her daughter who was living in church-owned property was treated unfairly when she was asked to leave her rented accommodation after she suffered from a mental illness. Her daughter was told by her landlord that 'real Christians can pray and therefore if you do have mental illness you're not praying hard enough'.

Housing and immigration

An issue that was not discussed during the field research completed in 2000, but which formed a significant strand of inquiry in the field research completed in 2011, was the relationship between immigration and housing. Concerns around immigration do not necessarily reflect concerns about religion and can, like other things, reflect overlaps between religion, race and ethnicity and also, perhaps, political rhetoric. Nevertheless the impact of immigration was something that a number of participants discussed. A Parish priest in Norwich described a huge change in the social demographics of his parish. For example he noticed that suddenly a large proportion of the social housing was taken up by Eastern European migrants. People were generally concerned that these 'newcomers' were 'taking over'. As a white, female, voluntary sector worker put it:

> You know all these people who, we understand, I mean people who are less interested in politics or at least listen to the politicians, we understand that our economy needs migrants or immigrants whatever but majority of people now believe that these newcomers they just take away from us jobs, wealth, housing and all other things. And that is a big threat to the society.

A number of participants stated that such concerns about social housing were being reported by all sections of society and that perhaps there was a problem of improper allocation and unfair or biased sharing of resources. One participant wondered whether councillors were 'favouring their own' while allocating social housing. Other participants also voiced concerns around the exploitation of immigrants, particularly with regard to housing, giving them properties of inferior quality.

Good practice

Alongside these continuing issues a large proportion of participants spoke about emergent good practice, especially in public sector provision. According to these participants, this improvement was at least partly attributable to legislation that allowed for inclusivity, increasing awareness of diversity and changed attitudes. In Blackburn, a Muslim man of South Asian heritage described this as follows:

> There's been great strides in that [housing] respect, yes. I've heard of a time when people would apply for state subsidized housing, in the form of council housing in the 60's and the 70's and such was the response from clerks within the council in certain areas that they were turned away at the door without any of their details being recorded. [. . .] but when you compare that situation that . . . to what the situation today is there is a stark contrast. Things have changed. Attitudes have changed. There's more procedures in place to regulate the way public sector workers operate and to ensure discrimination doesn't take place. It's not to say everything's perfect. [. . .] A lot of work still needs to take place but we can see that there's been great improvements over the years.

Another new strand that emerged was participants' narratives of good practice. For example, a public sector employee and equality and diversity specialist in the NHS (and who is a white Christian female) spoke about being more aware of the religion and culture of service users:

> Another one was staff going to people's homes and they [. . .] didn't know whether they should or shouldn't take their shoes off, and it got raised as a health and safety issue and I was asked to go along to a health and safety meeting [. . .] I knew it was predominantly in terms of going into people's homes who were of the Muslim faith and what had happened was, staff were coming on training and I was explaining about when you go into people's homes some people pray at home and you need to be mindful that when you're going into that house you may be going into the room where they pray.

Finally, an elderly white Christian man mentioned how the care home he lived in was being adapted to suit the needs of a more diverse population:

> I wanted to make sure that this new facility was compatible with a more diverse clientele using these facilities, whereas traditionally I suppose an Asian clientele would have been very rare. [. . .] they've specifically set out to try and make these facilities more compatible with people from different faiths.

Unfair treatment in health care

In the past have had GPs make comments such as I 'was ignorant' because I practised chastity. I don't think this would happen today – attitudes have improved. (Survey comment from Bahá'í respondent)

Introduction

Health and access to health services is a key aspect of people's lives and a basic human need. Religious identity and practice can affect people's behaviour and specific needs not only in terms of accessing health care, but also in the treatment they need and receive.

Reported experience of unfair treatment in health

The surveys completed in 2011 and 2001 collected the reported experience of unfair treatment of members of religious organizations in relation to: the attitudes and behaviour of general practitioners (GPs), NHS and private health care medical and non-medical staff and patients, as well as experience of unfair treatment in relation to public and private sector health care policies and practices.

As is the case across a number of other policy areas since the research completed in 2000, the level of reported unfair treatment on the basis of religion in the area of health care has on the whole declined.

In 2000, 20 per cent of responses indicated experience of unfair treatment, of which 4 per cent indicated unfair treatment that was frequent and 16 per cent that was occasional. In the 2011 survey (where, on average, these questions were answered by 434 respondents), overall 14 per cent of responses highlighted frequent or occasional experience of unfair treatment, of which 1 per cent indicated unfair treatment that was frequent and 13 per cent that was occasional. Despite the overall reported decline, the level of reported unfair treatment is still substantial, indicating the scale of its impact on people's lives, although for most religious organizations that reported unfair treatment on the basis of religion in the sphere of health care, it was occasional rather than frequent.

The reported incidence of unfair treatment on the basis of religion and belief in health care varied considerably across different religions from 0 per cent of the so-called 'Other religious' organization responses compared to 47 per cent of Sikh organization responses.

In the survey completed in 2011 the most commonly reported experience of unfair treatment concerned the attitudes and behaviour of NHS medical staff. In total 20 per cent of (343) organizations reported unfair treatment in relation to attitudes and behaviour of NHS medical staff. This compares to 26 per cent in 2000. Comparing types of health-care sector providers, lower levels of unfair treatment were reported in relation to private health care, private health-care staff and patients.

In terms of the policies and practices of NHS hospital trusts, higher levels of reported unfair treatment were reported in relation to Trust policies, at 15 per cent of (339) organizations compared to practices, at 18 per cent of (341) organizations. Though the difference is small, the pattern is still consistent with the findings in relation to other areas of people's lives.

We consider the issue of differences between an organization's policies and practices and the implications for policy-makers in more detail in Chapter 10.

Unfair treatment in health care: Survey findings by religion

It is important to consider in more detail, and by religion, the differences concerning reported experience of unfair treatment from responding organizations. Given the relatively smaller numbers of organizations responding to the survey from within some religious groups, some of these findings need to be treated with caution. Table 7.5 provides a summary of the responses by religion to all the questions in the sphere of health care.

As Table 7.5 highlights, Sikh and Muslim organizations were the most likely to report unfair treatment on the basis of religion in health care sectors. There are some parallels with the survey completed in 2000, with Muslim and Sikh organizations again most likely to report experience of unfair treatment from among their members, though NRM/Pagan organizations also reported comparably higher levels of unfair treatment in 2000 (44%). Higher levels of unfair treatment were also reported by Jain and Zoroastrian organizations in 2000, although the number of responding organizations upon which this is based was small.

In Table 7.6 we look specifically at reported unfair treatment in relation to the attitudes and behaviour of NHS medical staff (the overall area with the highest levels of reported unfair treatment). Considerable differences by religion can again be identified. As Table 7.6 highlights Sikh, NRM/Pagan and Muslim organizations were the most likely to report that their members experienced unfair treatment due to the attitudes and behaviour of NHS medical staff. Buddhist, Bahá'í and Christian organizations were the least likely to state that their members experienced unfair treatment. Unfair treatment is almost always occasional across all of the religions. From among those organizations that responded to both the surveys that were completed in 2000 and 2011, there is a

Table 7.5 Reported experience of unfair treatment across the sphere of health care as a whole, by religion

Religion	Frequent unfair treatment	Percentage	Occasional unfair treatment	Percentage	Combined percentage	No unfair treatment	Percentage	Total responses
Other	0	0	0	0	0	24	100	24
Bahá'í	0	0	3	1	1	334	99	337
Buddhist	0	0	6	2	2	308	98	314
Zoroastrian	2	5	0	0	5	42	95	44
Christian	6	0	88	6	7	1,299	93	1,393
Jain	0	0	7	8	8	81	92	88
Other Christian	6	3	23	11	14	176	86	205
Jewish	0	0	38	14	14	228	86	266
NRM/Pagan	0	0	20	17	17	101	83	121
Inter-faith	4	3	24	19	23	96	77	124
Hindu	0	0	56	27	27	154	73	210
Muslim	19	3	177	31	35	372	65	568
Sikh	13	9	53	38	47	74	53	140
Total	**50**		**495**			**3,289**		**3,834**

Note: All health-care question section responses are combined. The mean number of organizations responding to each of the questions in the health-care section is 430.

Table 7.6 Unfair treatment: NHS medical staff attitudes and behaviour, by religion

Religion	Frequent unfair treatment	Percentage	Occasional Unfair Treatment	Percentage	Combined percentage	No unfair treatment	Percentage	N
Bahá'í	0	0	0	0	0	30	100	30
Buddhist	0	0	0	0	0	29	100	29
Christian	0	0	15	12	12	114	88	129
Jewish	0	0	4	17	17	20	83	24
Inter-faith	0	0	3	27	27	8	73	11
Other Christian	1	5	5	25	30	14	70	20
Hindu	0	0	6	32	32	13	68	19
Muslin	3	5	22	39	44	32	56	57
NRM/Pagan	0	0	5	45	46	6	55	11
Sikh	1	8	7	54	62	5	38	13

Note: Where response numbers are low religions have been excluded from the table. Caution should be exercised where cell counts are low.

slight decline (from 22% to 16%) in the reported unfair experiences of their members from the attitudes and behaviours of NHS staff. However, of those organizations that reported their members experiencing unfair treatment in 2001, 30 per cent of (25) organizations continued to report experiencing unfair treatment in 2011.

Understanding unfair treatment in health care

Respondents were asked to provide details of specific examples of unfair treatment in relation to health care. These examples include: the attitudes and behaviour of medical and non-medical staff, health organization policies and practices, language issues, dietary requirements and chaplaincy services. Again, in general, the kinds of issues raised in 2011 were very similar to those in 2000. In Box 7.3, a selection is presented that highlights the everyday impact and/or complexity of unfair treatment on the grounds of religion or belief and what this means in people's lives.

Box 7.3 Unfair treatment in health care: Survey comments

Christian comments:

NHS staff suspended or disciplined for delivering care in keeping with their lived faith or for wearing religious jewellery.

Abortion has been pushed at someone.

Other Christian comments:

Paramedics and ambulance staff have to act quickly in emergencies and may not know a person does not want medical products derived from animal sources.

Prejudice over our position on blood transfusion is quite rare now.

Inter-faith comments:

Mental health services/practitioners unable/unwilling to recognise spiritual dimension of patients' lives/support system.

Jain comments:

Lack of vegetarian food made available to patients.

Jewish comments:

Lack of understanding regarding needs of Jewish patients religious practices/ traditions.

Muslim comments:

Delays in obtaining death certificates to register for burial in accordance with our faith.

In an X-ray dept a Muslim woman was asked to remove hijab in presence of male health worker (she refused and x-ray did not take place).

Some religious people reluctant to visit GP as wary of not being understood or treated with respect.

Assumptions that Asians and Muslims lack knowledge and are malingerers.

Zoroastrian comments:

Zoroastrian religion should be one of the recognized religions on the hospital database.

Unfair treatment in health care: Fieldwork findings

Introduction

During the qualitative process discussions were undertaken with non-medical staff members in hospitals including chaplains and equality officers. Other interviewees also sometimes referred to their experience of health care issues.

Generally improved but . . .

In general, and as also reflected in the reductions in unfair treatment shown in the survey findings, field research participants in all five field research locations on the whole felt that health care services had improved with regard to the understanding of religious diversity among staff members. However, a number of participants reported situations in which they felt they had been unfairly treated, but these were usually exceptions. Furthermore, these participants usually held individuals rather than organizations to be responsible for this unfair treatment.

For example, an elderly South Asian Hindu man described being treated rudely by a medical member of staff at a hospital when he accompanied his wife for some emergency treatment. He put the negative treatment down to himself and his wife having names that were distinctively Hindu. However, he did not blame the NHS for this and rather held the individual responsible: 'They can't change their nature because some people are very good and some people [are not]. I think not as an institution but individuals.'

In a similar incident narrated by the South Asian male chair of a Muslim organization, a young Muslim man was questioned by his heart surgeon who they stated asked him, 'why I am treating you if you are going to grow up and become a suicide bomber'. The young man and his family were offended by this comment and complained to the authorities, following which they received an apology. However the participant who narrated this incident remains concerned about the attitudes of individuals and concludes that:

> Now I am not saying that it is widespread, I believe he is an individual [. . .] what I am more concerned about is the mindset that has been created for an individual who is a professional who is there within the caring fraternity to actually speak in this particular manner. So obviously if an individual has spoken out like that I then question how many other people are thinking it but without actually expressing it.

Food and clothing in hospitals

Participants reported that dietary provisions had vastly improved in most hospitals around the country. They described how this had often been a gradual process of negotiation and consultation between hospitals and community groups in order to clarify their needs. In the field research completed in 2000, research participants reported that they had begun to initiate such channels of communication with their local hospitals (Weller et al., 2001: 73). A South Asian Hindu man in the 2011 field research describes this process of negotiation, emphasizing that sometimes the same word may be understood in different ways depending on cultural contexts.

> Being part of [. . .] the NHS advisory panel [. . .]. These issues have come out where our elderly ladies who are vegetarian and they don't get food in the hospitals. So we have raised that issue with them [. . .] But when we say vegetarian food . . . now vegetarian in the eyes of the English people means fish and eggs as well is vegetarian. Now fish and eggs are not vegetarian for us. We say look when we say vegetarian we mean Hindu vegetarian.

In this case the Hindu community was successful in convincing the hospital to provide vegetarian food. This participant also told us that since he lived in an area with a larger Muslim population *halal* food was easily available for Muslim patients. Noting that hospital menus normally reflect the population demographics in the area, it was realized that religious groups which are demographically small in a particular area may continue to have some difficulties. This was also expressed by a group of Jains in Leicester although Jain respondents (whose diet in addition to being vegetarian excludes onion, garlic and sometimes, root vegetables) also reported that as a community they were able to provide food to patients and were not stopped by the hospital.

With regard to dress codes, this was not reported as an issue during the 2011 field research except in instances where health and safety was a concern. A white Christian Equality and Diversity officer argued that it was important to understand people's reasons for various practices: 'it might not be a religion, it might be a philosophical belief and we need to check that out'. She described an incident in which an individual who was being interviewed for a health-service job and who wore a number of body-piercings was happy to remove them due to health and safety concerns. Hand-hygiene for members of staff was something that needed to be maintained and could occasionally lead to discussion in relation to sleeve lengths. In relation to requesting Muslim women to remove the *niqab* or face-veil she described developing a practice guidance booklet that provided information to patients and staff:

> I said well really, one we need to understand the context of that situation, was there a reason if for example she had a throat condition? [. . .]. The other thing is was it a male doctor or was it a female doctor? Is there a female doctor available at the doctor's practice? What we've done is we've investigated all those issues and drafted some guidance that can then be put into the practice information booklet.

She concluded that 'if people understand why you're asking them to remove the veil they're not going to be averse to doing so if it's about them getting better and they can understand why it is that you need to do that'.

Burials and cremations

In the report of the 2000 research, burials and cremations were highlighted as being a concern for a number of religious groups (Weller et al., 2001: 74). Muslims had reported that they had not been given immediate access to the body of the deceased. In Islam it is important that funeral rites are completed as soon as is practically possible following a death. In the field research completed in 2011, Muslims in particular reported an improvement with participants in all field research locations reporting that local hospitals now understood this urgency and normally released bodies to family members so that funeral rites could be completed. In most instances such provisions were also available when death occurred over a weekend.

Hindu and Jain participants also reported some improvement in this area, although some issues remained. For example, in Leicester, some Hindu participants reported, in separate interviews, that families were not being given access to bodies of the deceased when deaths occurred over a weekend and that they sometimes had to wait for up to four days for a time slot at the crematorium to become available. Moreover, they reported that the facilities at the crematorium were not appropriate.

According to one male Hindu participant, his local crematorium was perceived as 'Christian' so that when Hindu cremations were being conducted the family had to 'stick an OM mark' (the Hindu religious symbol) in the crematorium temporarily, which he felt was simply 'not good enough'. He felt that Hindus were a 'substantial part of the community' and 'put a substantial amount of money into the system'. His community requested the city council for space and permission to build either a multi-faith crematorium or a separate crematorium for Hindus, Sikhs and Jains who have cultural similarities. However, at the time that the research was conducted, they had not heard back from the council. Some Hindu participants felt this was unfair. Others, however, reported being satisfied with current facilities. In relation to Hindu funerals, a white Christian woman working for an inter-faith organization reported running an awareness course that included information about funeral rites in different faiths:

> What has been done on the faith awareness course when they were talking about politics and health and the way perhaps hospitals don't understand how different religions approach death for instance and they've recently given part of the river Soar over so that Hindus can have their relatives cremated here rather then flying them all to India.

Furthermore, some non-religious participants reported being uncomfortable about Christian symbols being displayed at crematoria.

Chaplaincy services

Chaplaincy services was one of the areas of health care that participants felt has seen considerable improvement over the last decade with most hospitals having multi-faith prayer rooms and chaplaincy services. However a small number of participants reported that this was not an 'even' service. As a white middle-aged Buddhist man put it:

> They've got hospital chaplaincies, they've got people of all various faiths to call upon and people of no faith as well. . . . I think they're probably a bit uneven I think in some places. They don't practice as well as they should be [and are not] trying to promote diversity.

Some non-religious participants stated they felt it was unfair and wrong for the NHS to fund chaplaincy services. As argued by a non-religious white man:

> . . . the money should be spent on nurses, on treatment, on other types of care and that a religious stance within the hospital is a personal thing and should be funded by the church or whichever religious bodies are wanting to intervene in the hospital care.

Residential care

No specific issues were reported about instances of unfair treatment in residential care within hospitals. Participants reported that there was significant good practice and that hospitals were culturally sensitive and generally aware of the religious and cultural needs of communities. Participants with specialized knowledge or experience in the area also reported on consultations and interventions being undertaken to provide for care homes for the elderly from South Asian backgrounds. Especially in Leicester, Blackburn and Cardiff it was mentioned that with a growing population and changing lifestyles, it cannot be assumed these elderly will be cared for at home, and it has become necessary to provide homes for the elderly that are culturally sensitive and aware of the religious (usually Hindu, Muslim and Sikh) affiliations of the service users.

Improving good practice

Overall, participants who worked in health care spoke about the good practices that were implemented in order to improve services provided to patients and their families. A doctor told us about the equality and diversity training that all medical and non-medical staff had to undertake and the rules that they had to abide by. A male Equality and Diversity officer in health care (who is also a Progressive Jew) also spoke about what had changed for the better:

> All hospitals will have a multi faith prayer room, and again if you go back maybe 10/15 years we wouldn't have that and you know, it's amazing how suddenly it's shifted. [. . .] and you have different [religious] books, they have chaplains in different religions available so it has made a big difference in the health service. Issues around dietary requirements, about food, it shouldn't be an issue [. . .] So I think that's been really beneficial. We've still got a long way to go but it's going in the right direction.

Participants described other good practices in which they had engaged either as members of staff at hospitals, clinics and surgeries, and/or also as interested members of the public. A Muslim organization in Cardiff reported running training days for members of staff from their local hospitals which was attended by everybody from 'porters to consultants'. Other participants mentioned health service-led initiatives such as Community Mental Health teams in Blackburn that provide culture-specific advice on mental health (which, in some communities, may have has cultural taboos associated with it). Similarly, two middle-aged South Asian Muslim women, also in Blackburn, described how they were trained as midwives after their local health services recognized a gap in provisions offered to women from both Muslim and also black and minority ethnic backgrounds.

Unfair treatment in social services, planning and other key services

> *Faith groups have special faith symbols and as such planning gets hard and bureaucrats cause problems.* (Survey comment from Sikh respondent)

Introduction

The survey completed in 2011 also collected respondents' experience of a range of other key services including: social services, benefits agency services, local authority planning services, local authority leisure services, public transport and shops and stores. All represent key aspects of people's public and private lives. While the services covered together here are in many ways very different from each other, they do represent services commonly accessed and used in people's everyday lives, even though some services are more likely to be used more frequently than others. As such this section is a useful calibration of the experience of unfair treatment across people's lives.

Reported experience of unfair treatment in key services

Overview

The surveys completed in 2000 and 2011 collected the reported experience of members of religious organizations in relation to: the attitudes and behaviour of social services staff, benefits agency staff, planning service staff, leisure services staff, public transport staff and shop staff. In addition, respondents were asked about experiencing unfair treatment in relation to policies and practices of these organizations.

The survey questions cover key areas of services and, as such, provide a valuable insight into the members of religious organizations who experience unfair treatment in relation to this area. As is the case across a number of other areas of peoples' lives since research in 2000, the level of reported unfair treatment on the basis of religion in the service areas considered has, on the whole, declined although the change is small.

In 2000, 22 per cent of the responses indicated experience of unfair treatment, with 5 per cent of these indicating that this was frequent and 17 per cent that it was occasional. In 2011 (where, on average, these questions were answered by 440 respondents) 16 per cent of the responses indicated unfair treatment, with 3 per cent of these suggesting that it was frequent and 13 per cent that it was occasional.

Especially in relation to this section, caution needs to be exercised in interpreting such data since such a wide range of services were covered in this part of the questionnaire. Nevertheless, there also appears to be a consistent pattern across the different key service. The reported incidence of unfair treatment on the basis of religion or belief in the sphere of services varied considerably across religions – for example, from 1 per cent of Bahá'í responses compared to 51 per cent of Sikh responses.

In the survey completed in 2011, the most common reported experience of unfair treatment in key services concerned the attitudes and behaviour of social services staff; social services practices; benefits agency staff; the attitudes and behaviour of planning staff; and the practices of planning organizations. Experience of unfair treatment in relation to shop staff, other customers and leisure services staff was considerably lower even though people are both in general more likely to use such services, and to do so more often.

As shown in Table 7.7, this pattern is similar to that in the survey completed in 2000 where the highest levels of unfair treatment reported were in relation to attitudes and behaviour of social services staff, social services practices, the attitudes and behaviour of planning department staff and the practices of planning departments.

Table 7.7 Reported experience of unfair treatment across key services, 2000–11

Key services, 2000/11	Yes frequently (%)	Yes occasionally (%)	Combined percentage	No unfair treatment %	N
Social service staff attitudes and behaviour					
2000	8	28	36	65	403
2011	5	24	28	72	286
Social service department policies					
2000	6	19	26	74	372
2011	3	18	20	80	280
Social service department practices					
2000	7	26	33	67	382
2011	4	21	25	75	279
Benefits agency staff attitudes and behaviour					
2000	4	17	21	79	364
2011	2	17	20	80	252
Benefits agency policies and practices					
2000	3	14	18	82	348
2011	2	10	12	88	244
LA planning staff attitudes and behaviour					
2000	9	23	32	68	350
2011	6	18	25	75	282
LA planning department policies					
2000	8	17	26	74	328
2011	6	11	17	83	272
LA planning department practices					
2000	9	21	30	70	334
2011	7	14	21	79	273
LA leisure staff attitudes and behaviour					
2000	5	14	18	82	365
2011	3	11	13	87	275
LA leisure service policies					
2000	5	10	15	85	351
2011	2	8	10	90	272
LA leisure service practices					
2000	4	13	17	83	353
2011	2	8	11	89	271
Public transport staff attitudes and behaviour					
2000	2	12	14	86	396
2011	3	9	12	88	312
Public transport providers policies and practices					
2000	2	9	11	89	374
2011	3	6	9	91	310
Shops and stores staff attitudes and behaviour					
2000	3	17	20	80	425
2011	1	13	14	86	326
Other customers' attitudes and behaviour					
2000	3	16	19	81	412
2011	2	13	15	85	314
Shops and stores policies and practices					
2000	4	12	16	84	405
2011	2	9	11	89	320

Note: Percentages may not total exactly 100% due to the cumulative effect of decimal point rounding.

In the surveys completed in 2000 and 2011, in terms of the policies and practices of organizations, and as also identified across other aspects of people's lives, higher levels of unfair treatment were reported in relation to the practices of organizations in comparison with their policies.

Unfair treatment in services: Survey findings by religion

It is important to consider in more detail, and by religion, the differences concerning reported experience of unfair treatment from responding organizations. Given the relatively smaller numbers of organizations responding to the survey from within some religious groups, this data needs to be treated with caution. What follows therefore focuses on the religions with larger numbers of responding organizations, namely: Christian, Hindu, Jewish, Sikh, Muslim and NRM/Pagan respondents, but other religions are included in the analysis where practical. Table 7.8 provides a summary of the responses by religion to all the questions across the services sphere.

As Table 7.8 highlights, taken as a whole, Sikh and Muslim organizations were the most likely to indicate unfair treatment on the basis of religion in the sphere of services. There are some parallels here with the results of the survey completed in 2000 when Muslim and Sikh organizations were also the most likely to report experience of unfair treatment from among their members alongside Hindu, Jain and Zoroastrian organizations. But overall, there has been a decline in the reported experience of unfair treatment since 2000 across the service areas in the field research.

Looking specifically (as in Table 7.9) at reported unfair treatment in relation to the attitudes and behaviour of social services staff (the overall area with the highest

Table 7.8 Reported experience of unfair treatment across the sphere of key services as a whole, by religion

Religion	Frequent unfair treatment	Percentage	Occasional unfair treatment	Percentage	Combined percenatge	No unfair treatment	Percentage	Total responses
Other	0	0	0	0	0	32	100	32
Bahá'í	0	0	3	1	1	371	99	374
Buddhist	0	0	7	2	2	348	98	355
Zoroastrian	0	0	2	4	4	49	96	51
Jain	0	0	10	8	8	113	92	123
Christian	9	1	136	8	9	1,525	91	1,670
Other Christian	3	1	17	7	9	207	91	227
Jewish	1	0	28	10	11	247	89	276
NRM/Pagan	0	0	21	14	14	134	86	155
Inter-faith	10	7	24	16	23	115	77	149
Hindu	12	4	63	21	24	232	76	307
Muslim	106	15	215	31	46	373	54	694
Sikh	6	4	73	47	51	76	49	155
Total	**147**		**599**			**3,822**		**4,568**

Note: All services question section responses are combined. The mean number of organizations responding to each of the questions in the services section is 440.

Table 7.9 Unfair treatment: Social services staff attitudes and behaviour, by religion

Religion	Frequent unfair treatment	Percentage	Occasional unfair treatment	Percentage	Combined percentage	No unfair treatment	Percentage	N
Buddhist	0	0	0	0	0	20	100	20
Baháʼí	0	0	1	4	4	23	96	24
Christian	3	3	24	21	23	89	77	116
Jewish	0	0	4	29	29	10	71	14
Hindu	1	6	4	24	29	12	71	17
Other Christian	0	0	5	38	38	8	62	13
Muslim	5	12	18	43	55	19	45	42
Sikh	2	22	3	33	56	4	44	9
NRM/Pagan	0	0	6	60	60	4	40	10

Note: Where response numbers are low religions have been excluded from the table. Caution should be exercised where cell counts are low.

levels of reported unfair treatment) considerable differences by religion can again be identified.

As Table 7.9 highlights, in relation to the attitudes and behaviour of social services staff, NRM/Pagan, Sikh and Muslim organizations were the most likely to report that their members experienced unfair treatment. Buddhist and Baháʼí organizations were the least likely to state that their members experienced unfair treatment. Unfair treatment was almost always reported to be occasional except for the members of Muslim and Sikh organizations. It is notable that in the survey completed in 2000 unfair treatment in relation to the attitudes and behaviour of social services staff was also the most frequent source of unfair treatment for religious organization members across the key service areas considered.

From among the organizations that responded to both the surveys that were completed in 2000 and 2011, there is a decline (from 33% to 25%) in the reported experiences of unfair treatment in relation to the attitudes and behaviours of social services staff. Of those organizations that reported their members experiencing unfair treatment in 2001, 37 per cent of (27) organizations continued to report experiencing unfair treatment in 2011.

Understanding unfair treatment in key services

Respondents to the surveys completed in 2000 and 2011 were asked to provide, on a write-in basis, details of specific examples of unfair treatment that their members reported having experienced in relation to services. Examples given included the attitudes and behaviour of service staff and customers and the policies and practices of organizations. In general, the kinds of issues raised were very similar to those in 2000. In Box 7.4, a selection is presented that highlights the everyday impact and/ or complexity of unfair treatment on the grounds of religion or belief and what this means in people's lives.

Box 7.4 Unfair treatment in key services: Survey comments

Christian comments:

Newer denomination/independent churches (often black-led and black majority) have great difficulty getting planning permission or change of use permission from planners.

A member in social care wanting to pray for a client met with opposition.

Strong antipathy in e.g. adoption agencies to committed Christian families.

Jewish comments:

One Jewish member has said she would like to be able to purchase Jewish festival cards in main stationary stores.

We felt badly served by the local council during a recent planning process connected with our application to convert a warehouse to a synagogue/community centre.

Muslims comments:

Within the social services there seems to be a preconception that all Muslim husbands are violent and purveyors of domestic violence. Many instances of social services getting unnecessarily involved in a family issue they have little or no understanding of.

Some Muslims being abused (verbally) by fellow customers. They sometimes feel that staff (some) are more smiling to others (!).

Bus not stopping for hijab-wearing woman.

NRM/Pagan comments:

Some printers/print shops have refused to print Odinist-related literature or other items (e.g. mugs, t-shirts).

Some social workers still believe the SRA [Satanic Ritual Abuse] myths and try to use those beliefs to justify placing children on child protection/safeguarding lists.

Unfair treatment in social services, planning and other key services: Fieldwork findings

Introduction

Participants in the field research were asked about their experiences and perceptions of discrimination and equality with regard to religion or belief in accessing services. In the survey this included questions about social services, benefits agency services, local authority planning services, local authority leisure services, public transport and shops and stores. However, in the field research, apart from in relation to social services and local authority planning services, it was evident that the term 'services' was open to interpretation and was understood in a variety of ways. Narratives about these areas are highlighted in the various sections that follow in this chapter.

Experiences of unfair treatment in social services and other key services

In a general sense, when asked about 'services', a large proportion of participants in all five field research locations usually felt that this was an area that had seen considerable improvement over the last decade, with service providers being more aware of diversity and that the needs of diverse users were usually catered for. However, there were a number of instances in which participants felt that they were treated unfairly. While these experiences may be understood as infrequent and occasional (which mirrors survey findings), they are nevertheless significant in that they reflect areas where further work needs to be undertaken.

That these occurrences are infrequent may also be indicative of the issues being located in the attitudes of individuals rather than the policies of organizations. It is also important to note that, although an occurrence may be rare, it can negatively impact the lives of those directly concerned, and also upon wider perceptions within their communities. There is also the problem mentioned by a young Muslim male public sector employee in Blackburn about the possibility that unfair treatment with regard to services go unreported due to fears especially among the elderly in some ethnic minority communities 'because they feel that the next time round the service that they're going to get is going to be bad because they've complained'.

The examples of unfair treatment described here are quite varied and have occurred in all five field research locations. However, these were not felt to be representative of general practice in these areas. A disabled Pagan participant mentioned that she once had a new support worker who made inappropriate comments about the participant's Pagan beliefs and lifestyle along the lines of 'Oh why can't you get your Pagan friends to help you out with things like this. They do things like that don't they?' When she complained, the support worker was taken away, and the participant was left without support for six months. However, she now has 'great carers' who are interested in her beliefs.

With regard to fostering and their religious beliefs, two participants in Cardiff described experiences of what they identified as unfair treatment. In the first case an elderly white Bahá'í couple said that while fostering a second child, they were questioned about their 'morals being too high' and their ability to deal with this child (who in the past had displayed some challenging behaviour) as he grew up. They felt this was discriminatory as 'they don't call Christians in to ask them about their understandings of morality'. In another instance, also in Cardiff, a white parish priest narrated the experiences of two couples in his parish. In one of these couples, the man involved was a convert to Christianity from Islam and his conversion and faith were questioned by social services. According to the Parish priest, such instances were leading to a sense of marginalization within the Christian community: 'Yes, I think a part of the issue was that the Christian population and particularly Evangelical Christians could not understand why everyone else had to be tolerated but suddenly they weren't tolerated.'

In relation to public places, a number of Muslims mentioned issues around unfair treatment that they felt were perhaps a result of Islamophobia. A young Muslim man of Arab origin described how his wife, who wore a face-veil, was regularly verbally abused in the city centre. A number of turbaned Sikh men mentioned being the target of 'displaced Islamophobia' in city and town centres, because they were mistaken for the Taliban. A Muslim woman of Somali heritage described an instance in which a bus driver refused to help two women he knew who were travelling to Heathrow Airport. He helped all the other passengers with their bags but when they asked for help he replied, 'I'm not going to help you because I don't know if there's any bombs in there.' They complained about this and received compensation. However, the participant reporting this instance felt that this was not sufficient as the bus driver was still working for the bus company. She concludes: 'but those kind of incidents are obviously triggered by the media and Muslims are just viewed as ... [extremists] ..., and it may not always be Muslims it could be other visibly ethnic minority'.

Some religious communities that are smaller in number have concerns around not being recognized. A group of Jains in Leicester spoke about their dietary needs not being catered for, not being mentioned in the census form. A member of this group summarized their situation: 'the sense that we don't have the man power, we haven't got that capacity, and then there hasn't been that support from that wider world to really bring us into the mainstream'. Finally, from among the non-religious there was a general sense that they were marginalized in a number of different ways. As a white, non-religious man in Cardiff put it:

> Just on the employment legislation when I signed up to a National Secular Society newsletter it's full of examples of faith schools and academies or welfare services being taken over [by religious groups]. I'd like in the age of the Big Society to see more robust protection of non-religious people in accessing jobs and services.

Good practice in relation to social and other services

Against the background of the kind of continuing issues noted above, a Hindu man of South Asian origin living in Blackburn, describes what he perceives as 'tremendous improvement':

> Quite often when there is a new service about to be launched either with the council or social services or national health services they always keep us in touch [. . .] with us saying this is what we are doing, we have got leaflets in such and such language. [. . .] Hindi, Gujarati and Urdu, and Bengali as well . . .

> I can remember that when you said ten years ago. I must say as a result of what was been complain or what's been brought up in the Parliament and the things which were sort of been asked by all the statutory bodies including the NHS, the social services, the council, to make improvements. [. . .] That's a tremendous improvement, not just slow improvement but tremendous improvement.

On the other side of the provider–user relationship, a number of public sector workers described the impact of legislation around equality and diversity on their work and obligations to address the needs of diverse populations. These workers spoke about having more diverse workforces that reflected the diversity in communities. Also in this context representatives of religious organizations, and particularly from minority religious groups, described liaising with local authorities to create awareness of their specific religion and the needs of their religious community. Such awareness had become central to the kind of planning that went into the provision of such services. As a Muslim woman local authority employee in Cardiff put it:

> . . . people get along fine, it is about knowing that you belong here, this is where I live, this is my city, this is my country I belong here and the way I can show you that is because when I go somewhere and I need things being given to me as a Muslim Welsh person those things are available for me so when services are designed they take into consideration that the services are going to be used by Muslims, Jews, Sikhs.

Furthermore such diversity and 'ownership' of diversity is in general reflected in English and Welsh high streets, shopping centres and shops. A number of participants commented on how shop assistants reflected ethnic demography of the local area. A young male Muslim public sector employee comments about his positive experiences in his town of Blackburn with Darwen:

> . . . so like I said in Blackburn with Darwen we've got a great community that works very closely. They've got a large number of people who are working in services across the borough. You walk into the town centre, you walk into 90% of shops you will see people from different backgrounds working together and I think another one of the great things about Blackburn with Darwen, it's not like [. . .] larger city areas where you've got massive populations. It's a small population compacted in such a concise area where [. . .] communities are so tightly knit, closely knit together that you'll tend to find that you've got your white, your Indian, your Pakistani . . .

Unfair treatment in planning

The experience of organizations

As noted in the section above in this chapter on housing, in contrast to the reported experience of individuals, religious organizations, including places of worship, community centres and religious charities reported that they continued to experience various forms of unfair treatment in relation to their buildings and to matters of planning. This was reported across all field research locations.

A young South Asian woman who worked with a Muslim charity in Cardiff said that when trying to run a fund-raising event at a local park, she was told that the park could not be hired for an event as this was not a facility provided by the city council. However, a few weeks later the park was being used by another charity to run an event similar to the one that her organization had planned. Similarly, Pagans and members of the NRMs in Cardiff and Norwich continue to describe problems in securing venues to run events. As a white Pagan woman put it: 'in this day and age for someone to turn their nose up at you when you want to hire a venue because you're Pagan is ridiculous'.

Other religious organizations identified some of the source of the difficulties that they face due to having limited resources of their own, thus making them dependent on being able to hire facilities from others. This issue, which has long been identified in relation to predominantly black Christian Pentecostal groups was identified in the field research by a black Christian Pentecostal woman in Leicester:

> So what you have, you have struggling Pentecostal churches, not able to own their own buildings, so they don't have their own places of worship, so they look to community centres, or other centres to hire to hold the services, and there's always a problem.

In other instances religious groups that were not well known described difficulties in hiring facilities for religious events and this was attributed to not enough being known about their faith. As narrated by a Bahá'í (male and female) couple, there was a perception that it was easier for Christian groups to hire venues than it was for non-Christian groups:

> We have occasionally run into people who have said, 'well what's that, what then is the Bahá'í?' And then I say okay let's go through some of the basic teachings of the Bahá'í faith and see if you can find anything in those that you would find would stop you from allowing us to hire the hall and you go through a few of the basic concepts of the Bahá'í faith and usually that is fine and okay.

Such experiences of unfair treatment of one religious or belief group by another was reported during a number of interviews. For example, it was reported that a Pagan group was told that it was not welcome at an inter-faith event being run in a Cathedral. Similarly a Sikh community centre had indicated that it was not given the opportunity to buy their Muslim neighbour's property when it was put up for sale.

From spires to minarets and other planning permission issues

A number of participants described concerns about churches which were closing down due to not having large enough congregations. This mirrors concerns raised during the field research completed in 2000. Some of the concerns were due to empty churches being vandalized. A middle-aged Methodist woman in Leicester explained:

> Well I think that church is up for sale is [. . .] which is opposite where I live. Now what was very sad is that it got broken into by somebody, person or persons unknown, and there was particular desecration, bits of the font got smashed and some of the robes in the vestry got slashed and people have been sort of living in it, living rough. And I find that sad in terms of a lack of respect.

In other examples participants were unsure what the future of these buildings should be. Was it better for them to be converted into a block of flats? Or was it better that the building's tradition of worship should continue, albeit through the language and forms of an other than Christian religious group? This was a debate that participants could not agree upon. There were also concerns that the skyline of British cities and towns in some instances was changing. During field research in Blackburn, the field researcher often picked up such sentiments in public discussions on internet forums and also offline, which reflected concerns about the growing number of mosques in the city. A South Asian Hindu man summarized this sentiment:

> So in the last ten or last I would say like twenty years, things have been changing. Now there are some people in the society, I mean in the host community, who have got some sort of why? why are they here? why this? why have they got too many temples? why have they got too many mosques? what they do? And that is the part of their thinking. At the same time because they are not used to these things, the elderly people, they are not used to these things, they are feeling a bit strange.

Inconsistencies in planning permission were reported as a problem in the 2001 research report (Weller et al., 2001: 67), and these continue to be problematic. According to a white male Parish priest who is also a local councillor:

> People feel they are unhappy with certain groups moving in, whether it's Christian or if it's Hindu or whatever, when it's religious buildings there is still always conflict around that. What gets in meetings in planning terms, it isn't the Tesco or Westfield, the largest shopping in the whole of Europe or whatever it is, didn't get one objection. If you try to put a Mosque beside my church there would be 300 objections. I know because I led a campaign for a Gurudwara in my parish [. . .], I got in all sorts of trouble. [. . .] So to say it doesn't happen nowadays, of course it will happen every single time.

A Muslim chaplain described the disagreements that his regional Muslim association was having with their local authority after purchasing a disused pub in order to convert it into a mosque. After their purchase, the property was deemed to be listed, which led to further problems for the conversion. In other instances it was perceived that local authorities made allowances for groups that were more articulate and forceful in arguing for their needs.

Neighbourhood traffic and parking issues continued to be reported as a problem. For example, a leader of the Hindu community told us that his temple was not given permission or space for worshippers to park outside the temple during festivals – which occurred only a few times a year. By contrast, he drew attention to parking restrictions having been lifted every Friday for the local mosque and identified this as unfair. Finally, a Hindu woman in another field research location, described problems with securing planning permission to build an extension and car park for her local temple. She contrasted this with the experience of Muslims who, according to her, had been allowed to build a mosque on 'each and every road'.

The above examples of perceived inconsistencies of planning permission were located across all five field research locations, although we do not locate specific quotations in order to preserve anonymity.

Vandalism and/or specific attacks on places of worship

As in the 2000 research, a number of religious organizations reported instances of vandalism such as graffiti, windows being smashed, intruders and desecration (see Weller et al., 2001: 68). However, in both our 2011 research and the 2000 research, it was often acknowledged that the problems of vandalism were possibly more the result of general anti-social behaviour rather than being a consequence of specific targeting on the basis of religion.

Often, this was not even described as unfair treatment due to religion or belief. In the case of a Gurdwara which had all its windows smashed, this was not even reported by the Sikhs who were interviewed. Rather, it was other participants (in this particular case Christians) who mentioned this act of vandalism. Similarly, participants at a Sri Lankan Buddhist Vihara initially said that they experienced no unfair treatment at all. They later described instances of vandalism that were serious enough for metal grills to be installed on all the windows of the Vihara. Nevertheless, they did not feel that this was discriminatory or that this was unfair treatment directed specifically at their religious beliefs. Instead this was described more generally as anti-social behaviour and also perhaps some amount of racism. Similar examples of vandalism were described by a number of religious organizations.

All the Jewish participants interviewed mentioned the increased security provisions including CCTV cameras, which were either already available or which were being provided in all synagogues. This was in order to address antisemitism and threats of vandalism which seemed to directly correlate with events in the Middle East.

A number of participants mentioned vandalism at their mosques and community centres. The chair of a Muslim umbrella organization described how the windows of his office were smashed every week. A South Asian Hindu male reported that a Hindu temple reported experiencing some unfair treatment, which he identified as being the result of misplaced Islamophobia rather than being due to any negative perceptions of Hinduism:

> This is a very burning issue at present. I mean if there is anything happens in Leicester, there is one white community and one is Asian community. I am sure they will throw stone at the temple because some of these people they don't know the difference of temple and the mosque. [. . .] These people are ignorant you see, you understand.

Planning and the non-religious

Non-religious participants did not describe any issues specific to religion or belief in relation to meeting places. Non-religious groups generally meet wherever convenient and so this was not generally seen as problematic. Where issues relating to non-religious beliefs are mentioned, it is with regard to the presence of religious symbols in public places like crematoria. We now turn to examine unfair treatment in funding.

Unfair treatment in funding

Local authorities have myths and misconceptions of Jewish organizations and charities. They are perceived to be 'wealthy' or because the mission is working directly for Jewish communities they are perceived to be acting without 'equality of opportunity'. Jewish charities are treated homogenously and without an understanding of needs and requirements. (Survey comment from Jewish respondent)

Introduction

This section examines issues of funding in relation to charities, trusts and local and central government sources. Such issues are closely related to the legal recognition an organization has in terms of charity law and more generally in terms of how funding structures impact on how religious organizations define their work and how they present themselves publicly. We also consider reported experience of unfair treatment in relation to donations from the public.

Survey findings in relation to funding issues

Reported experience of unfair treatment in relation to funding

The surveys completed in 2000 and 2011 collected the reported experience of unfair treatment of members of religious organizations in relation to: the attitudes and behaviour of staff from charities and trusts and from local and central government. Respondents were also asked about unfair treatment in relation to the policies and practices of these organizations. Finally respondents were asked about their experiences of unfair treatment in relation to the attitudes and behaviour of the general public with regard to making donations.

Since 2000, the level of reported unfair treatment on the basis of religion in the area of funding has on the whole declined. In the survey completed in 2000, 33 per cent of the responses indicated experience of unfair treatment, of which 12 per cent indicated that unfair treatment was frequent and 21 per cent that it was occasional. In 2011 (when, on average, these questions were answered by 435 respondents), overall 26 per cent of the responses highlighted experience of unfair treatment, of which 7 per cent indicated that the unfair treatment was frequent and 19 per cent that it was occasional. For most religious organizations that reported unfair treatment on the basis of religion in the area of funding it was occasional rather than frequent.

Again, the reported incidence of unfair treatment on the basis of religion or belief varied considerably across different religions. For example, 0 per cent of Zoroastrian responses compared to 50 per cent of Sikh responses indicated unfair treatment.

In the survey completed in 2011, the most commonly reported experience of unfair treatment in funding concerned the funding practices of local authorities – 32 per cent of (280) organizations, though only slightly lower levels of unfair treatment were reported in relation to central government and charity funding practices. Overall, the lowest levels of unfair treatment were reported in relation to the attitudes and behaviour of charity staff – 17 per cent of (296) organizations.

These findings broadly reflect the patterns found in the 2000 survey. Forty-one per cent of the religious organizations reported unfair treatment of their members in relation to local authority funding practices and this was the most frequent source of unfair treatment in relation to funding that was reported in 2000 (Weller et al., 2001: 173, 178). In 2011, in terms of the attitudes and behaviour of the public and public donations, 24 per cent of (281) organizations indicated experience of unfair treatment. This compares to 2000 when 29 per cent of organizations reported unfair treatment. It seems that there has been no increase in this area in terms of unfair treatment experienced in relation to public donations – in fact quite the opposite.

It is important to look further at the differences between reported experience of unfair treatment in relation to policies and practices with regard to informing discussions about the development and implementation of policy, law and practice. Across the sphere of funding, although the differences are small, there is a consistent pattern of higher levels of unfair treatment reported in relation to organization practices compared with organization polices.

Unfair treatment in funding: Survey findings by religion

It is important to consider in more detail, and by religion, the differences concerning reported experience of unfair treatment from responding organizations of different religions. Given the relatively smaller numbers of organizations responding to the survey from within some religious groups, some of this data needs to be treated with caution. Table 7.10 provides a summary of the responses by religion to all the questions in the funding sphere. Sikh, NRM/Pagan and Muslim organizations were most likely to

Table 7.10 Reported experience of unfair treatment across the sphere of funding as a whole, by religion

Religion	Frequent unfair treatment	Percentage	Occasional unfair treatment	Percentage	Combined percentage	No unfair treatment	Percentage	Total responses
Zoroastrian	0	0	0	0	0	24	100	24
Other Christian	0	0	2	3	3	62	97	64
Bahá'í	0	0	7	5	5	129	95	136
Jain	0	0	6	12	12	44	88	50
Buddhist	0	0	24	13	13	154	87	178
Jewish	5	2	31	15	17	177	83	213
Inter-faith	9	5	31	18	23	135	77	175
Christian	70	6	226	21	27	800	73	1,096
Hindu	14	8	40	24	33	111	67	165
Other	0	0	7	35	35	13	65	20
Muslim	67	18	77	20	38	238	62	382
NRM/Pagan	14	16	24	28	44	48	56	86
Sikh	11	10	42	39	50	54	50	107
Total	**190**		**517**			**1,989**		**2,696**

Note: All funding question section responses are combined. The mean number of organizations responding to each of the questions in the funding section is 435.

Table 7.11 Unfair treatment: Local authority funding practices, by religion

Religion	Frequent unfair treatment	Percentage	Occasional unfair treatment	Percentage	Combined percentage	No unfair treatment	Percentage	N
Bahá'í	0	0	1	7	7	13	93	14
Buddhist	0	0	2	12	12	15	88	17
Jewish	0	0	3	14	14	19	86	22
Inter-faith	1	5	3	16	21	15	79	19
Christian	8	7	35	30	37	72	63	115
Muslim	6	14	11	26	40	25	60	42
Hindu	4	24	3	18	41	10	59	17
Sikh	2	18	4	36	55	5	45	11

Note: Where response numbers are low religious traditions have been excluded from the table. Caution should be exercised where individual cell counts are low.

report unfair treatment on the basis of religion in the funding sector, with Muslim and NRM/Pagan organizations being the most likely to report frequent unfair treatment. Although Christian and Hindu organizations also reported considerable unfair treatment, it was more likely to be occasional than frequent. There are some parallels here with the results of the survey completed in 2000 when Muslim and NRM/Pagan organizations were the most likely to report experience of unfair treatment from among their members (Weller et al., 2001: 173–9).

Looking specifically at reported unfair treatment in relation to local authority funding practices (the area in the funding sphere with the highest levels of reported unfair treatment) considerable differences by religion can again be identified.

Table 7.11 highlights that Sikh, Hindu and Muslim organizations were the most likely to report that their members had experienced unfair treatment due to local authority funding practices. Unfair treatment is, on the whole, occasional for all organizations, though Hindu organizations were the most likely to report frequent unfair treatment in relation to funding. From among the organizations that responded to both the surveys that were completed in 2000 and 2011, there is a decline (from 39% to 32%) in the reported experience of unfair treatment of their members in relation to local authority funding practices. However, of those organizations that reported their members experiencing unfair treatment in 2001, 48 per cent of (25) organizations continued to report experiencing unfair treatment in 2011.

Understanding unfair treatment in funding

Respondents to the surveys that were completed in 2000 and 2011 were asked to provide details of specific examples of unfair treatment that their members reported having experienced in relation to funding. Examples given included: attitudes and behaviour of staff, funding application processes and the general lack of funding for religious organizations. In general, the kinds of issues raised in 2011 were very similar to those in 2000. In Box 7.5, a selection is presented that highlights the impact and/

or complexity of unfair treatment on the grounds of religion or belief and what this means in people's lives.

Box 7.5 Unfair treatment in funding: Survey comments

Baháʾí comments:

Funding less likely to go to 'other' religious organizations.

Buddhist comments:

Mistrust based on misunderstanding and assuming we are proselytising.

Christian comments:

Christians have to be non-religious to receive funding.

There is an unrealistic expectation that churches can separate out mission/ evangelism from social care and service.

Often funding is refused to anything that has a non-secular connotation. Churches are forced to change the name of building from 'Sunday School' to 'Community Centre' in order to be able to apply.

Most secular charities unwilling to accept any social action project from a church due to 'promotion of religion'.

Hindu comments:

Local government plays numbers game and sometimes smaller communities do not get a fair share of grants.

Muslim comments:

'Prevent' policy serves to demonise Muslims as a 'security' issue. Muslims seem only to attract funding for addressing 'extremism', which has attracted people who want to make a career of talking up 'extremism' and denies funding to more needed and constructive projects.

Pagan/NRM comments:

We have a basic problem in that we are having great difficulty in acquiring charity status which would allow us to apply for funding from other sources.

Inter-faith comments:

We found it hard to get funding as most charities were not willing to give to any religious enterprise, even interfaith. More recently the (previous) government encouraged giving for the purposes of community cohesion and faith and interfaith groups.

Unfair treatment in funding: Fieldwork findings

During the field research, participants were asked about gaining access to funding and any experience of any unfair treatment on the basis of religion or belief.

From exclusion towards inclusion in funding for religious organizations

As in the field research completed in 2000, a number of participants reported being excluded from applying for funding on the basis of them being religious organizations (Weller et al., 2001: 83). According to one male Evangelical Christian pastor in Norwich, this is discriminatory:

> It's so hard. And that I get angry about. Whereas I've got . . . loads and loads of funding organizations that are more than happy to throw money at any people that are doing parent toddler groups, that are involved in schools, that are doing life skills training amongst benefit culture, that are running youth groups but as soon as you get to the point where you say oh by the way we're Christian, we're a church . . . all doors are shut, no. And I say . . . I've said to people you are actually, you are discriminatory.

Religious, and particularly Christian, organizations felt that such exclusion was mostly due to concerns about religious organizations using the funding to proselytize under the guise of running community services and/or events. This was seen as problematic because many participants stated that religious organization usually had strong links and ties within local communities and that naturally they were well placed to provide communities with the services that they needed. Also, they felt that because of the religious nature of these groups they also had motivated volunteers. Furthermore, the environment had changed and people were not volunteering to convert people, they volunteered to serve needs and often did not talk about faith at all, unless the subject came up. According to a male Salvation Army employee, decisions about funding religious organizations should be judged based on the merit of the services they provide rather than on their religiosity:

> Almost every church, every faith organization that was represented there, actually were saying to the local government; do not judge us because we are people of faith, but judge us on the quality of the goods that we provide. And if they are suitable, if they are good quality goods, then continue to provide the funding.

A key difference between participants' narratives from a decade ago and in the field research completed in 2011 lies in the difference in the religious backgrounds of those raising this issue. In the previous work such issues were raised mostly by Christian groups (Weller et al., 2001: 83), but in the field research completed in 2011, participants from a number of different religious groups reported reduced access to funds for religious organizations as an issue of concern. A number of respondents felt that there were problems of 'recognition' as mentioned by this middle-aged white Buddhist female:

> Thinking in terms of not getting funding because we're Buddhists and not getting grants whereas Churches will, that does happen occasionally. . . . I've heard of it happening to people in this movement where it's accepted that a Church is a

religious body but it's not automatically assumed that a Buddhist centre is a religious body. It's changing a little bit now because people are a bit more aware, especially since the discrimination [law] changed.

A small number of participants identified what they felt was a clear shift in government policy to supporting different religious groups to now supporting mostly inter-faith and inter-community activities. As a Muslim woman from Norwich explained:

Previously there wasn't a problem they did fund individual groups but now it is getting tough to get funding. So now they are trying to say OK we won't fund Muslim group or Hindu group or Asian group or Chinese group we would like to fund you, if you are working together in collaboration then we will fund the whole group so you have to show that you are working in partnership.

Religious organizations were divided about the benefits or limitations of this inter-faith agenda, with some feeling that it would bring communities together and promote cohesion. Others – such as in the following view articulated by a male Evangelical Christian participant – felt that it would dilute the quality and impact of work being undertaken and therefore viewed these new policies with suspicion:

Now the interfaith agenda we engage with that, like I go along to meetings, I've got relationships with the leaders of the different faiths involved [. . .] what's the motive behind it, there's something good coming out of the faith community and you're trying to sort of squash it, and control it.

Other funding strategies and problems

Some religious participants in the field research were simply unaware and naive about the processes of applying for funding or suspicious of the process, assuming that there would automatically be nothing in it for their religion. As reported by a middle-aged Sikh man in Newham:

Sikhs . . . will come and talk to me and ask if they can do this or that and I tell them that yes there is a grants programme and they will say straight away, 'I'm not a Muslim, I'm not going to get any money' and I will say 'have you tried?' A lot of them I think do not actually apply for things.

However, a number of religious groups were addressing funding issues in other ways with many taking an approach of self-sufficiency. For example, during the field research, on a visit to a temple it was observed that it had a plaque outside that included the names of people who had made significant donations towards the building of the temple. These were all Hindu doctors working in hospitals in one of the local fieldwork areas. In another similar example a white male representative of the ISKCON movement mentioned running a vegetarian café and also running fund-raising campaigns. Although he had previously considered applying for funding, he had realized that seeking funding would entail making compromises that he and his religious group were not prepared to make:

> Because we have only so much funding from the government we mostly fund ourselves. This small business ventures (like this café) we are more kind of more self-sufficient, so that we don't rely upon the government [. . .] I know we've started to look into funding but one thing that was just staring at us was how it might compromise our practice, compromise our principles so no [. . .] We asked for funding but we had to, I can't remember what they wanted, we had to make a list of compromises.

Similar experiences were reported by other groups who were small in number such as the Bahá'ís or Jains who, in general, did not feel the need to seek external funding and who raised resources and funds from within their communities.

Non-religious participants did not report any issues around funding that impacted directly upon them. However, as mentioned in the section about health care, they felt that too much public sector funding was made available to religion and religious groups.

'Prevent' and perceptions of increased funding to Muslims

A large number of participants either themselves felt or knew others who felt that there were increased funding opportunities for Muslim groups that were resulting in reduced access to funding for other groups. An example of this was a white Pentecostal Christian minister in Blackburn who spoke about a feeling of marginalization:

> People feel that the Muslims are getting more funding than the white population. Just whether that's true I don't know. I don't have the statistics but I have heard that said, where the white community feels that Muslims get better treatment than we do.

This perception was articulated by many participants while others felt that they were the result of what was described as 'stupid *Daily Mail* type stories which have sort of affected public perception'.

The field research was conducted just after a period during which funding had been allocated to local authorities and community groups under the Prevent agenda, a significant proportion of which was then invested in work relating to Muslim communities. This led to considerable criticism for mixing community cohesion issues with issues around preventing violent extremism and thereby, it is argued, fuelling stereotypes of Muslims. Moreover, among Muslims themselves, there were accusations that groups that had access to this funding were 'spying' on the wider Muslim community, which meant that for many groups, this source of funding was unattractive. However others took a different stance:

> Well to be honest [. . .] Prevent was mishandled from the beginning [. . .]. In Wales particularly we had some funding from the Government for training but it

wasn't from Prevent funding it came from Community Cohesion funding. [. . .] In England particularly people were dead against taking money from Prevent. Our approach, was anything which benefits the community we should do it and all these [claims] that they just want to spy on your community and everything, our approach was that they know more about us then we do, right, what difference would it make.

The economic crisis and funding

One concern that extended across participants from all backgrounds and in all five field research locations, was the economic uncertainty in the United Kingdom and beyond, which had led to a general reduction in funds for which organizations could apply or bid. Individuals were losing jobs, and communities were generally feeling under pressure, which was leading to tensions. A white female Christian minister described this feeling as 'a climate of fear' within which 'if people are feeling threatened then they will pick up bits of rumour then they will construct a case from it'. She felt that this could lead to suspicions of discrimination, allegations of particular groups being favoured and a general increase in tensions within communities. A middle-aged male Muslim researcher in Leicester commented about the challenge of maintaining positive community relations in economically strained times:

> I think there is a very real challenge there in terms of getting the message of positive relations, harmony imbedded into grass root communities. . . . and of course as economic times become harder as the economy becomes worse it's going to create more and more tension at a local level and people will compete for even more resources. . . . and I can only see things getting worse in the short term.

Another impact of the current economic downturn that was evident in the field research were the budget reductions being reported by local authorities in all five field research locations. A large number of public and voluntary sector workers mentioned cuts in resources and staffing. For example, a small team of three individuals who worked for a local authority race and equality unit reported that following on from the *Equality Act* of 2010 their remit had being widened to include all the equality strands and not just race – a task for which they felt understaffed.

The majority of participants who worked in areas of equality and diversity or reducing inequalities were concerned that such cuts were coming at a time when issues around discrimination are likely to increase. In all five field research locations public and voluntary sector participants and those who were representing religious organizations unanimously expressed concerns about the economic situation and budget cuts in a time of increased inequalities.

However, reactions to this varied considerably between the field research locations. So, for example, in Leicester where considerable amounts of funding had been previously available, participants reported that budget cuts and understaffing has already led to a number of public funded initiatives either having already closed down and/or being in the process of doing so. As expressed in the opinions quoted above, there was a concern that this would have a significant impact on social relations in the city.

In Cardiff all participants were concerned about reduced budgets and the situation of public sector workers and initiatives was similar to those in other cities. However, when it came to participants representing religious organizations, in general, they felt that given a relative lack of previous government funding, communities had learned to fund themselves and undertake projects using community volunteers and that, because of this, the cuts would not significantly impact upon community relations.

This kind of sentiment was articulated by an elderly Jewish man in Cardiff who stated that there was 'no' feeling of concern in Cardiff and that 'the Assembly for Wales, are very conscious of the various religions [it was] supporting'. He reported that an inter-faith forum had recently been awarded a significant grant to continue their work despite reduced Welsh Assembly budgets. Furthermore, a number of participants reported that organizations would continue their work with reduced resources – that metaphorically speaking, 'the show would go on', as articulated by an Evangelical Christian minister:

> We are aware of a lot of churches, or Christian individual projects that are mainly reliant on funding, because of the current economic climate they'll have to cut back on staff, I don't think this will have a negative effect on community relations, I hope you'd find the same, you'd get the same answer talking to, Muslim or Hindu or Jewish groups with that. But I think Wales is a place where is certainly good interfaith relations.

Conclusion

Having presented the survey and field research findings for these areas of society, the next chapter goes on to explore unfair treatment on the grounds of religion or belief from other religion or belief groups as well as that from other than religion or belief groups such as political, community and other pressure groups.

8

Experience of Unfair Treatment from, between and within Religious Groups and from Political, Community and Pressure Groups

I had a colleague . . . he was Church of England, very Evangelical hard line and he was totally convinced in his own mind that all 700 million Roman Catholics in the world were evil . . . I said well have you ever actually talked to a Catholic, been to a Catholic Church, listened to a Catholic service? And the answer of course is no because 'I don't mix with them.' (Interview with male, Anglican Priest)

Introduction

Religion and belief discrimination and unfair treatment is not only something that is experienced by religion and belief groups. It also occurs within and between religion and belief groups, as well as being experienced from political, community and other pressure groups in the wider society.

Unfair treatment from other religious groups

Fundamentalists of any kind – most frequently Christians. . . Constantly refer to Paganism being either 'Devil worship' or in some way 'dark' or 'dangerous'. (Survey comment from Pagan/NRM respondent)

Inter- and intra-religious relations in social and religious context

This section examines reported experience of unfair treatment from other religious groups. Many organizations report having experienced unfair treatment from other religious groups and traditions both within and outside their tradition.

Survey findings on unfair treatment and other religious groups

Overall survey findings on other religious groups

The surveys completed in 2000 and 2011 collected the reported experience of unfair treatment of members of religious organizations by other religious groups. Respondents were asked to state which groups were the source of this unfair treatment and to provide an example of it.

In 2011, 23 per cent of (452) organizations reported that their members experienced unfair treatment from other religious groups. This compares to 29 per cent in 2000 and therefore marks a reduction in such reported unfair treatment. However, the level of reported unfair treatment is still substantial, indicating the scale of its impact on people's lives.

Unfair treatment from other religious groups by religion

It is important to consider in more detail, and by religion, the differences concerning the reported experience of unfair treatment from responding organizations. Given the relatively smaller number of organizations responding from within some religious groups, some of this data needs to be treated with caution. Table 8.1 provides a summary of the responses by religion.

As Table 8.1 highlights, NRM/Pagan, Other Christian and Sikh organizations were the most likely to indicate unfair treatment from other religious groups, and all religious groups were stated to be the source of some unfair treatment. There are some parallels here with the results of the 2000 survey where NRM/Pagan organizations were the most likely to report unfair treatment from other religions. However, overall and across most religions there would seem to have been a decline in the reported experience of unfair treatment since 2000. In some instances reported experience of unfair treatment from other religious groups has declined considerably such as for

Table 8.1 Reported experience of treatment: From other religious groups, by religion

Religion	Yes	Percentage	No	Percentage	N
Christian	19	11	155	89	174
Hindu	3	13	21	88	24
Buddhist	8	22	28	78	36
Muslim	15	25	46	75	61
Inter-faith	6	26	17	74	23
Bahá'í	10	31	22	69	32
Jewish	12	33	24	67	36
Sikh	6	40	9	60	15
Other Christian	12	60	8	40	20
NRM/Pagan	12	80	3	20	15

Note: Where response numbers are low religions have been excluded from the table. Caution should be excercised where cell counts are low.

Christian organizations being down from 25 per cent to 11 per cent of responding organizations. However, for others the reported experience of unfair treatment has increased – including 80 per cent of NRM/Pagan organizations in 2011 compared with 64 per cent in 2000. However, it should be noted that only 15 Pagan/NRM organizations responded to this question.

Given what is reported here about unfair treatment on the basis of religion or belief, it is notable that it is exemption from equalities legislation in relation to religion or belief is one of the most frequently cited issues (39% of organizations). The main concern here is thought to be focused on their religious freedom to determine the internal religious life of their own religions and associated organizations, though there are some implications for policy agendas and laws relating to equality, which we consider in more detail below.

From among the organizations that responded to both the surveys completed in 2000 and 2011, there is a decline (from 31% to 25%) in the reported experience of their members in relation to other religions. However, of those organizations that reported of their members experiencing unfair treatment in 2001, 50 per cent of (56) organizations continued to report experiencing unfair treatment in 2011.

Understanding unfair treatment from other religious groups

Respondents to the surveys completed in both 2000 and 2011 were asked to provide, on a write-in basis, details of specific examples of unfair treatment that their organization members reported having experienced from other religious groups. These examples included: general ignorance/indifference; verbal abuse; physical abuse; damage to property; general practices; exclusion/lack of acceptance; use of facilities and attempted conversion. In general, the kind of issues that were raised are very similar to those raised in 2000. In Box 8.1, a selection is presented that highlights some of the everyday impact and/or complexity of unfair treatment on the grounds of religion or belief and what this means in people's lives.

Box 8.1 Unfair treatment from or within religious groups: Survey comments

Bahá'í comments:

Bahá'ís have not been invited to the main interfaith organization and are 'relegated' to a second group of faith groups.

Muslims do not feel Bahá'í faith should exist. For some Muslims this is a big problem though most are tolerant.

Buddhist comments:

At multifaith events there is often a Christian bias (perhaps understandable). Even where this is addressed there is generally still a 'Theistic' assumption.

Christian comments:

A member from a Muslim background is routinely harassed and verbally abused by Muslim groups when engaged in public Christian activity.

Converts from other religions (especially Islam) are subjected to abuse and even violence. Churches are subject to vandalism in some areas for religious reasons. Confidentiality does not allow one to name individuals.

'Other Christian' comments:

Church of England is the main one but other mainstream churches have been guilty of misrepresenting our church. We have sought to rent halls/other premises for meetings and been rejected and even without warning had premises we have been using closed on us.

Hindu comments:

Leafletting and high pressure evangelism during a recent Hindu festival right inside the festive area.

Muslim comments:

The Wahhabi sect regard some other Muslims as heretical and in this way they justify their harassment and ill treatment of our sect and its members.

Pagan/NRM comments:

The Interfaith Network have refused us membership – predominantly Christian groups.

Zoroastrian comments:

A Zoroastrian couple in refugee accommodation near Birmingham were regularly attacked by their Muslim neighbours who had assumed that because they are Iranian, they MUST be Muslim.

Unfair treatment from other religions: Fieldwork findings

As part of the discussions, both religious and non-religious participants invariably volunteered information about experiences in their interactions with members of religion or belief groups different from their own. There was some evidence of discrimination or unfair treatment caused as a result of these interactions, although there was also evidence of good practice and inter-community dialogue.

Conflict between religion groups

A Bahá'í participant described extremely difficult relationships with her Christian family who sought to limit her rights and role within the family. Her mother, who was also Bahá'í, had recently passed away. She was denied a Bahá'í funeral, and when this participant tried to challenge this, she was subjected to verbal abuse. Other Bahá'ís explained that some of the issues they faced were because they were not always recognized as a religious group. For example, an instance was mentioned about problems in not being able to hire a venue for an event where the difficulty was not specifically because they were Bahá'ís, but 'it's just that you are not Christian'.

A large number of Pagan and NRM participants reported that, although they were generally more accepted in society as compared with a decade ago, they still experienced occasional unfair treatment – mainly, but not only, from Evangelical Christian groups. As noted by a white male Druid: 'I do know people who have expressed that they have come across prejudices from mainly Evangelical Christians who try and convert [them] over to their way of thinking.'

Among the examples relating to other traditions of Christianity are those of a Pagan prison chaplain who described an incident in which a Catholic prisoner with whom she was working told her, after he discovered that she was a Pagan, that she should die and go to hell. In another example, a group of Pagans explained how they were not allowed to book a room in a Cathedral which was available to all faith groups except the Pagans. At the same time, this group also noted that, more recently, the same cathedral had organized an inter-faith event in which all groups including the Pagans were invited. A small number of individual Pagans and people from NRMs also reported that their events were sometimes picketed by Christian groups.

Christian migrants and asylum-seekers who had migrated to the United Kingdom from predominantly Muslim countries such as Pakistan reported discrimination from Pakistani communities in Britain. Since Pakistani Christians share a similar cultural and linguistic background with Pakistani Muslims, they are often assumed to be Muslim, and discrimination occurs after they are identified as Christian by the Muslim groups with whom they interact.

Jews and Muslims reported experiencing respectively, antisemitism and Islamophobia, from the people of the other religious group in response to events in the Israeli–Palestinian conflict in the Middle East. Similarly many Hindus and Muslims reported tensions that flared up between them following communal rioting in the Indian subcontinent.

Racism and antisemitism

In the 2001 research, participants continued to report experiences of racism and antisemitism (Weller et al., 2001: 95). A small number of Jewish participants reported that cemeteries were often desecrated and that extra security measures including CCTVs were provided in synagogues for added security. Issues usually flared up after tensions/conflicts in the Middle East leading to perceptions being reported that activities leading to damage to property were carried out by, among others, Muslim groups.

Many members of Black-led Pentecostal churches described tensions with Anglican Christian churches that tended to avoid sharing church space with them. They felt that this was partly due to racism but also due to the rapid increase in the congregation sizes within Pentecostal churches that were attracting more worshippers, as well as concerns about the more charismatic style of worship within their Pentecostal Christian practice.

Ethnicity, racism and 'South Asian religions'

During the fieldwork, tensions were evident across the visible religious minority communities with predominantly South Asian profiles, specifically: Hindus, Muslims and Sikhs. The existence of such tensions was especially the case in areas with high proportions of these groups – Newham, Leicester, also in Blackburn where there is a large Muslim population but extremely small Hindu and Sikh communities, and to a lesser extent in Cardiff and Norwich. There was also thought to be an element of racism to these tensions. As the Chair of a Sikh community group in Norwich put it:

> ... discrimination within Asian communities has always been there and the most important reason for this discrimination is faith. Different religions don't tally with each other. Muslims don't like Sikhs, Sikhs don't like Muslims, and within the Muslims some don't like Bengalis.

Such tensions may partly be attributed to competition for resources and a perception among some sections of Hindu and Sikh communities – partly based on the Prevent funding that has been focused on addressing radicalization and violent extremism among Muslims – that Muslims have more access to funds and resources as compared with other groups.

Similarly, there was a perception among a group of Hindu participants in a local fieldwork area that Muslims were more freely given resources and planning permission for mosques and community centres. A Hindu woman in this group questioned why there were so many mosques in her area whereas planning permission to expand the temple had, for the last five years, repeatedly been turned down by the local council, with the implication of there having been undue influence upon the local authority from Muslims.

An elderly Sikh man who ran a community group cited the example of his Muslim neighbour who was keen to sell her home but refused to sell it to his Sikh community centre. A Muslim policy researcher based in Leicester explained the reasons for such strained relationships:

> There is some anecdotal evidence of significant frostiness at best, tension at worst even animosity at worse between . . . Hindus and Muslims, Sikhs and Muslims. I don't think there's a big problem between the Hindus and Sikhs but it's more with the Muslim dimension of the minority communities and that goes back, partly back to historical relationships between those religions back in India and the Indian subcontinent but also partly due to competition for resources here.

Furthermore, some of these tensions were exacerbated by events such as 9/11, which led people with a shared 'South Asian' ethnic heritage to differentiate more among themselves. As a male Sikh university student in Cardiff explained:

> [E]veryone came here in the 70s/80s everyone was one community, although you were Sikh, Muslim, Pakistani, or Bengali you were a brotherhood, a community,

we had the same understanding. But after 9/11 here everyone was like 'Oh, I'm Sikh, you're Muslim, you're Hindu,' and everything spread and there goes that brotherhood we had back in those days, not there anymore, everyone has split.

Religious conversion

As also reported in the fieldwork completed in 2000, conversion from one religion to another remained a sensitive subject for individuals and communities alike (Weller et al., 2001: 97). A Muslim community sector worker in Cardiff reported that a small number of converts to Islam with whom he worked reported changed attitudes from colleagues. Male and female converts had told him about problems at work and in social circles after they started keeping a beard or wearing *hijab*. This was corroborated by another example in a different fieldwork location in which a number of participants described the experiences of a female police officer who they felt was treated unfairly by her colleagues after she converted to Islam and started wearing a *hijab*. A number of converts also reported that their relatives refused to talk/interact with them after they had embraced Islam. As a white male convert in Norwich put it: 'There is a whole series of things there, was I a traitor, had I betrayed, had I signed over to, you name it you know, all these things are embedded in you know, way, way back.'

In the report of the 2000 research, members of the Church of Jesus Christ of Latter-day Saints highlighted that converts to their Church sometimes faced unfair treatment from their families and communities (Weller, 2001: 97). In the fieldwork completed in 2011 a local representative of the church stated that this situation had somewhat improved: 'it's not really very common in the UK . . . We usually find that if that happens, over time people see that it's only improved that person who's been converted [. . .] and often they're accepted back in their families, reconciled again.'

A white male convert who joined ISKCON recounted how he was initially not accepted by his community who perceived him to be different. However, 20 years later he feels that the choice he made is now respected. He also stated that because he was white, he was not always accepted by Hindu communities either:

> . . . everybody thought that I had lost my mind, cos it was such a turning away from my previous existence, the way I lived my life to the way I live my life now. It was a contrast and you couldn't get a wider contrast. [. . .] But one interesting thing is that people come up to me after 20 years and they see me and say 'So you're still into it then, then there must be something in it', so I feel slightly more accepted in this town anyway.

A humanist man also reports discrimination in the context of 'converts' to secular/ humanistic stances:

> I can give a number of examples where a number of secular Muslims were beaten up for not fasting. Or have been abused for not wearing cultural clothes or have

received threatening phone calls. So its beyond prejudice or discrimination, its taking an air of violence to get people to conform.

Unfair treatment within religious groups

A small number of people from within a number of different religious groups reported unfair treatment between different denominations and/or ethnic groups within the same religion. For example some Roman Catholic Christian participants in all five fieldwork locations reported that although the situation had generally improved, prejudices still existed about their faith. As a Catholic voluntary sector employee explained:

> I was just going to say, Tony Blair had to wait until he resigned to convert [to Catholicism]. Yes, so there are still those things which annoy me, that's [discrimination] too strong a word but sometimes I'm surprised that they're still there, I'm surprised they still exist.

A participant from the Church of Jesus Christ of Latter-day Saints reported that although their church was growing in size, she felt that other Christian groups set up barriers which prevented their participation within the wider Christian community. She reports that members of her community are seen as 'weird' both by secular society and by other Christian groups:

> Perhaps because it's becoming an increasing secular society and anybody who practises a religion daily is looked on as slightly weird perhaps, no matter what your persuasion but I think that's perhaps part of it but strangely enough a lot of the discrimination we meet is from other Christian religions who don't see us as Christian because our beliefs don't quite chime with theirs.

Similarly members of a Unitarian church described occasional concerns with Anglicans:

> I wouldn't say great issues but we have had [. . .] an Anglican vicar who refused to come in here, though we have equally had an Anglican vicar with whom we have close collaboration and who has worshipped with us. We could say that the evangelical wing of Christians do not like us.

A member of the group who understand themselves to be 'Messianic Jews', reported some tensions between his community and Orthodox Jews, although he did not feel that this translated into unfair treatment:

> There's a lot of suspicion by and large between it. I mean, on an individual level the contacts we have [. . .] tend to be quite open and friendly so far, without too much

of a problem. There's a kind of suspicion about us which they, you know: 'OK, Jews, but really?!' [. . .] But it's not, it's not open hostility or anything.

A group of Muslim women in one of the fieldwork locations reported that there were tensions between them and another Muslim community that had different denominational and ethnic backgrounds. They therefore did not usually socialize together and prayed in different mosques. Similar disconnections were reported between Sikh groups that had originally migrated to the United Kingdom from the Indian subcontinent and those that had migrated from Africa – these groups had similar cultural and linguistic backgrounds and, according to a female Sikh, these tensions were largely due to socio-economic differences. Finally, a white female participant who belonged to a Nagarjuna Kadampa Buddhist centre reported that some of her friends were excluded from Buddhist events in which organizers had felt their beliefs were incorrect. This she felt was discriminatory.

Unfair treatment: Religion and migrants

While the impact of immigration on religion may not be immediately visible, there are a number of ways in which it interacts. In the long term this is reflected in the establishment of religious practice and worship as migrant communities become 'settled' as is evident in the experiences of Muslim, Hindu and Sikh communities.

In the shorter term, the influence of immigration is evident in the efforts being undertaken by Catholic churches in all five fieldwork locations to be more inclusive towards Eastern European communities, particularly of Polish and Lithuanian origin and that are predominantly Catholic. Measures being undertaken include Polish masses, providing space for Polish community groups to meet, language classes in both English (for adults) and in Polish (for children).

Gender and sexuality within religious groups

Some other aspects of identity and equality interact with unfair treatment experienced from religious groups. Issues of discrimination around gender and sexuality remain a sensitive area for some religious groups and can become controversial, especially when heightened by media sensationalism. As a white Anglican woman put it: 'I think certainly in Christian debate what's recently been in the media, the Church of England thing, tearing itself apart over the role of women and the role of gay people.' Such situations also present interesting examples for exploring the overlaps between different equality strands.

A female Christian parish priest reported how she was discouraged from applying for a vacancy within her church primarily because of her gender. Another Christian woman told us how she left the Brethren church, in which she was brought up as a child, because she felt it was too patriarchal. She chose to join a more ecumenical church instead, in which she felt she had more of a role to play as a woman. In separate interviews, two Muslim women who did not wear headscarves or *hijabs* reported that they occasionally faced prejudices. These women also reported that sometimes there was resentment within wider Muslim communities towards their career choices, although they had both had the support of their immediate families. A homosexual man told us about prejudices that he was sure existed within all major religions:

> I think there is a homo-negativity, I don't like the word homophobia because that is a pseudo clinical term, but I think there is a homo-negativity inside almost all the religious groups even including the Buddhists, the monotheistics, Judaism, Christianity and Islam [. . .] And I wouldn't call it discrimination easily, but I do think it is prejudice.

He said that these prejudices had prevented him from becoming ordained as a Christian minister. Another male homosexual couple described that when they had their civil partnership, although most of their community supported them, they also experienced prejudices from some sections of their local church.

Non-religious experience of unfair treatment from religious groups

Non-religious individuals who participated in the focus group discussions in all five fieldwork locations described a number of incidents in which they faced unfair treatment, mostly from interaction with Evangelical Christian groups. Different participants reported how they felt themselves to be either 'looked down upon' or 'perceived as lesser human beings' or especially that they were seen as being 'somehow less moral'. As a white, non-religious woman described it, there is a 'default position that you are supposed to be religious preferably Christian in this country and if you're not you are in some way a bad person, or a deficient person or a dodgy person in some shape or form'.

A humanist man described how he met a Christian Evangelical group in his city centre. When this group realized that his belief was a non-religious one and when he refused to 'convert', he stated that he was told that he would 'burn in hell'. His 5-year-old daughter was with him and she was extremely upset by this statement. Most of the atheist or humanist participants who were in their late teens also reported similar experiences where they felt they were bullied because of their non-religious stance. As a white non-religious woman put it:

> What amazes me is how angry people of faith get about your lack of faith. I have had people ask me 'how can you not believe?' As far as we are considered we don't take the short cut and don't believe in a religion because your parents do. Some people get so irate about your lack of belief.

Such attitudes impact upon relationships, and one non-religious man reported getting into difficult situations with friends and/or family who were religious. Such attitudes were also identified as leading to issues in social and employment contexts. For example, a small number of non-religious applicants felt that they experienced direct or indirect discrimination when seeking a job in a religious school/organization. Another participant reported that since she was white, assumptions were made about her beliefs and it was assumed that she would feel able to attend a church service as part of a work celebration. Other assumptions are also made, as this non-religious male community worker explains:

> Most of the people who do community work like me are not religious.. . . and if they are it's never been an issue that we have had to discuss. I think somehow a big, big assumption is made that you don't contribute to the local community unless you are religious.

Inter-faith and inter-community dialogue

Alongside the kind of issues reported above, during the fieldwork completed in 2011 there was considerable evidence of good community relationships being fostered through macro- and micro-level inter-community and inter-faith dialogue events. All fieldwork locations visited had at least one inter-faith body which regularly ran dialogue events. Many participants from these bodies as well as other participants who had attended/heard about these events reported about the positive outcomes.

A large proportion of representatives of both religious and non-religious organizations reported that they often engaged in inter-faith activities, spoke in public forums about their religion or belief and, in the case of religious participants, encouraged students and other groups to visit places of worship. Such activities were thought to be contributing to better relationships with communities and, in the long run, to be reducing discrimination. For example, a member of the Unitarian Church described how her community shared its space with other religious groups:

> Not so long ago we were very happy for the Buddhists to come here, they wanted to have a big funeral and they haven't a suitable place and we were very happy that they should come and do that. We have had people from the Muslim community come on a Sunday morning to talk to us, less recently but certainly we are on good terms with them. We did for a while offer the liberal Jews a home. And we are represented on the interfaith group.

An orthodox Jewish woman reported about her *Mitzvah* day celebrations, which had included a strong inter-faith element:

> *Mitzvah* is a Jewish word [. . .] in this context it means good deed and we stood outside two supermarkets asking people not for money but for things to do a good deed [. . .] and people gave us most generously, it was across the faiths. We had people from other faiths, particularly the Muslim faith, there was women's organization which brought us enormous amounts of stuff to donate to our charities, [. . .] and it was most heartening to see the support and the understanding that we received for that day.

A young Sikh man commented that he thought that such dialogue activities took place because 'because there was a recognition within communities to create an atmosphere of respect and mutual friendship that would allow each community to have their rights and their beliefs respected, but also respect the beliefs of others'.

The next section of this chapter goes on to look more closely at the unfair treatment reported by religious groups as coming from a range of specifically organized groups such as political, community and other pressure groups. But it is clear from the findings of the fieldwork (including especially the focus groups held with the non-religious) as reported in this section that, while religion and belief groups face considerable unfair treatment within the structures and processes, attitudes and behaviours of the broader society, non-religious people also experience considerable unfair treatment on the grounds of religion or belief, including directly from religious people or groups.

Unfair treatment from political, community and other pressure groups

BNP. Arson attacks on our mosque/grafitti/door to door petition against the new plan for our mosque. (Survey comment from Muslim respondent)

Introduction

This section examines reported experiences of unfair treatment of people of various religious groups from political, community and other pressure groups in the wider society.

Survey findings on unfair treatment from political, community and other pressure groups

The surveys completed in 2000 and 2011 collected the reported experience of unfair treatment of members of religious organizations from political, community and pressure groups. Respondents were asked to state which groups were the source of the unfair treatment and to provide an example of it.

Unfair treatment from political, community and other pressure groups

In the survey completed in 2000, 21 per cent of responding religious organizations reported unfair treatment from political, community and other pressure groups compared to 19 per cent of (452) responding organizations in the survey completed in 2011. The level of reported unfair treatment is still substantial, indicating the scale of its impact on people's lives. It is nevertheless notable that the incidence of this reported experience of unfair treatment from political, community and other pressure groups is lower than that of the reported experience of unfair treatment from other religious groups.

It is important to consider in more detail, and by religion, the differences concerning reported experience of unfair treatment. Given the relatively smaller numbers of organizations responding to the survey from among some religious groups, some of this data needs to be treated with caution. Table 8.2 provides a summary of the responses by religion.

Table 8.2 Reported experience of treatment: From political, community and other pressure groups, by religion

Religion	Yes	Percentage	No	Percentage	N
Hindu	1	4	25	96	26
Bahá'í	2	6	30	94	32
Sikh	1	7	13	93	14
Buddhist	3	8	35	92	38
NRM/Pagan	1	8	12	92	13
Christian	25	15	145	85	170
Other Christian	4	21	15	79	19
Inter-faith	8	32	17	68	25
Muslim	25	41	36	59	61
Jewish	16	42	22	58	38

Note: Where response numbers are low religions have been excluded from table. Caution should be exercised where cell counts are low.

As Table 8.2 highlights, overall Jewish and Muslim organizations were the most likely to report unfair treatment from political, community and other pressure groups. In this, there are some parallels with the findings from the survey completed in 2000, where Muslim organizations in particular were the most likely to report unfair treatment.

From among the organizations that responded to both the surveys completed in 2000 and 2011, there has been very little change (20% and 19%) in the reported experience of unfair treatment of their members in relation to political, community and other pressure groups. However, of those organizations that reported their members experiencing unfair treatment in 2001, 31 per cent of (35) organizations continued to report experiencing unfair treatment in 2011.

Understanding unfair treatment from political, community and other pressure groups

Respondents to the surveys completed in 2000 and 2011 were asked to provide, on a write-in basis, details of specific examples of unfair treatment that their members reported having experienced from other than religious groups, including the types of groups perpetrating this unfair treatment. Examples of the kinds of unfair treatment given included: verbal abuse; physical abuse; damage to property; exclusion; lack of acceptance; hostility and bias. The groups identified as perpetrating this unfair treatment included: Right-wing groups; political parties; pressure groups; government/ local council; health and social services the general public and gay and lesbian movements. In general, the kind of issues that were raised were very similar to those in 2000. In Box 8.2, a selection is presented that highlights the everyday impact and/ or complexity of unfair treatment on the grounds of religion or belief and what this means in people's lives.

Box 8.2 Unfair treatment from political, community and other pressure groups: Survey comments

Buddhist comments:

Tarring Buddhists with the same brush as the Theists they object to.

Christian comments:

At Alcohol Anonymous two members have been denied permission to speak about Jesus when asked to speak about their higher power in meetings.

Militant atheists or secularists. Disguised as politically correct 'liberals', these people attempt to drive Christianity out of the public view by posing as the defenders of minority religion. They attempt to stir distrust between faiths.

British Humanist Society; National Secular Society; Stonewall and other political groups hostile to religion. These groups maintain a constant campaign to marginalize religion from public life. The humanist groups mainly exist for this purpose.

Jewish comments:

We have on occasion received letters with antisemitic insults and denying the Holocaust.

Too numerous to list, everything from Socialist Workers' Party to the BNP.

Muslim comments:

The BNP and EDL are increasingly taking over the community and promoting an incorrect extremist agenda against long established local Muslims.

Other religions comments:

Using private photos to anonymously post on internet denegrating people for being from our religion.

We have been subject to a campaign of harassment from a few anonymous students organized on the internet. Abusive phone calls and emails. These acts seem intended to terrorise us.

Inter-faith comments:

(Jewish members) stated that anonymous, but investigation suggested perpetrator(s) not religious, just antisemitic, anti-Israeli. Blown up photos of civilian victims in Gaza of Israeli military action fixed to synagogue doors, i.e. photos of women and children who were killed.

Unfair treatment from political, community and pressure groups: Fieldwork findings

During interviews, participants occasionally spoke about unfair treatment from political, community and pressure groups. Such discussions usually formed part of general narratives about discrimination.

Far-right groups

Echoing what was identified and reported above from the survey of religious organizations, in the fieldwork completed in 2011 both religious and non-religious participants described 'concerns' and 'tensions' around the activities of far-right groups such as the EDL (English Defence League), WDL (Welsh Defence League) and the BNP (British National Party).

For example, a voluntary sector worker described an incident in which a group of Sikh children aged 6–7 were picketed and threatened by a group of EDL supporters while on a summer camp. Participants in three case-study areas also reported concerns about marches conducted by the EDL or WDL and the build up to these events, which led to considerable tensions about security and harmony within cities. Concerns were voiced more specifically about the increased potential of violence towards Muslim residents during these events. A Muslim student stated that her mother refused to let her attend university classes on the day of a march. A community leader from a Muslim umbrella organization described his concerns about 'follow-on violence':

> Obviously you have the EDL Welsh version of that which is WDL, Welsh Defence League. So they kind of stir up you know issues within the community and that's that quite targeted at Muslims obviously so it's religious discrimination and belief discrimination. Although they say you know they're just against extremists, you know, their rhetoric and the things they say sometimes are targeted at mainstream Muslims as well. So as a community we try to calm things and tell people not to go out and protest against them, otherwise it's gonna cause a conflict and a clash.

With regard to the policing of such events, many participants in fieldwork locations where such events occurred (Leicester, Blackburn and Cardiff) reported efficient and effective actions by the police, local government and community organizations in order to reduce tensions. As a Muslim male working with the Blackburn local authority said in relation to an EDL march that took place there: 'so basically right up until that march, we were meeting regularly with the community, giving them messages and assurance from a policing perspective and messages of togetherness from a cohesion perspective and that was really helpful'. In Leicester, a majority of participants described the 'One Leicester' event which was organized that day after the EDL march, as a response to it and as a show of solidarity across different religious and non-religious groups in Leicester. As a Hindu man expressed it:

> But we have shown a very good show when there was the EDL march in Leicester last time and all the faiths got together with the council, police and all and said

this is not right, Leicester is not the right place for you to come. So at that time we were all together.

Some participants discussed the need to hear and address the views of EDL supporters who often come from deprived areas. A male Muslim inter-faith worker in Blackburn stated the views of a colleague who volunteered as a marshal during an EDL march:

> She was one of the marshals at the EDL march and she was based in an area which is a white indigenous deprived community and youths were coming out, you know, in big numbers and were already marching down the main road, [. . .] she was kind of worried that this is the situation with our youth at this day and age. These youth will be our backbone for our town and city, work desperately needs to happen with these youths so it eradicates all those issues. So you've got both sides of the spectrum of how it is.

'Spontaneous' and 'randomly' experienced unfair treatment

As also reported in responses to the survey completed in 2011, a number of participants described incidents of unfair treatment that occurred in city centres, street corners, etc., which usually consisted of name-calling and verbal abuse. Participants who were visible in any particular way, either because of their religious practices or symbols, faced such spontaneous and random unfair treatment. For example, a female Anglican vicar reported that a street vendor of the *Big Issue* magazine shouted 'And you call yourself a Christian!' when she declined to buy a magazine. She was recognized as a Christian because she was wearing her 'dog collar'. A pastor reported being called 'Jesus man' outside a school by students who recognized him because he regularly presented sessions on Christianity, although he did not consider this offensive.

A majority of Muslim participants reported quite a few examples in the general public sphere of random name-calling and hate crime such as women's headscarves being pulled on the street. They added that frequency of such incidents usually increased in the aftermath of acts of terrorism internationally and also in the United Kingdom. Sikh and Hindu participants also reported being mistakenly identified as Muslims and having had to face such attacks. A young Sikh man reported that stones were thrown at him quite soon after the events of 9/11 when he was mistakenly identified as a member of the Taliban. Buddhists, Hindus, Muslims and Sikhs also reported vandalism of places of worship and graffiti which was discussed earlier in more detail in the section on 'Housing and planning' (see Chapter 7).

Many Jewish participants reported incidents that seemed to correlate with developments in the Israeli–Palestinian conflict in the Middle East and associated organized protests in the United Kingdom, which sometimes did not distinguish between the state of Israel and Jewish religious belief. A rabbi reported that he was concerned about the Anti-Israel/Pro-Palestine groups that held their events in the city centre and which sometimes picketed the synagogue. He felt threatened by them and felt that they misrepresented events in the Middle East, although what really surprised him was that this group was led by a Jewish woman.

Conclusion

Having explored in detail the key quantitative and qualitative findings of our research in Chapters 6, 7 and 8, in Chapter 9 we present an overview of our findings and go on to explore an analytical continuum that might enable a more sophisticated understanding of religion or belief discrimination and unfair treatment on the basis of religion or belief.

9

An Analytical Spectrum for Understanding the Evidence

Unfair treatment and discrimination: Actual or perceived?

Chapters 6-8 have presented a large body of reported evidence in relation to unfair treatment on the grounds of religion or belief. As noted in Chapter 1, one of the aims of the 2011 research (building on one of the terms of reference of the 2000 research) was to make an assessment of evidence of religious discrimination 'both actual and perceived'. Put as simply and as clearly as possible, not everything that individuals or groups identify as discrimination or unfair treatment can safely be presumed to be either discriminatory or unfair, since even a deliberate act which is perceived by others as unfair does not necessarily constitute discrimination.

At the same time, in law (and certainly in relation to 'indirect discrimination'), unfair or discriminatory treatment does not have to be deliberate, or even detected by the victim, in order to constitute discrimination. Nevertheless, from the perspective of those who report unfair treatment and discrimination on the grounds of religion or belief, their subjective experience is very relevant. As powerfully highlighted in the research completed in 2000, a mixed group of Hindus and Jains expressed the anguish that suspicion or scepticism in relation to belief or acceptance about their reported experience can cause for those who seek to articulate it to a wider audience, in ways that then further compound the pain of the original experience:

> Discrimination is difficult to prove. It can always be said that it was an individual's attitude rather than an inadequate or discriminatory policy; as a result, you can't get action taken. People are laughing in your face: discrimination is an experience, the experience of a slap in the face. (Weller et al., 2001: 115)

As was argued in Chapter 1 in relation to the concepts of 'religion' and of 'belief', when trying to understand the individual and personal reported experience of discrimination and unfair treatment, the self-definition of those researched is arguably the best place to begin. At the same time it is unlikely also to be the place to end, either in terms of the law or of research. This is because, in legal terms, claims need to be tested in relation to relevant evidence; considered in the context of the letter of the law; the intentions of the lawmakers; and the interpretations of those applying the law within the context of due process. In terms of research, the reported experience of both individuals and groups needs to be critically scrutinized in a way that goes beyond the mere recounting of it by individuals and groups and the purely descriptive reporting of it by researchers. It is with this attempt to differentiate and understand the diversity of the reported experience of unfair treatment that this chapter is concerned.

The analytical spectrum of unfair treatment: An overview

In their review of 'belief' within religion or belief discrimination, Woodhead with Catto (2009: 4) suggested, as a starting point, the possibility of distinguishing between three kinds of religion or belief discrimination. In this, they identified socio-economic or 'material' discrimination (e.g. in employment), cultural or attitudinal discrimination (e.g. ignorance, ridicule, distortion, trivialization of religious commitment) and religious 'hatred'.

However, a more complex and multidimensional approach was developed by the 2000 research project (see Weller et al., 2000: 14). In the 2011 research, this has now been developed further in the form of an analytical spectrum in which we have identified seven (as compared with an original six) aspects of unfair treatment that can be distinguished from each other but between which there can also be overlaps.

As compared with the earlier version of the spectrum in the *Interim Report* (Weller et al., 2000) of the 2000 research, that which is used in the 2011 research has been articulated in terms not only of religion, but also in relation to 'religion or belief'. In part, this reflects the changing legal and policy framework since 2000 in which, because of the introduction of the HRA (informed as it was by the provisions of the ECHR) 'belief' equally forms part of this 'protected characteristic'. In *substance* this was not different from the intention of the 2000 research and its analytical framework since, as the *Interim Report* of that research explained it:

> Although the research concentrated on the views and experiences of people who identify themselves with a religion, this is not to ignore the possibility that secularists, humanists and agnostics may also experience discrimination on the basis of religion. Such experience also needs to be taken into account in framing policy in this area. (Weller et al., 2000: 2)

At the end of the 1990s the language of 'religious discrimination' reflected a period in which its use was arguably a necessary part of bringing into focus a dimension of personal and social experience to which, until then, relatively little policy attention had been given compared with other aspects of identity such as ethnicity, gender and social class. But the relationship between the use of language and the framing of policy is an important one, and the fact that the 2000 research had to spell out a more 'inclusive' explanation of the terminology it used at the time is indicative of the substantive importance of moving from the previous language of the analytical spectrum to its current formulation.

This development of the analytical spectrum is, however, also reflective of the nature of the 2011 research and its findings which, distinctively and importantly, have included the specific aim of capturing aspects of the experience and perspectives of those who understand themselves to be 'non-religious'. The seven identified aspects of the spectrum are therefore in principle equally applicable to framing and understanding unfair treatment on the grounds of religion or belief of those who are 'non-religious' as well as those who are 'religious'. They can also be applied equally to understanding the experience of unfair treatment in relationships between and within the 'religious' and the 'non-religious', as well as to these groups in relation to the structures and sectors of the wider society.

Because of this, we have created an analytical spectrum to aid a properly nuanced understanding of the diversity of the reported experience of unfair treatment on the basis of religion or belief. It is also hoped this can act as a 'bridge' between the descriptive findings of the project; the identification of possible measures for tackling such unfair treatment; and our evaluation of the implications of our findings in terms of identifying signposts for future law, policy and practice.

The analytical spectrum provides also a practical tool that can inform those who hold responsibility for the internal life and external service provision of organizations (including religious organizations) in the decisions that they make concerning how, in their sphere of responsibility, to tackle unfair treatment on the basis of religion or belief. For civil servants and politicians its distinguishing between different kinds of unfair treatment can inform both a more grounded and more nuanced approach to developing appropriate legal, social and policy instruments.

The analytical spectrum of religion or belief discrimination in its various aspects

'Religion or belief naivety'

In 'unpacking' the spectrum we begin with an aspect that has been added as a direct result of our further reflection on the findings of the 2011 project and especially of its fieldwork. 'Religion or belief naivety' is here defined as a lack of basic religion or belief literacy that sometimes leads to actions that can be seen as and/or result in unfair treatment. During the fieldwork completed in 2011 and across all five fieldwork localities, among those who were interviewed or who were part of focus groups, participants spoke of there being a lack of knowledge relating to religion or belief. This was particularly, but not only, in relation to lesser known religious groups such as the Jains or the Bahá'ís. In many situations it did not have any apparent directly negative impact on the lives of individuals or groups other than (the effects of which should not itself be underestimated) perpetuating a status quo where not enough was known about these religions.

Thus, as reported in Chapter 6, a Bahá'í woman felt that the level of awareness of her community was that of 'put it in the pending tray'. Similar perceptions were also reported by Jain participants. Such a lack of knowledge can lead to unfair treatment, where a particular service is denied or not provided. Examples of this were noted in Chapter 7 where it was highlighted that a range of religious groups found they were unable to hire venues for their religious events because venue administrators simply did not recognize who they were or what their religion entailed.

We have adopted the terminology of 'religion or belief naiveity' in preference to that of 'religion or belief ignorance' because what is identified here is not a more settled state of 'ignorance' in relation to which some individuals/organizations do not wish to be challenged or to change their attitudes, behaviour or policies and practice. Rather, 'religion or belief naivety' can also encompass the effects that occur even where there is an intention to be inclusive. A poignant example of this was described by a retired Anglican Christian woman chaplain when she spoke of what happened during a lunch that she otherwise said had been an extremely fruitful inter-faith event for leaders of a range of different religious groups:

> and they had organized a beautiful and I think quite expensive buffet and no-one but the Christians could eat anything because the vegetarian option, the vegan option for the Buddhist, was on the same plate as the ham sandwiches. The Jewish person couldn't eat anything because they had mixed meat and milk and they had put the ham sandwiches alongside the egg sandwiches. The Muslims couldn't eat anything [. . .] it was just pure lack of thought because they had obviously gone to town and provided this lovely spread and spent money on it wanting to sort of do a nice thing and actually only the Christians could end up eating and everybody else was just on coffee or tea, it was appalling.

In this and other similar instances, the organizers were clearly well-intentioned but their apparent lack of knowledge of basic information led to what could be both perceived and experienced as unfair or, at very least, what she additionally described as 'appalling impoliteness'. According to a female voluntary sector employee such things occur 'from lack of knowledge I would say not actual prejudice more a lack of understanding and I would say that that happens a lot in religious context that a lot of people don't understand and don't realize different things'. A non-religious woman also spoke about her experiences of what she termed the assumptions that people made:

> An example not of discrimination but the assumption that everybody is religious – as part of a winter celebration there was a religious service afterwards and we were invited to recite a prayer sort of thing and people just went along with it. I was thinking – I'd bet you any amount of money that 50% of the people are not religious but are just getting on with it. I did not like the assumption that I being a non-religious person was expected to do that without even being asked my preferences. I left and then did speak to them afterwards and told them they had made a grave assumption. I don't think this was prejudice or discrimination. I think it was quite lazy.

Such instances may be understood, in part, as a byproduct of society's growing religion or belief plurality feeding into an inevitable unfamiliarity with the religion or belief norms of at least some groups. Thus, the key aspect of 'religion or belief naivety' is to be seen not in the intentions of those whose actions might be characterized in this way, but rather in the effects that this naivety can have on others. Some of these effects can be similar to those of 'religion or belief prejudice', although the characteristics of this are different as explored next.

'Religion or belief prejudice'

'Religion or belief prejudice' involves the stereotyping of particular religion or belief groups through attitudes that can wound or hurt individuals and form a basis for exclusionary unfair treatment, harassment or victimization. While it shares some of the features of 'religion or belief naivety', it has become a more settled/entrenched attitude of mind, emotion and will, and involves at least some stereotyping of the religion or belief 'other' often, but not always, associated with a negative evaluation of them.

As something fundamentally attitudinal, 'religion or belief prejudice' may not necessarily result in unfair or discriminatory actions. However, as with attitudinal prejudice in relation to other 'protected characteristics', prejudice on the grounds of religion or belief can translate into behaviours that clearly constitute direct discrimination. As seen in Chapters 6-8, the results of the survey completed in 2011 reveal a generally consistent pattern in which the attitudes and behaviours of individuals were identified as a more frequent source of unfair treatment than the policies and practices of organizations. What attitudes of prejudice might mean were highlighted by a white Muslim convert who defined it in the following way:

> Prejudice to me is to judge in advance, in advance of the facts if you like on the basis of a preconception and I dare say that's a factor sometimes, that people have a preconception immediately the moment [they see a] Muslim, that conjures up something. In the current context [. . .] that's fixed in the [mind] you know Muslim equals terrorist [. . .] or a common one would be alien or foreign automatically and here am I and I am native [. . .] prejudice you know it's like blanket statements which are very risky, all or none or never, always and you know that kind of thinking excludes the middle.

Thus while 'religion and belief prejudice' may, like 'religion or belief naivety' involve a lack of information, in addition it entails the presence of *mis*information that is demeaning; which *inferiorizes* the different other (Contractor, 2012); and which sets up barriers between the *us* and *them* (Hinton, 2000; Hussain, 2004; Pickering, 2001). In principle, 'religion or belief prejudice' can be found in relation to all religion or belief groups, including that which is generated within and targeted at one religious group from another as was explored in Chapter 8.

Such prejudice may be perpetuated in the media and popular discourses in ways reported in Chapter 6. It is often, but not always, rooted in the historical inheritance of conflictual relationships that have developed over many centuries involving the overlapping of religion, belief, politics and warfare. For example, in relation to Muslims such stereotyping it is argued that this is deeply and historically entrenched in Western societies (Daniels, 1960, 1969; Hussain, 1990). With regard to Jewish communities, a Progressive Jewish man interviewed in Leicester commented that such stereotypes are fuelled both by historical prejudice and also current affairs around the conflict in the Middle East:

> I think Jews have historically faced clear discrimination you know, in Europe massive discrimination and prejudice and [. . .] and so there's always been that weariness of antisemitism which does manifest itself in British culture from time to time but then increasingly over the last 20 years the situation in Israel Palestine then impacts on relationships between communities in a city like Leicester. [. . .] Certainly (inaudible) when Israel invaded Gaza then there was an increase in attacks well you know, prejudice attacks, name calling and that was noticeable across the country.

According to fieldwork participants, prejudices of these kinds can include 'deep suspicion', 'communities feeling under siege' and 'paranoia' and can feed into concrete actions of unfair treatment and discrimination. For example, the white female chairperson of a regional Pagan group discussed such prejudice in the light of the changing contexts and experiences of the people in her group. The experiences of her community have changed from a 'quite serious fear of prejudice' in the 1970s to a situation that is more bearable now:

> [P]eople make comments about all sorts. They might make comments about being a witch or something like this. But on the whole it's only verbalised it's not the physical prejudice anymore, it doesn't stop people getting jobs anymore, I've not really heard of anyone being beaten up because they are Pagan for instance anymore.

Similarly to what was articulated by this participant in relation to a longer historical period, the results of the survey completed in 2011 show a general reduction in the reporting of unfair treatment since the survey completed in 2000. This is not, however, to underplay the significance of such prejudice in the lives of individuals and groups. Thus, in relation to Pagans it is important to note that this participant's observation was made relative to what were historically extremely difficult experiences of unfair treatment. Therefore, even in the light of improvements reported by Pagans in both the survey write-in comments and in the fieldwork, the results of the 2011 survey show that Pagans and people from NRMs continue to have high levels of reported experience of unfair treatment.

As noted in Chapter 8 a number of non-religious participants also described how such prejudice impacted in their lives, reporting that they were perceived as 'immoral', 'dodgy' and 'lesser human beings'. In a particularly graphic instance cited in Chapter 8, a non-religious father described the serious impact of prejudice when he explained how, in front of his 5-year-old daughter, he was told by a religious person involved in street proselytizing that he would 'burn in hell'. Thus, when 'religion or belief' prejudice informs actions that, for their recipients can become start to become intimidatory it begins to shade over into some of the characteristics of 'religion or belief' hatred, as explored next.

'Religion or belief hatred'

'Religion or belief hatred' can occur when prejudice intensifies into a settled attitude of mind, emotion and will that can spill over into intimidatory and/or violent behaviour towards the religion or belief 'other'. In other words, this is related to the legally recognized phenomenon of harassment on grounds of religion or belief. Such phenomena can be very serious, threatening and destabilizing in their consequences for individuals and groups.

Across Europe in general, such 'religion or belief hatred' that has traditionally been directed towards the Jewish people has, more recently, also become directed towards Muslims as representatives of what is often perceived as an alien civilization that is fundamentally at odds with the European heritage and is identified as a specific category of 'undesirable other'. Indeed, it is this kind of deep-seated prejudice that has led to the characterization of these specific attitudes as being examples of 'Islamophobia' (Allen, 2010; Commission on British Muslims and Islamophobia, 1997). Similarly, the specific form of it that affects Jews is antisemitism, while more recently the term 'Christophobia' has been coined in relation to Christians (see Weiler, 2003). In each instance it is arguable that some identifiable dynamics are at work (Weller, 2007), but that these forms of hatred are also clothed in particular characteristics that relate to specific groups.

Religion or belief hatred has a specific meaning within legal frameworks as defined by the *Racial and Religious Hatred Act*, 2006. However, within the fieldwork, many participants expressed a more general understanding and also some confusion about what exactly hate crime entailed. Local Authority Hate Crime Officers and Equality and Diversity Officers offered clearer understandings. Thus a public sector employee in Leicester provided a link to the Leicestershire County Council 'Report Hate Crime' webpages which, together with procedures to report hate crimes, also describes such crimes as:

> A hate incident is any incident where you or someone else has been targeted because you or they are believed to be different, this may be motivated by: age, disability, gender identity, race, religion/belief or sexual orientation. An incident/ offence may be physical, verbal or written and can take many forms including physical attack, threat of attack, verbal abuse or insults, offensive leaflets and posters, harassment, bullying and victimisation. (www.leics.gov.uk/reporthate)

A number of public sector and local authority employees commented about under-reporting of hate crime, which they identified as being partly because not only people do not really recognize what a hate crime is, but also because they are not aware of the procedures for reporting such crimes.

According to a survey conducted by the South Wales Police Authority in Summer 2011, 11 out of 114 victims of hate crime said they felt the reason for the crime was religion. Similarly, when people who had witnessed a hate crime were asked, 36 out of 138 said they felt the crime was motivated by the victim's religion or belief (www. southwalespoliceauthority.org.uk/en/content/cms/consultation/previous_survey/ hate_crime/hate_crime.aspx).

In describing their experiences around hate and hatred, religious and non-religious fieldwork participants often associated 'religion or belief hatred' with activism by far right groups such as the EDL or in Wales, the WDL. According to a South Asian Muslim male participant living in Blackburn, such groups are 'are spewing hate across the length and breadth of this country'. For many Muslim and other than Muslim participants, these activities appeared to be targeted particularly at Muslims and Islam. As a male Brahmakumari of South Asian background put it:

> . . . we had the EDL come and I think it was more about to incite hatred, especially against the Muslims because . . . You know what happens in society everybody paints everybody with the same brush, but everybody is unique, everybody's different. [. . .] People didn't see it as having a go at the Muslim community, what they thought it was, was basically they were just spreading hatred. Hate for the sake of hate and they just happened to be using the Muslim community as a point of sort of venting their discrimination.

Moreover, as explained by a South Asian middle-aged male Muslim participant and active researcher, such acts of hatred could also include, 'vandalism, hate mail, pigs blood and pigs heads outside mosques, all of those sorts of things, you know women with headscarves being attacked, abused on the streets, those things are all there'. Another South Asian elderly Muslim man who was a legal professional spoke about the 'mind boggling ignorance coupled with genuine hatred towards Islam' and that the 'two rammed together, ignorance and hatred'.

As another example, but concerning a different religion or belief group, a Jewish man in Leicester reported concerns within the Jewish community 'that a Synagogue could get vandalised, could get graffiti, could get bombed or something like that' and he also reported 'Swastikas painted on the synagogue walls'. The following comment from an elderly white Jewish man in Cardiff is reflective of concerns about such hatred that were raised by the majority of Jewish interviewees, and which have led many Jewish organizations to install strict security measures at synagogues, cemeteries and other Jewish community centres:

> So Jewish people tend to be very unpopular and therefore we have security on both synagogues and if you go to the orthodox synagogues the security there is enormous. There are huge railings, every window is reinforced, in other words they are bullet proof and there are alarms on every entrance and every window, you can't get in let's put it that way.

The non-religious can also face 'religion or belief hatred'. Thus, a middle-aged non-religious man of South Asian background described how those whom he called 'secular Muslims' may also face such hatred from Muslims who strongly identify with their religion: 'Secular Muslims were beaten up for not fasting. Or have been abused for not wearing cultural clothes or have received threatening phone calls. So it's beyond prejudice or discrimination, its taking an air of violence to get people to conform.'

Many fieldwork participants across all the fieldwork locations associated an increase in hate crimes with the current economic and unemployment situation in the United Kingdom. As one participant put it, this meant that 'people are getting more frustrated', also in relation to increased competition for jobs and resources as a result of new migrant communities. Other participants linked it with visibility. As a Unitarian woman said, 'the more visible you are the more likely you are to attract hatred'. But, speaking out of his experience as a middle-aged white homosexual Christian, a man in Leicester also made the point, albeit with also broader reference to many aspects of Christian Church history and practice that, 'religion has had a lot to answer for in undergirding discrimination and hatred'.

This participant made particular reference to the historical roots of some of the 'religion or belief' hatred about which he spoke and which he located in aspects of the historical relationships between religion, power and law. At one extreme, this can feed into the kind of active persecution of 'the other' on religious grounds that is manifested in political projects of 'religious cleansing' that can be a systematically violent manifestation of religious hatred. But in much less dramatic and destructive ways, other forms of the relationship between religion, power and law can lead to a reduction of social space for the religion or belief 'other', as in the phenomenon of 'religion or belief' disadvantage, which is explored next.

'Religion or belief disadvantage'

'Religion or belief disadvantage' is a more structural instance of unfair treatment that affects groups and organizations as much as individuals. In this it differs from the more individual forms of unfair treatment, although the way it operates may also be associated with aspects of, for example, 'religion or belief prejudice'. However, even if it is not informed by such prejudice, it is very real in its structural effects.

In at least some measure, such 'religion or belief disadvantage' can be experienced by all minority religion or belief groups in relation to the relative position (and sometimes privileges) of majority groups. Such disadvantage can occur as a result either of historical factors and/or from specific constitutional, legal and social relationships that underpin a number of privileged alignments between a particular religion or belief group or groups, the state, the law and various social institutions (Madeley and Enyedi, 2003). Such disadvantage can, to some extent, be understood by analogy with socio-economic disadvantage in relation to access to employment, housing, education and other similar factors. But in this context it occurs when a particular group or groups of people considered in relation to their religion or belief identification do not have the same rights of presence and access available to another dominant tradition within their own religion, or to another religion or belief group or groups.

As noted in Chapters 2 and 3, disadvantage of this kind can be a part of the position of all non-established religious groups in relation to those which have a so-called special relationship with the state and many institutions of society. At the same time, it is also clear historically that particular political and legal interpretations and applications of the contested concept of 'secularism' can impact significantly upon the possibilities of social inclusion that are open to religious minorities (Weller, 2006).

Evidence from the fieldwork completed in 2011 suggests an increasing complexity and degree of nuance in relation to this aspect of the spectrum as seen in England and Wales, in which there seems generally to be an understanding and acceptance among most minority religious group interviewees that they live in a country whose predominant religious and cultural heritage is Christian. According to a South Asian elderly Muslim legal professional and community leader who migrated to Britain from Uganda:

> [O]f course this is a Christian country, we know, and our monarch is the head of the Anglican Church, the Queen is head of the Anglican Church and although the whites may not be all practising Christians, it nominally is a Christian country. We are a small minority the Muslims, Hindus, Sikhs etc.

Sometimes members of minority religious communities report having to make compromises with regard to the values of their religions, but these are not always seen as being problematic. As expressed by a South Asian Hindu woman in Leicester:

> We've chosen to come to this country which is predominantly a Christian country and so it is for us to work around it because we've chosen to live here and work around the things, the values that are happening here. So I will give you one example . . . As a Hindu I'm a strict vegetarian but that doesn't mean everywhere I go they should provide me with a vegetarian meal, although if there's a choice I would say I want a vegetarian meal, [. . .] So I think that's the attitude a lot of us have adopted, and erm I'm happy to live by it.

At the same time, there were fieldwork participants who identified Christianity as being privileged. This was especially the case in relation to education, where a large proportion of both Sikh and Jain participants argued that in schools there was too much education about Christianity relative to a very small amount of education about their own religions. This is despite the fact that, as identified in Chapter 6, the fieldwork completed in 2011 has suggested significant improvements in inclusivity within the sector of education. But as expressed by a young Jain woman of South Asian ethnic origin working in Leicester, problems of disadvantage remain:

> You learn about Christianity and you learn about, God there's so many, you've got the Roman Catholic and then you have the Protestants and you have to learn that so much and then you learn a little bit of the Hinduism, and then you hear very little about Sikhism and then very little about Muslims. Jainism doesn't exist because it just didn't exist.

Secondly, and reflective of the 'secular' and 'non-religious' dimension of what was argued in Chapter 3 is a 'three-dimensional society', the identification and criticism of Christian privilege (and especially of the established religion aspects of that) are increasingly coming from the non-religious sections of society. Indeed, the fieldwork evidence suggests that the perception of religion or belief disadvantage was more acute among the non-religious than among minority religious groups.

According to the non-religious focus group participants in all five fieldwork locations, they are disadvantaged by the structural forms of RE and observance in schools; by the special place given to Bishops in Parliament and when applying for jobs in organizations that work with the wider public but have a religious foundation. Such participants identified a corollary of disadvantage in terms of what they saw as the privileges of Christian groups.

Among things of this kind identified by non-religious fieldwork participants one stated that: 'UK and Iran are the only two countries where religious representatives get automatic rights in terms of the state'; that education includes the RE of a kind that some non-religious participants described as 'indoctrination'; and that there are 'self-appointed bishops in Parliament'. A non-religious participant in Leicester identified such issues in the structural composition of the component parts of SACREs: 'One the Church of England has it entirely to itself, the second it's all the other religions, then there are the representatives of the local authority and then there are the representatives of the education organizations. So there's an obvious privilege.'

In 'mirror image' to the broad perception from non-religious participants and against the background of the increasing religious diversity and secularity of society underlined by the most recent Census data, a number of Christian participants reported a sense of Christianity becoming marginalized. According to these participants society has departed from what was once perceived as its Christian foundations. As articulated by this Presbyterian minister:

> We feel as Christian people, because in its earlier days was really based upon the Word of God what we considered the Bible, and that's the foundation but now they've departed from that and therefore inevitably we are going to be discriminated against. We were known at one time as a Christian country.

At the same time, not all Christian participants agreed that Christianity was being marginalized. A few felt that this was a view that was being actively encouraged by a small minority of Christians. Nevertheless, a very evocative comment from a Christian minister (already noted in Chapter 6) highlights not only the deep sense of loss being experienced by some Christians, but also the connection of that loss with a previously relatively more powerful position in which Christianity could be assumed to be predominant by saying: 'It's almost like losing the empire all over again, its just that it's the empire of your own country.'

One of the historical and continuing aspects of religion or belief disadvantage is that the relationships involved within it between religion, the power of the state and the law. Chapter 2 highlighted the ways in the history of England and Wales in which the law itself acted as an instrument of discrimination on the grounds of religion or belief. But within the legal and policy frameworks for equalities and human rights, the law has been important in providing a measure of protection and redress for individuals facing specific and individual direct discrimination on the grounds of religion or belief, and it is such 'religion or belief direct discrimination' that is explored next.

'Religion or belief direct discrimination'

'Religion or belief direct discrimination' occurs in deliberate exclusion of individuals from opportunities or services. This aspect of our analytical spectrum overlaps with the legally defined meaning of discrimination which, in England, Wales and Scotland is now, as set out by the EHRC (2011): 'the less favourable treatment of a person compared with another person because of a protected characteristic' (which, as explained in Chapter 4 also includes: age, disability, gender reassignment, pregnancy and maternity, race, sex or sexual orientation).

In Chapters 6–8 a number of instances were reported which might, prima facie, be considered possible examples of what is meant, also legally, by 'religion or belief direct discrimination' – although it is not known whether these instances would be legally determined as such if tested in the context of a legal process. For example, in Chapter 7, the narrative was cited of a Muslim man whose CV was not shortlisted for interview. He suspected this was because of his Muslim name. When he applied using another name but the same qualifications and experiences, he was shortlisted. Similar mechanisms have historically been used by equalities bodies in order to identify both direct and indirect discrimination on the part of employers, service-providers and other institutions.

Other examples cited in Chapter 6 include that of the Sikh man who felt he was denied the opportunity to work in a bar on the grounds that his turban might not be acceptable to patrons. There was also an instance of the Christian who, in the context of being a member of a shortlisting panel for a job, reported that other members of the panel cited mention in an applicant's CV of her being 'very active in her local parish' as a reason for excluding her. Non-religious participants also reported issues, as for example the non-religious woman whose husband was a teacher and who lived in an area with a high proportion of faith schools and who felt that her husband's job prospects were greatly reduced as a result of him being non-religious. At the same time, in this instance the legal provisions for exempting religious bodies from aspects of the equalities framework highlight a distinction (as discussed in Chapter 4 and again in Chapter 10) between the generally applicable meaning of discrimination and the qualifications to that which can be found in the law, especially in relation to religion or belief exemptions.

While only employment examples are cited above, throughout Chapters 6-8 instances have been described in other sectors of life and in which both religious and non-religious participants report having encountered what they believe to be outright 'religion or belief direct discrimination'. The manifestations of this ranged in severity and frequency from name-calling or banter that participants felt they could live with, through to bullying and other more serious instances for which participants could seek recourse through legal action. For example, as discussed in Chapter 6, the young Muslim man who stated his CV was not originally shortlisted for interview reported having taken his case to an employment tribunal from which he received an out-of-court settlement.

In other instances, participants in the fieldwork completed in 2011 may not always have been sure whether or not they have been discriminated against, or what action could be taken. As in one example given by a male Sikh interviewee, individuals may be too angry and/or lacking in confidence for any meaningful action to be taken. An important aspect of the social experience of 'religion or belief direct discrimination' is that it is not always evident to either the complainant or anyone assessing their case, whether any discrimination that might have occurred was based primarily on the religion or belief of the person; on another of the equality strands (such as ethnicity); or on a combination of several (for example, religion or belief, ethnicity and gender). Evidence from the fieldwork completed in 2011 (as in the 2000 fieldwork) suggests that it can be particularly difficult to distinguish between discrimination on the basis of 'race' or ethnicity and that of religion or belief. As a white Christian man interviewed in Cardiff put it:

> [W]ithin education, within society, it's very, I think it's very difficult [. . .] to identify whether discrimination is about race and colour as opposed to religion [. . .], and whether that's based on religion or whether it's based on colour and race is, the two are so intermixed when you look at the kind of conflicts that go on in the rest of the world they appear to be religious conflicts but underneath it all there are often racial and tribal conflicts going on.

As explored in Chapter 8, it is important also to note that religion or belief direct discrimination can occur not only as a result of the treatment of religion or belief groups by either the state or the institutions of the wider society. Also, it does not only occur due to the actions of various non-religious community, political and pressure groups. Rather, such treatment may occur from within one religion or belief group in relation to another, as well as within such groups. Discrimination and unfair treatment within religion or belief groups can also be either on grounds of religion or belief itself, or in relation to other 'protected characteristics'. In particular, gay and lesbian participants in our fieldwork reported concern about prejudice and unfair treatment towards themselves expressed by religious, and mostly Christian, groups.

However, alongside direct discrimination, unintended and indirect discrimination can extend beyond individual instances affecting single persons to impact upon the experience and opportunities of whole groups. It can therefore be at least as significant, and perhaps even more so in its effects, than 'direct religion or belief discrimination'. It is to such 'religion or belief indirect discrimination' that we now turn.

'Religion or belief indirect discrimination'

'Religion or belief indirect discrimination' can occur where the effect of historical decisions, contemporary structures or patterns of behaviour have not been reconsidered in the light of current religion or belief plurality and result in unintentional discrimination. The EHRC (2011) describes indirect discrimination as: 'The use of an apparently neutral practice, provision or criterion which puts people with a particular protected characteristic at a disadvantage compared with others who do not share that characteristic, and applying the practice, provision or criterion cannot be objectively justified.'

Such discrimination can therefore be understood in terms of the exclusionary effects of historical decisions, contemporary structures or patterns of behaviour and organization that may not be informed by attitudes of 'religion or belief prejudice', although they may be related to aspects of 'religion or belief disadvantage'. Where such historic patterns have not been explicitly reconsidered in the light of the implications of contemporary religious plurality, they can unintentionally result in discrimination against people of various religion or belief groups. Examples of this can include culturally exclusive requirements and provisions in terms of diet, clothing, religious festivals and a range of other matters.

In the fieldwork completed in 2011, a Hindu participant in Norwich spoke about different types of discrimination: 'subtle discrimination', 'open discrimination' and 'indirect discrimination'. However, very few participants in the fieldwork spoke about the concept of indirect discrimination, and those who did so, spoke in very general terms. Nevertheless, from the narratives of participants there seem to be examples of what might be considered to be 'religion or belief indirect discrimination'. For example, as noted in Chapter 6 some fieldwork participants reported that a number of schools in Blackburn do not allow the wearing of the *niqab*. As reported by these fieldwork participants, this appears to have had the by product of excluding some Muslim mothers who wear a *niqab* from visiting the schools to discuss their children's performance. However, since this is justified by reference to school uniform policy, this example also illustrates the difficulty involved in evaluating indirect discrimination.

Also in Chapter 6, it was reported that a Christian man cited his son as not being offered a job when he refused to work on Sundays – which was a requirement of the job. Similarly, non-religious participants described not being given jobs because they would not fit into the religious ethos of a faith school or other faith-based organization. Many Muslim respondents and a number of Bahá'í participants reported that due to their avoidance of alcohol, they felt a sense of being excluded because team meetings took place in pubs and places which served alcohol.

Many fieldwork participants from minority or BME religious groups and whose religious beliefs were visible, felt that they encountered a 'glass ceiling'. From the evidence, it was not clear how far this was due to their religion or belief backgrounds, their 'race' or ethnicity or other factors. Thus a public sector employee in Blackburn who is an expert in equality and diversity issues noted that indirect discrimination is 'much harder to prove and less tangible' and therefore:

> You can be in an organization or glass ceiling all your life where people will come in and shoot up much faster than you have because they're in the right social circles or they're from the right backgrounds but in the same token it's when you're looking at indirect discrimination [. . .] people can just come up to you, ask you what you do and then walk away and not bother.

In some institutional settings there is a sense that the permeative nature of the barriers to participation is so extensive that what is being experienced might be analogous to the kind of 'institutional racism' identified in the Macpherson Report on the Metropolitan Police (Home Office, 1999). It is therefore to the example of 'religion or belief institutional discrimination' that we now, finally in this chapter, turn.

'Religion or belief institutional discrimination'

'Religion or belief institutional discrimination' can develop when unfair treatment becomes endemic and structurally embedded in organizations leading to a collective failure to provide equitable treatment. Because this is a form of unfair treatment on the grounds of religion or belief that manifests itself in this way, its key characteristic is that it can include many of the other aspects of our analytical spectrum, concerning which it would be superfluous to repeat again here.

As with 'religion or belief indirect discrimination', only a small number of fieldwork participants themselves talked about 'religion or belief institutional discrimination'. It is possible that this to some extent reflects the overall reduction in reported experience of unfair treatment on the basis of religion or belief seen in the results of the survey reported on in Chapters 6-8, and in the many improvements indicated in the fieldwork. However, for example, in relation to some aspects of the media relatively higher levels of reporting of unfair treatment continued to be reported in comparison with that from other sectors of society. In the fieldwork, too, certain areas of the media were continually cited as being very problematic. Thus a Bahá'í woman articulated what quite a large number of other religious group fieldwork participants were saying: 'In institutional terms, the one big thing that we suffer from, I think, that all the faith communities suffer from is we can't get decent coverage in the media.' Non-religious people also identified substantial problems with media representations of them.

In an issue related also to 'religion or belief disadvantage', numbers of non-religious participants described how religion, particularly the Church of England, was embedded within government in ways that might not only inform 'religion or belief disadvantage' but could furthermore be characterized as 'institutional discrimination'. The following reflection from a white non-religious man in Leicester specifically used this terminology:

> When government documents come out saying we've got that money available for capacity development, it's usually addressed to faith groups and in the small print somewhere it says 'and the rest' or words to that effect. Now that's not the right way of going around developing capacity in the voluntary sector. So there are many institutional discriminations against people who do not belong to a religious group.

Applications of the spectrum of unfair treatment

The analytical spectrum that has been introduced and discussed throughout this chapter has been applied to examples from the evidence of the survey and fieldwork completed in 2011 in order to gain a more nuanced understanding of the varied aspects of unfair treatment and discrimination on the grounds of religion or belief. It is not the only way of approaching this and, like the relationship between all models and the inevitably more 'messy' realities which they seek to illuminate, it is not always fully adequate to the evidence. However, the strength of the spectrum lies in its capturing of the differently nuanced expressions of unfair treatment that people report experiencing. In illuminating the raw findings from the survey, fieldwork and Knowledge Exchange Workshops, the spectrum contributes to an appropriate and balanced understanding of possible measures to tackle unfair treatment on the grounds of religion or belief.

Because the spectrum applies generically across the reported experience of all religion or belief groups, it can also effectively integrate with an understanding of society and an approach to policy, law and practice which recognize that discrimination and unfair treatment can at least in principle be experienced by all parts of what our project has articulated as a 'three-dimensional' policy context with its Christian, secular and religiously plural dimensions. At the same time, the flexibility of the spectrum allows for the recognition that, in specific geographical and historical circumstances, different parts of the spectrum may be more relevant to the experience of one or other part of the 'three-dimensional society' and/or specific sub-groups within this. Because of this, it is likely that the development of specific measures to tackle unfair treatment will need careful calibration to both the kind of unfair treatment being reported and the religion or belief identity of those experiencing it, and it is to these measures that we now turn.

10

Evidence-based Signposts for Future Policy, Law and Practice

Context for the evidence, analysis and signposts for the future

The first decade of the 2000s in England and Wales and across Britain has been a time of transition in policy, law and practice relating to religion and belief, discrimination and equality. In this period there have been elements of both continuity and change that have significantly impacted the lives of individuals, groups, the state and the wider society in negotiating a way through the changing contexts of policy, law and practice.

The conduct of the research completed in 2011 straddled a change in the UK governing political parties from over a decade of New Labour government to those of the current Conservative-Liberal coalition and also the impact of the global economic crisis in the rolling back of the welfare state, public spending cuts and politics of austerity (Taylor-Gooby, 2012). This has also included debates concerning the government's ongoing commitment to the HRA and related EU legislation in this area through to the ECHR.

This final chapter of the book begins by summarizing the context, evidence and analysis of discrimination and unfair treatment on the basis of religion or belief and law relating to it. Through the application of the analytical spectrum to differentiated aspects of unfair treatment, appropriate measures to tackle such unfair treatment on the basis of religion or belief are discussed. Finally, through critical interaction between our findings and discussion of recent relevant policy, law and practice, we identify some signposts for the future in these distinct but related areas.

The key findings from the research

Context for research findings

Religion and belief are important aspects of people's lives, informing how they see and live in the world, both as individuals and as part of groups. Issues around discrimination and equality on the grounds of religion or belief (including non-religious beliefs) are sensitive and sometimes highly contested. These issues involve matters of individual freedom of conscience and of collective organization and expression in public life and the role that the state can, or should, play in protecting aspects of people's identity.

Religion and belief also exist alongside, and are interlinked with, other aspects of people's identity, many of which have achieved legal recognition as 'protected characteristics'. Conflicts between these can result in claims and counter-claims about whether these can or should be balanced. The issues also involve relationships within and between religion or belief groups and between these groups and the wider society, including debates about the nature of a 'secular society'.

Key findings: Continuity and change (2001–11)?

A decade ago in England, Wales and Scotland unfair treatment on the basis of religion or belief had little scope for domestic legal redress. Since then, equality legislation such as the *Employment Equality (Religion or Belief) Regulations*, 2003, the *Incitement to Racial and Religious Hatred Act*, 2006, and the *Equalities Acts*, 2006 and 2010, came into force. These laws are designed to protect the holders of religious and non-religious beliefs from unfair treatment.

The findings of the project survey completed in 2011 suggest that there is evidence that over the past decade there has, in general, been a reduction in the reported experience of unfair treatment on the basis of religion or belief. The findings of the fieldwork completed in 2011 suggest there are indications that the introduction of law has been associated with changes of policy and practice, particularly in the public sector. For example, Pagan organizations, in particular, have cited human rights law as having opened up the possibility of more equitable participation in aspects of public life.

However, both the survey and the fieldwork results continue to highlight substantial levels of reporting of unfair treatment on the basis of religion or belief in important areas of people's lives. With regard to its impact, the survey findings indicate that, in most areas and across most religious groups, the unfair treatment is more often reported to be occasional than frequent. The unfair treatment is generally reported to be more to do with the attitudes and behaviour of individuals (including within employment in relation to managers and colleagues) than with the policies or practices of organizations.

Certain religious groups continue to report experience of higher levels of unfair treatment than others – in particular Muslim and Pagan and NRM organizations. Jewish organizations also continue to report significant experience of antisemitism, including stereotyping and targeted attacks on Jewish property.

High profile controversies and legal cases reflect continued experience of what is felt to be unfair treatment with regard to employer dress codes in relation particularly to Muslim women using head coverings and to Christians wearing crosses. In schools such issues affect pupils as well as teachers, and in comparison with a decade ago, the research contains some indicative evidence of what might be more widely spread difficulties for Sikhs in the wearing of 'the 5Ks' of their religion.

It is clear that the relationship between the perception and reporting of unfair treatment on the basis of religion or belief and the legal determination of it remains complex and open to contested interpretations. The introduction of new laws has not been a panacea. Moreover, the fieldwork findings suggest that many religious people are only very generally aware of their new legal rights. At the same time, many non-religious focus group participants had a sense that, despite a broadening of the meaning of 'belief' in recent case law, these laws do not work equally for them especially in the areas of education and of governance where religious, and especially Christian, bodies play significant institutional roles.

Unfair treatment in various areas of life

Findings from the survey indicate a general reduction in the incidence of reported unfair treatment since 2001. This is especially so in the areas of criminal justice and employment. However, fieldwork research evidence points to continuing unfair treatment in implementing immigration controls. Evidence from interviews with research participants in the fieldwork suggests that where there is an awareness of them, legal changes have contributed to a sense of improvement among religion or belief groups in terms of their being consulted on a more inclusive basis, especially in relation to public sector policies and practices. Examples of this include liaison between the police and religion or belief groups. At the same time, during the fieldwork, concerns were expressed about some of the concepts involved in, and aspects of the implementation of, the Government's Prevent initiatives designed to tackle violent extremism.

Also from within the fieldwork, education (and especially RE) was identified as having become more inclusive of diversities of religion or belief (including humanist views). These developments were especially linked with the work of SACREs, despite the fact that some SACREs still do not accommodate non-religious participants. But, Knowledge Exchange Workshop participants expressed concern that such gains could be undermined by policy developments around Academies and Free Schools in which RE is not required to have an integral place in the curriculum.

Participants in fieldwork research reported that, overall, relations between different religious groups have improved since 2001. Survey results also show a reduction in reporting of unfair treatment from other religious groups since 2001. However, levels of reported unfair treatment from other religious groups were substantial and religious organizations were more likely to identify other religious groups as being a source of unfair treatment compared to non-religious groups. At the same time, some political groups including Right-wing groups were frequently cited in both the survey and the fieldwork as a source of hostility and insecurity.

Similar reported patterns of unfair treatment

Education, employment and the media remain key areas of people's lives in which they report experience of unfair treatment. Although there has been an overall reduction in the reported experience of unfair treatment in education and employment, evidence relating to the media suggests considerably high levels of unfair treatment. However, as in 2001, experience of unfair treatment is more strongly identified with national rather than local media. But the fieldwork findings also suggest that the 'new media' is seen as bringing both benefits and new problems.

As in 2001, higher levels of unfair treatment were reported in relation to employment in the private sector than the public sector. Overall, even where there have been positive policy developments in organizations, there remain issues of consistency in translating policy into practice. Individual prejudicial attitudes can still create impacts that go beyond the individual, both internally within organizations and in their delivery of goods and services.

There is continuing complexity around the intersections between religion or belief and ethnicity in relation to claims of unfair treatment, with evidence that 'visible' religion or belief minorities continue to experience patterns of unfair treatment through a combination of factors that can also involve gender, ethnicity and other aspects of identity.

New forms of reported unfair treatment

New forms of unfair treatment are being reported – particularly, but not only, by Christians. For example, both the project's survey and fieldwork research evidence point to a greater reported incidence of Christian employees concerned about employer policies and practices on Sunday working. Some Christians also articulated a sense of the marginalization of Christianity compared to its historic position in society and spoke of what they felt was a now comparatively fairer treatment of other religion or belief groups compared to Christians. At the same time, the project focus groups highlighted the degree to which non-religious people feel that Christianity and religion in general is privileged in ways that are structurally embedded in the society and can result in unfair treatment for others, especially in education and governance.

In both the fieldwork and survey evidence it was clear that people from a number of other religious groups (including especially, but not only, Sikhs) were being misidentified as Muslims and thereby becoming the target for unfair treatment and a particular hostility that was clearly intended to be directed towards Islam and Muslims. This highlights not only the unfair treatment Muslims have encountered, but also how this affects other groups.

Ways of tackling unfair treatment on grounds of religion or belief

Suggestions from the survey and fieldwork evidence

In the light of the summary findings of the 2011 research presented above, we go on now to consider ways of tackling unfair treatment. In the research completed in 2000, the terms of reference from the Home Office precluded the making of any recommendations, allowing only the identification of a range of possible options. The 2011 research was not constrained in this way. But it is important to ground any evaluation of our own in a proper engagement with the range of relevant options and possibilities that respondents to, and participants in, the survey and fieldwork completed in 2011 themselves proposed. In both the 2000 and 2011 research, respondents and participants were asked about the most appropriate ways of tackling discrimination and unfair treatment.

Survey and fieldwork approaches

In the survey completed in 2011, those completing questionnaires on behalf of religious organizations were also asked for their personal views about the measures that should be considered in order to combat unfair treatment. As in the 2000 research, each respondent was asked to identify up to three measures from the same list of eight options (to which they could also add their own suggestions) or to indicate that they did not think any new measures were necessary.

The survey results have the limitation of representing the views of respondents from religious and inter-faith organizations. They therefore need to be complemented by evidence from the fieldwork interviews and focus groups, which also include the perspectives of the non-religious.

Measures to tackle unfair treatment

Table 10.1 sets out the cumulative responses from the respondents in relation to preferred measures for combating unfair treatment. As this shows, there is consistent support across the decade for education and training-based measures. Strong support for educational measures was also identified by participants in the fieldwork interviews. This included support from focus groups with the non-religious, as well as from individuals and groups who considered themselves to be religious. In the fieldwork,

Table 10.1 Measures to combat unfair treatment on the basis of religion, 2000 and 2011 (all responses)

Measures to combat unfair treatment on the basis of religion	2000		2011	
	N	%	N	%
Other	24	1	11	1
Take no new action	27	2	26	2
Changes in the law/introduce new law	152	9	79	6
Voluntary codes of practice	190	11	99	8
Policy reviews in each service area to promote equal treatment	254	15	182	15
Better training of staff	318	19	263	21
Public education programmes	359	21	280	23
More teaching of comparative religion in schools	370	22	297	24
Total	**1,694**	**100**	**1,237**	**100**

the importance of examples of good practice was cited, particularly in relation to a more inclusive approach to consultation with religion or belief groups and improved public literacy concerning religious perspectives on life.

We now consider the measures in more detail alongside developments in relation to equality. In discussing these it is important to bear in mind the relationship between each measure and what has been found about discrimination and unfair treatment on the basis of religion or belief. In 2011 there is still substantial reported experience of unfair treatment in many sectors of social life, as also between religious groups and between political, community and other pressure groups and religious groups. Therefore, in considering what measures and approaches might be most appropriate and effective for the future, it is important to bear in mind the question of how effective such measures have been over the past decade.

The role of the law in tackling unfair treatment and promoting equalities

The law and tackling unfair treatment

As can be seen in Table 10.1, in the survey completed in 2011 there was a small reduction in responses (from 9% to 6%) advocating further new laws or for changes to existing law, as compared with the survey completed in 2001. In itself this is not sufficient for drawing any secure conclusions. In addition, the results for the survey completed in 2011 need to be seen in the context of the substantial development of new legislation that has taken place between the two surveys. It is also important to consider the varied aspects of the new legislation and how it might have been seen as a help or a hindrance to religious organizations.

The survey completed in 2011 also collected the views of respondents on the impact of new legislation in reducing unfair treatment in relation to people of their religion, as set out in Table 10.2.

Table 10.2 Helpfulness of legislation to reduce unfair treatment for people of your religion

Legislation	Very helpful (%)	Somewhat helpful (%)	Neither helpful nor unhelpful (%)	Somewhat unhelpful (%)	Very unhelpful (%)	Don't know (%)	Total N
Human Rights Act, 1988	13	24	28	6	3	27	437
Employment Equality (Religion or belief) Regulations, 2003	14	27	25	7	3	23	430
Religious and Racial Hatred Act, 2006	13	22	28	8	5	25	437
Equality Acts, 2006 and 2010	14	20	25	10	5	25	436

Only a small proportion (between 9% and 15%) of respondents thought the new equality and human rights laws unhelpful, while between 34 and 41 per cent of respondents thought them helpful. Around a quarter of all respondents indicated that, for their religion in general, these laws have been 'neither helpful nor unhelpful'. Those responding 'Don't Know' may be indicative of some broader ambivalence among respondents from among religious organizations towards the helpfulness of the new equalities and human rights laws in relation to their own religions and/or a lack of awareness of the law. It is important to note that the question as asked in the survey was not about the value of the law in reducing discrimination in general, but rather asked only about this in relation to the respondents' own religions.

The law, the equalities agenda and 'protected characteristics'

In addition to questions about the helpfulness of the laws in reducing discrimination as experienced by religious groups, respondents were also asked about the impact of equality laws and policies across the eight 'protected characteristics', and specifically in terms of the helpfulness to how their own religious organization works (Table 10.3).

Respondents viewing equality laws and policies for protected characteristics as 'unhelpful' range from 3 per cent in relation to 'age', up to 24 per cent in relation to 'sexual orientation' and 26 per cent in relation to 'marriage or civil partnership'. In terms of actual reported experiences of unfair treatment as a consequence of the equality laws it is notable that overall 5 per cent of the respondents reported that their members had experienced unfair treatment. A further survey question asked about the extent to which respondents felt that religious organizations should be exempt from equalities legislation. Table 10.4 summarizes the responses.

A substantial proportion of respondents from religious organizations clearly favour exemptions from equality laws on matters of gender, marriage and civil partnership, sexual orientation and religion or belief itself. There is also some support for exemptions from equalities legislation in relation to the longer established legally 'protected characteristics' of 'race', age and disability.

The high proportion of respondents arguing for exemptions from the religion or belief protected characteristic is striking but perhaps not surprising since this kind of response may relate to the concern of religious organizations to be able to operate without what they might see as external interference. The role played by many religious organizations is given in, for example, the solemnization of marriage and their likely wish to arrange such ceremonies according to what might be termed their 'own norms and values' even if those differ from those found in wider society. Again this highlights one of the tensions in the current equality legislation which accords religious organizations some specific exemptions of a kind not accorded to other kinds of organizations or areas of life (see Chapter 4).

The law and other measures to combat unfair treatment

Overall, then, the 2011 research evidence has shown that new laws have not been a panacea. At the same time, although reporting of direct discrimination continues, the

Table 10.3 Helpfulness of equalities laws and policies in relation to how your organization works

Changes in equality laws and policies	Very helpful (%)	Somewhat helpful (%)	Neither helpful nor unhelpful (%)	Somewhat unhelpful (%)	Very unhelpful (%)	Don't know (%)	Total N
Changes in equality laws and policies in relation to age	10	18	68	2	1	2	401
Changes in equality laws and policies in relation to disability	14	26	55	3	1	2	406
Changes in equality laws and policies in relation to gender reassignment	6	14	63	9	6	2	399
Changes in equality laws and policies in relation to marriage or civil partnership	6	15	52	16	10	1	399
Changes in equality laws and policies in relation to race	12	22	61	3	1	2	405
Changes in equality laws and policies in relation to religion or belief	13	23	49	9	4	2	409
Changes in equality laws and policies in relation to sex	7	16	65	7	4	2	399
Changes in equality laws and policies in relation to sexual orientation	8	12	55	15	9	2	401

Table 10.4 Desire for exemptions for religious organizations from the requirements of equality laws in relation to 'equality areas'

Exemption from equality laws	Yes (%)	No (%)	Don't know (%)	Total N
Equality laws in relation to disabilities	8	78	14	422
Equality laws in relation to age	9	76	15	424
Equality laws in relation to race	9	78	13	421
Equality laws in relation to sex	23	61	17	418
Equality laws in relation to gender reassignment	31	47	23	411
Equality laws in relation to religion or belief	39	47	14	420
Equality laws in relation to sexual orientation	39	43	19	419
Equality laws in relation to marriage or civil partnership	41	41	18	424

fact that discrimination is illegal and gives individuals opportunity to seek recourse in law has acted as a stimulus to quite widespread changes in policy and to some change in practice.

In our analytical spectrum, 'religion or belief direct discrimination' occurs in deliberate exclusion of individuals from opportunities or services, and 'religion or belief indirect discrimination' can occur where historical decisions, contemporary structures or patterns of behaviour have not been reconsidered in the light of current religion or belief plurality and result in unintentional discrimination. Together with 'religion or belief hatred' these aspects of our analytical spectrum overlap with legal understandings of discrimination and related legal mechanisms. So, although dialogue, training and education continue to be important in reducing inequality based on religion or belief, as articulated by a male Muslim fieldwork participant:

> Education and awareness is a way of possibly starting to redress the issue, but certainly will not eliminate it, in fact nothing will eliminate it but at least there has to be some recourse in law to give some protection. At least the community will feel confident that it is there, if everything fails legislation is there.

In this context, one legally related measure to which the UK government might give consideration is (as discussed in Chapter 4) to sign up to the Optional Protocol to the ICCPR as an additional means to support legal redress in relation to civil and political rights, including matters of discrimination, equality and religion or belief.

Nevertheless, training and education remains a priority measure which must also include clarification and discussion of the new laws and the new challenges and complexities to which these laws have given rise. This is especially the case with regard to the contestations that have emerged around the intersectionalities within people's everyday lives and experiences and other (sometimes conflictual) relationships between the different 'protected characteristics'. Both domestic and international jurisprudence reflect a wider and still ongoing public and political debate about how best to achieve the law's formal intentions to exclude discrimination and support equality for all, while doing so in a way that does not place people whose identity is more closely related to one or more of the 'protected characteristics' at a disadvantage compared to those whose identity is most closely related to a different 'protected characteristic'.

Emblematic of this complexity have been the high-profile legal cases of what eventually became *Eweida and Others (Chaplin, Ladele and McFarlane) v. the United Kingdom* (as discussed in detail in Chapter 4) which were heard in the ECtHR in 2012 following a series of domestic tribunals and appeals, leading to a judgement in early 2013. It is clear that legal judgements such as those from the ECtHR are unlikely finally to resolve these issues. It is also unlikely that they can be resolved by other policy instruments alone unless at least accompanied by training and educational measures. This is because these can, in principle, engage individuals and promote change in ways that law and social policy instruments usually cannot achieve on their own. This is especially the case in the context of a broadly democratic social and political framework as distinct from one that seeks to develop policy and law without regard to public consent.

It is therefore to the training, public and school education and inter-faith/inter-community dialogue measures for tackling unfair treatment on the grounds of religion or belief, which were prioritized by the 2011 research respondents and participants, that we now turn. Such approaches need to take account of the wider equality framework and overlapping aspects of identity.

As highlighted by the survey completed in 2011, ethnic or 'racial' aspects of people's identities continue to be perceived as an important part of the reason for unfair treatment in relation to religion, especially in relation to some religious groups. Overall in 2011, 45 per cent of (438) religious organization respondents stated that they felt that ethnic or racial aspects were at least some part of the reason for unfair treatment on the basis of religion in relation to their own religion. (25% felt that it was a large part or the main reason). Moreover, a further 15 per cent of respondents stated they 'Didn't Know'. Looking back to 2000, the evidence was very similar. Then, 47 per cent of respondents stated that they felt that ethnic or 'racial' aspects were at least some part of the reason for unfair treatment on the basis of religion although at the same time, in both the 2000 and 2011 research, unfair treatment on the basis of religion or belief was also being reported by people who were not of minority ethnic heritage.

Formal education and in-context training

In the surveys completed in 2000 and 2011, as can be seen from Table 10.1, respondents strongly supported the role of formal education and in-context training in tackling unfair treatment, while in the fieldwork participants noted that much had already been achieved in this regard. For example (as noted in Chapter 6) participants said that RE syllabi were more inclusive, including information about most religions as well as non-religious perspectives and that curricula are working towards developing values of citizenship, community cohesion and pluralism.

Participants in the fieldwork recommended that, in the future, the educative approaches already begun needed to be enhanced and rolled out more consistently across the country. Thus, a county council employee whose portfolio of work included equality and diversity, inclusion and schools pointed out that, while schools in urban areas with high levels of religious diversity had good access to external speakers and places of worship which students could visit, this was more difficult in rural areas. He concluded that much more needs to be done 'to ensure their students get a rich diverse learning of different cultures' but that 'I think we need to do more of that because the county is less diverse than the city.'

A small number of non-religious participants argued to 'ban religion from schools'. However, on the whole, non-religious participants articulated a more inclusive vision of RE and philosophy in schools that included information about religions presented in an objective manner and which also equipped students with morals and values that were not dependent on religious perspectives. A white humanist woman expressed it as follows:

> I'd like to see more teaching of how you debate, how you come to your own moral values without religion so that's not to say humanist teaching but the idea that you, ethics yeah, ethics and personal development, that you come to your own understanding through engagement and work.

In relation to our spectrum of unfair treatment, measures of this kind would be appropriate for engaging with 'religion or belief naivety' – which is a lack of religion or belief literacy and can sometimes lead to actions that can be seen as and/or result in unfair treatment. But it cannot be assumed that any style of education will automatically produce the further step of the kind of 'attitudinal change' necessary for tackling 'religion or belief prejudice'. Much depends on the kind of educational approaches used which, especially in contexts of formal school education, can be very constrained by examination and qualification-related requirements.

Public education and increasing the awareness of law

In broader public education, opportunities can be created to take a more developmental approach using participative adult education methodologies that take full account of the complex identities (often including more than one of the 'protected characteristics') and integrity of those who freely agree to participate in the learning process. Within such approaches, 'safe spaces' can be created to facilitate the kind of dialogical and transformational learning that enables engagement with sensitive issues on the basis of mutual respect among participants (for an example of which, see further below on Belieforama). Such learning opportunities are important because in the fieldwork completed in 2011 it was recognized that legal frameworks alone were not sufficient. As a Bahá'í man put it:

> Legislation is never going to change people's attitudes, that has to come from somewhere else, in them, it is a question of awareness and provision of knowledge of course. If they actually know what something is then they are no longer afraid of it, or no longer feel as if they have to attack something.

At the same time, while generally being aware that discrimination is illegal, participants from religion and belief groups in the fieldwork completed in 2011 were themselves not always aware of what exactly discrimination is under existing law, nor of the procedures for reporting it. This suggests the need for further public education and development of awareness also about the laws themselves, including among the intended beneficiaries of these laws while recognizing that the legal implications of the new laws are still being established. As a middle-aged Christian man from Blackburn put it:

> There needs to be an awful lot of education and some of the laws which have been passed which are there to protect people, they've got to be rightly interpreted and we've all got to understand what they mean and understand when we're over – reacting or when we're helping. It's a very complex thing really.

One area in which over-reaction can be possible concerns the dividing line between criticism robustly or sharply expressed and the expression of 'religion and belief hatred' through the use of 'hate speech'. In our analytical spectrum, 'religion or belief hatred' can occur when prejudice intensifies into a settled attitude of mind, emotion and will that can spill over into intimidatory and/or violent behaviour towards the religion or belief 'other'. For reducing unfair treatment of this kind, part of the solution includes better clarification to the general public about what 'hate crime' consists of, along with the creation of increased awareness of the frameworks within which such unfair treatment can be reported.

More broadly, training which increases understanding and awareness of equality and human rights law is likely also to form part of any successful strategy to try to address the phenomenon of 'religion or belief institutional discrimination' which, according to our analytical spectrum, can develop when unfair treatment becomes endemic and structurally embedded in organizations leading to a collective failure to provide equitable treatment. While legal and perhaps internal disciplinary measures may also be needed to tackle such institutional discrimination, from the parallel experience of institutional racism identified in the MacPherson report (see Home Office, 1999) into the Metropolitan Police, it is likely that internal education and training would also need to continue to play a substantial role.

Finally, since religious organizations themselves form a substantial part of the wider civil society and public life, one priority for broader than formal educational measures includes the need for such education to take place within religion (and belief) groups and organizations themselves. The results of the survey questions discussed above indicate at least some ambivalence and some resistance to the law being seen as an appropriate instrument for enforcing equalities policies in relation to the internal life of religious groups and organizations. The findings also suggest some further differentiation within this in relation, in particular, to the 'protected characteristic' of sexual orientation.

This therefore suggests that, within the overall broad public education measures concerned with embedding the equality framework in society, there may be a special need for some specific work to take place within religious groups and organizations, and especially around the relationships between the equalities and human rights adhering to religion or belief itself, and the equalities and human rights that adhere to other 'protected characteristics'. The raw and painful nature of the kind of conflicts that can occur was sharply articulated by a fieldwork participant who is a gay Catholic Christian:

> I have spent the last forty years, more than that, battling for civil rights for lesbian and gay people and also inside the Churches, Christian Churches and inside the Catholic Church particularly, because the Catholic Church has a particular set of attitudes which I don't agree with. [. . .] For example, the right to hold very discriminatory views against lesbian and gay people and to express them and somehow they think they should be enshrined in law to protect the particularly religious and I don't think they should. They are anti things like gay marriage and civil partnerships which I think is appalling and at the employment level it is almost as if you are out as a gay or a lesbian person in the Roman Catholic Church you can be sacked just for being gay or lesbian which I think is appalling.

As discussed in Chapter 4, Hepple (2010: 14–15) has argued that, 'there must be no hierarchy of equality. The same rule should be applied to all strands unless there is convincing justification for an exception. To a large extent, the Act achieves this aim'. Therefore, when it comes to the internal life and organization of religion or belief groups, at present it could be said that the Act only partially 'achieves its aim'. In specified and circumscribed ways, Parliament has determined that when the rights adhering to the 'protected characteristic' of religion or belief intersect with those relating to sexual orientation and to gender, 'there is convincing justification for an exception' for religion or belief groups. This is especially so in the context of the characteristics of religiously inspired and based associational social forms which exist with civil society between the private sphere of the individual and the family and the more completely public sphere of commercial organizations, the state and the public sector.

Thus in advancing an ultimate social policy goal and equality principle, the state is at present exercising a reticence in using the instrument of the equalities law to enforce social change in relation to a recognition of some limited autonomy within which, on the basis of their human right to manifest religious freedom, religious groups are allowed some significant scope to determine their own internal rules and practices.

Neither religion or belief groups nor groups constituted in other ways should be, or are, immune from the possibility of change. But especially where potentially competing beliefs and values are concerned, it is important to try to create safe educational and dialogical spaces within which (particularly) individuals can personally meet one another in the integrity of their complex identities. In the context of such meeting, tried and tested adult education and diversity education pedagogies can facilitate a transformational learning that leads to change in attitudes in ways that can bring about social benefits.

The creation of such opportunities is not easily achieved, nor can such learning be achieved through a 'quick fix' approach to the development of religion and belief competence. Rather, the secure development of religion or belief literacy both for religious and non-religious groups alike in interaction with other equality and diversity learning needs time as well as space, both of which are challenging in the context of economic crisis and downturn. However, concrete examples of what can be achieved do exist. One such example is the European programme 'Religious Diversity and Anti-Discrimination Training' developed by Belieforama (www.belieforama.eu). This has been developed with both religious and non-religious input and which has been used for adult training and education among both religious groups and (especially) in mixed religious and non-religious groups. Since 2004, over 2,000 people have engaged with this, including large numbers of people from England and Wales. Among the training that it offers is a module on Reconciling Religion, Gender and Sexual Orientation, which was collaboratively developed by religious, non-religious, gay and heterosexual people. This training operates on an inclusive basis of transformative learning aiming towards equality and diversity, but in a way in which all involved can express their full identity with shared respect for mutual rights and responsibilities.

Research into the learning achieved by participants and trainers in these programmes has shown evidence of the change that can occur. As explained by a white female participant in the training who is from the Netherlands and has what she described as spiritual beliefs, but who is not aligned with one religion:

> I believe strongly that one of the strong points of this training, and the philosophy of Belieforama is especially [. . .] that there is a space, a way of working, a very clear didactic approach, that in group that feels okay with the fact there is difference – we have to start at that point. We then create a space where people learn to listen to themselves about their own identity and to listen to others and to confront issues in order to be a more able citizen and go into social action. (quoted in Weller and Contractor, 2012: 21)

Belieforama thus demonstrates an approach to policy implementation that does not rely on the direct force of the law alone but can work with the impetus for social change generated by law and social policy; respond in ways that create opportunities for transformational learning; and in turn contribute to the further development of a more nuanced and successful policy implementation.

During the project fieldwork completed in 2011, other examples of transformational learning focused strongly on the possibility of people of diverse backgrounds and identities becoming engaged in common projects in a way that mediates between adult learning and initiatives in inter-faith and inter-community initiatives of the kind explored in the following section. For example, as explained by a Muslim male public sector employee and community cohesion specialist:

> A lot of our projects are aimed at interaction usually to develop understanding and mutual respect and it's like exposure to each other [. . .] the 100 Voices project [. . .] What we found very quickly within the voices was people very soon did not focus on the race and faith issue, they moved in to areas of commonality, so things they had in common. [. . .] All of those common problems were shared with people in the community. Nobody focused on the differences then and that was something positive for us. [. . .] We've done various other work like we've commissioned

cohesion residentials where young people go away, have an informal active panel maybe do something like a series of activities or working together on problem solving activities, something like that where you are forced to work together. We've got a stream here we've got to cross it how do we do it? [. . .] We come back away from that and we open a dialogue up around it [. . .]. That's been really powerful.

Inter-faith and inter-community dialogue

The final grouping of measures proposed by participants for tackling unfair treatment on the basis of religion or belief emerged strongly out of the fieldwork completed in 2011. It revolves around support for inter-faith and inter-community dialogue activities. A white humanist participant in Leicester stated that such dialogue could be helpful on the level of information. But he also noted that information would not be enough since 'you know, I think it's about understanding and respecting each other as much as possible as well'. As a young Sikh man and voluntary sector worker concluded, dialogue activities and education are interlinked, with the process of one feeding into the other:

> The first process is learning about the different faiths and learning, and from learning you get understanding, and from that understanding you can actually respond to the needs of the different faith communities and by that you will actually make better community cohesion . . . creating dialogue it is always the best starting place to create better community cohesion.

It is arguable that, in some instances, 'religion or belief prejudice' like 'religion or belief naivety' may be resolvable through dialogue as well as through education, as already discussed. However, as explained by a middle-aged Christian fieldwork participant, this is a much harder process:

> All religions have the power to do that, connect us at the human level if done in a way that isn't dismissive of people of other faiths or no faith. So there is the potential there but it is so hard to move beyond prejudice.

A white male Christian public sector employee of a city council stated, 'I'd like to see political correctness removed in many ways because I think it's stopping freedom of speech.' Linked with this he added, 'I would also like to see far more inter faith dialogue taking place between the day to day adherents rather than the leaders.' In other words, he was advocating a more open form of communication in a supportive context which would not need to shy away from engagement with difficult issues.

In relation to more structural issues, it is possible that more institutional forms of inter-religious and inter-community dialogue can make a contribution towards moving away from the 'religion or belief disadvantage' aspect of our analytical spectrum. But as noted by respondents to, and participants in, our research, even the mechanisms for dialogue themselves can reproduce aspects of 'religion or belief disadvantage'. Thus, examples exist of well-established bodies for inter-religious dialogue, such as the Inter

Faith Network for the United Kingdom (Weller, 2013) that have been able to facilitate real engagement, both between religious organizations and institutions themselves, and also with government departments and agencies. But at the same time, there are those (and especially Pagans) who express concern that their organizations are not able fully to participate in such organizations on the same basis as those from other religions.

On a European level, there has been the recent development of an embryonic initiative called ENORB (European Network on Religion or Belief at: www.enorb.eu/). Its approach goes beyond that of the Inter Faith Network for the United Kingdom due to its explicit aim to engage with not only religious organizations, but also with those of a non-religious philosophical and ethical orientation. In the wider European context this takes account of the strong French tradition of laïcité and reflects the historic patterns and contemporary practice of countries such as Belgium and the Netherlands, where consultation from public bodies has, for many years, structurally involved both religious and non-religious philosophical-ethical groups.

A policy context for change

'Twin-track' policy developments

Building on its description in Chapter 3 of England and Wales as a 'three-dimensional society': Christian, secular and religiously plural, this chapter and book goes on to argue for what it calls a 'three-dimensional' approach to policy, law and practice. But in order to locate this proposed approach, it is necessary first, briefly, to examine two main tendencies in social policy as they have impacted on matters of religion or belief, discrimination and equality over the past decade.

Religion and belief groups: Social capital and civil society

Governments of all political positions have, in the early twenty-first century focused on reducing the scale and scope of the state and public services. Partly as a by-product of this, governments are increasingly looking for partners in civil society with which to develop appropriate social policy and deliver social services. Because religions and religious organizations involve substantially more people than other sectors of civil society, or indeed, political parties, they have increasingly become involved in such provision (Smith, 2002, 2003, 2004). The recognition of this can also play into the current government's promotion of the idea of the 'Big Society', in which religion and belief and wider voluntary sector groups are encouraged to play a major role.

An early example of partnership between government and religious groups was the formation, in 1992, of the Inner Cities Religious Council (ICRC) which was created as part of the then Conservative Government's response to the issues raised by *Faith in the City* report produced by the Church of England Archbishops' Commission Urban Priority Areas. Over the subsequent years, an extensive range of structures and initiatives emerged at the local level that have been concerned with facilitating interaction between the Christian, secular and religiously plural dimensions of the UK religious landscape.

During the period of New Labour government, its approach to these matters was informed by the concept of social capital drawn from the work of American political scientist, Robert Putnam (1995, 2000). For Putnam, religious groups can produce both bonding social capital (the kind of energies that create solidarity within a particular group) and also bridging social capital (the kind of energies that link groups to the broader society) that can benefit the wider society (Furbey et al., 2006). In the context of the New Labour government's strongly regional focus, religious groups and public authorities increasingly collaborated at both regional (Northwest Regional Development Agency, 2003), county (Bates and Collishaw 2006) and local city/town levels (Ravat 2004) to document and further engage the contributions of religious groups to the wider society.

From this period a series of good practice guides that are still in use today were produced on which national and local government units worked together with the Inter Faith Network (IFN), the ICRC and also the Faith-based Regeneration Network (FbRN). These include the IFN's and ICRC's (1999) *Local Inter-Faith Guide: Faith Community Co-Operation in Action*; the Local Government Association's (2002) *Faith and Community: A Good Practice Guide for Local Authorities*; and the IFN's (2003) *Partnership for the Common Good*.

The UK Coalition government has promoted an ideology of 'localism', including the right of individuals to provide service provision (Cabinet Office, 2010). In part this policy shift is linked to initiatives under the Big Society agenda, public spending cuts and the restructuring of the welfare state (Taylor-Gooby, 2012). Citizens are being encouraged and, in part required, to take a greater role in looking after themselves, those around them and the areas where they live (Dorey and Garnett, 2012). It is notable that the revised UK Citizenship/Live in the UK Test introduced in 2013 includes a new focus on the responsibilities and expectations of being a citizen. It also includes wider coverage of religion and other 'protected characteristics' identified in British equality and human rights law.

From multiculturalism to 'extremism', conflict and terror and responses to them

Since the mid-1960s, the social policy and political consensus in the United Kingdom that has underlain the equality and diversity policies of central and local government and other significant social institutions, as well as equality law, was predicated on the promotion of multiculturalism (Parekh, 2000a; Rex, 1985). This was classically articulated by the former Labour Government Home Secretary Roy (later Lord) Jenkins, the architect of the UK's 1968 *Race Relations Act*. Jenkins (1967: 269) argued, 'I do not think that we need in this country a melting-pot, which will turn everybody out in a common mould, as one of a series of someone's misplaced vision of the stereotyped Englishman'. Rather, he set out the aim of government policy being to support 'integration' (understood in those days as the opposite of 'assimilation') which he defined as, '. . . equal opportunity, coupled with cultural diversity, in an atmosphere of mutual tolerance'.

During the 1990s, the adequacy of this vision of multiculturalism came under strain relative to emergent developments. An early sign was during the controversy that developed around Salman Rushdie's (1988) book, *The Satanic Verses*. In response to this even Roy Jenkins (1989) was recorded as saying, 'In retrospect, we might have been more cautious about allowing the creation in the 1950s of substantial Muslim communities here.' The writer Fay Weldon (1989: 31) put it even more starkly, claiming that, 'Our attempt at multiculturalism has failed. The Rushdie Affair demonstrates it.' While that controversy was still resonant came the disturbances in the summer of 2001 in some northern mill towns, followed by the seismic global shock of 11 September in the United States.

As a response, policy development informed by the notion of social cohesion became very much a part of the agenda of national and local governments. Some of the issues involved were explored in the Denham (2001) report on *Cohesive Communities* and the Cantle (2001) report on *Community Cohesion*. The reference to 'cohesive' and to 'cohesion' in these report titles in many ways contrasted with the emphasis of the earlier, independent 'Parekh Report' (2000b) of the Commission on the Future of Multi-Ethnic Britain, which advocated a vision of the United Kingdom based on the notion of a 'community of communities'.

This emphasis on cohesion gathered pace and intensity following the Madrid train bombing of March 2004 and the London Transport bombings of July 2005, which resulted in the deaths of 52 people and the injury of 700 others. This tragedy in London, followed two weeks later by a further failed attempt, resulted in what Weller (2008: 195) has described as a 'social policy shock' arising from the realization that these first suicide bombings in Europe were carried out by young men brought up in the United Kingdom who were, to all outward appearances, integrated members of British society, including within their local Muslim communities. As a consequence of this the spotlight of public discourse and of new policy (including security developments) was shone onto concerns about religious 'extremism' and religious 'radicalism', supplemented by a wish to identify the shared values of what, increasingly, became called 'Britishness'. The concerns which this generated were articulated in a statement released by the (then) Chair of the (former) Commission for Racial Equality (and until Autumn 2012 Chair of the EHRC), Trevor Phillips who, in 2005, argued that:

[T]he aftermath of [the bombing of July 2005] forces us to assess where we are. And here is where I think we are: we are sleepwalking our way to segregation. We are becoming strangers to each other, and we are leaving communities to be marooned outside the mainstream.

Phillips' statement led to widespread and sharp public and political debate. Analysis using UK Census data by Finney and Simpson (2009) claims ethnic residential clustering can be driven by positive forces of community building and sharing but that it is not increasing. Where there is such evidence, it is related to population growth rather than in-migration of minorities clustering in particular areas. A concern identified by Finney and Simpson is that the language often used in these debates is one in which the discourse is focused on minorities rather than discussing how populations move, migrate and mix, and/or it is based on the presumption that areas should be majority 'white'. However, while it might not be true in terms of actual numbers or in terms of movement patterns, there is a *perception* of segregation related to minority population growth among certain populations. Aspects of this, and of the need to address it, are tackled in a very recently published piece of research for the think tank Demos (see Kaufmann, 2013).

The general emphasis on cohesion led to the establishment of a Race, Cohesion and Faiths Directorate in what became the newly created Department for Communities and Local Government (DCLG). Building on work initiated by the former Faith Communities Unit in the Home Office, the new Directorate also took on the wider agendas of 'race' and cohesion, being made responsible for tackling racism, extremism and hate, while working closely with the Home Office on the Prevent agenda developed to counter radicalization. A Commission on Integration and Cohesion was convened and published a 2007 report entitled *Our Shared Future*. With this, the emphases on integration and cohesion might be seen as coming almost full circle around 40 years after Jenkins' classical articulation of multiculturalism, resulting in that is now being called 'integration' having a meaning that is quite close to what used to be meant by the 'assimilation' that Jenkins originally rejected.

Government policy focus and participation in British society

In considering policy foci, it is important to consider the link with perceptions of citizenship, being British and aspects of liberal democracy, such as freedom of speech. In the survey completed in 2011, respondents were asked about the government policy initiatives listed in Table 10.5 and how helpful they felt them to be to the participation of people from religious groups in the wider British society.

From the survey completed in 2011, among policy emphases for assisting the participation in society of people and organizations of various religious groups, the policy emphases such as equal opportunities and community cohesion were seen as being the most helpful for creating a context in which unfair treatment on the grounds of religion or belief might be reduced. Relative to these, the idea of 'Britishness' was

Table 10.5 Helpfulness of government policy emphases to the participation of people and organizations from religious groups in British society

Policy emphases	Very helpful (%)	Somewhat helpful (%)	Neither helpful nor unhelpful (%)	Somewhat unhelpful (%)	Very unhelpful (%)	Don't know (%)	Total N
Citizenship	20	34	26	5	1	15	433
Britishness	10	23	33	15	3	18	430
Community Cohesion	21	41	20	4	0	14	427
Multiculturalism	20	38	18	9	3	11	431
Equal opportunities	26	39	20	4	1	10	431
Freedom of speech	27	30	22	7	4	12	432

not seen to be very helpful to the participation of people and organizations from religious groups in British society. From the fieldwork completed in 2011, a public sector employee explained how historic foci on 'race' and ethnic relations had now been broadened to include also religion or belief:

> I think there's been a lot of work around cohesion and I think people often mistake community cohesion to just being about racial issues. [. . .] they've [local council] been very much looking at cohesion in a wider context so religion and belief and looking at how the different religions can work together on common causes has been something that has been quite refreshing.

At the same time, as noted already in Chapter 7, a small number of fieldwork participants reported concerns about government funding going only to 'certain groups' and not others. A participant from the public sector explained that:

> The main criticism has been that they mixed community cohesion funding and community cohesion events with preventing violent extremism and then there have been accusations of spying, accusations of 'oh you know we are all not terrorists and you're brushing us with the same brush, sweeping generalisations etc.'

However, on the whole, religious and non-religious participants in the fieldwork commented about the positive impacts of the broader initiatives in support of cohesion. At the same time, as highlighted in contributions to the project's Knowledge Exchange Workshops, due to the current economic downturn, funding sources were being cut and a number of community initiatives reported having had funds reduced or completely withdrawn. Many fieldwork interviewees were unsure as to whether or not their work could be sustained. At the same time, many interviewees commented that it is possible, even without funding, for people from diverse backgrounds to 'get on' and 'get along' with each other. A humanist respondent stated:

> . . . I am fairly relaxed about religion – I can see its positive aspect and I can live with it. I can see a woman going down a street in a *burqa* or *hijab* and I take positive pleasure from that – I feel this is a liberal society and she's allowed to dress like that whereas I get angry about France that says you can't wear that. I don't feel discriminated against. I see the values of my grandparents or leaders in other countries that are religious and I can see that it has a sort of community cohesion influence.

Finally, a Muslim equality and diversity expert working in the public sector summarized that to her community cohesion means 'to belong' and also that her needs and the needs of diverse communities are all catered for by a pluralist and inclusive society:

> . . . as far as I'm concerned community cohesion is not about getting on together, people get along fine, it is about knowing that you belong here, this is where I live, this is my city, this is my country I belong here and the way I can show you that is

because when I go somewhere and I need things being given to me as a Muslim Welsh person.

'Three-dimensional' policy, law and practice

Towards a 'three-dimensional' balance

In tackling unfair treatment, rather than attempting to add to or change the law, the primary need now is to build on the impetus that law has given to recognizing the impact of these issues in society including for religious groups themselves. The best way in which to approach doing this is especially by educational measures within the formal education system; in broad public education; and in training connected with specific roles and responsibilities within religion or belief groups themselves and in the wider society.

That such initiatives should be inclusive of religion or belief groups themselves as well as of organizations, sectors and institutions in the wider society, is an integral part of the argument presented here for a 'three-dimensional' approach to identifying signposts for the future overall direction of policy, law and practice in relation to religion and belief, discrimination and equality. By a 'three-dimensional' approach, we mean one which enables connection with the Christian, secular and religiously plural realities of the society in which policy, law and practice seek to operate and in which they seek to bring about change. This is because each of these dimensions reflects and embodies social forces and claims that have a bearing upon policy, law and practice. As argued in our 2001 report, 'For policy to be effective, it needs to be grounded in the experiences and worldview of those most likely to be affected' (Weller et al., 2001: 159).

The 'three-dimensional' approach to policy-making that we advocate is also informed by the approach taken in our analytical spectrum, which is designed to be equally applicable to understanding unfair treatment on the basis of religion or belief as experienced by religion or belief groups from the wider society; as perpetrated by religion or belief groups in relation to the wider society; and as experienced between and/or within religion or belief groups. To fail to take sufficient account of one or the other of the 'three dimensions' is likely to lead to directions in policy, law and practice that will fail to connect with a broad enough base in society to secure the kind of consent that, in a democratic polity, is necessary for the effects of policy, law and practice to be constructive. By contrast, the absence of such consent could at the least compromise the intended aims of policy, law and practice, while at the worst it might even create potentially destructive side effects.

In summary, this means that with reference both to the context and the content of the research evidence, it is important to develop an approach to policy, law and practice that is able to facilitate the kind of development that can mediate between factors of continuity and change. It is this which, when combined with specific measures for tackling unfair treatment on the basis of religion or belief that promote education and dialogue, a 'three-dimensional' policy approach can facilitate. Because of this, each of the three dimensions are considered further, below, in terms of their specific relevance for signposting towards future policy, law and practice.

The 'Christianity dimension'

From evidence in the Census and other survey data as discussed in Chapters 3 and 5, it is clear that, in headline terms, England and Wales and Britain can be described as 'less Christian' now than ten years ago. From our research Christian voices appear increasingly to be identifying a sense of marginalization in comparison with their previous social position. Along with this, is a growing sense that people of other than Christian religious groups might now be being perceived by some Christians as being treated more fairly, in some instances extending to a quite sharp sense of unfair treatment, which is even occasionally articulated in the more active and extreme language of 'persecution'.

At the same time, it is also important to understand that the reported experience and structural position of different Christian groups is internally differentiated. Indeed, as explained in Chapter 2, Catholic and Free Church Christians have been more removed from this kind of relationship with the state and until the late nineteenth century were, in many ways, excluded from full participation in the structures and institutions of the wider society. In relative terms this historic differentiation continues today, albeit that the development of ecumenical relations has taken on some features of a kind of 'extended establishment'. Nevertheless, similar experiences remain for those sectors of the Christian community associated with the 'New Church' movement and with churches of migrant origin (and especially the development of predominantly black-led churches among people of African and African-Caribbean heritage), all of which are important to bear in mind for a rounded assessment of the 'Christian dimension'.

Not least because of the growth of these sectors of Christianity, it is important not to overstate the argument in relation to the 'less Christian' context. This is because, even within a clear scenario of overall decline, in both absolute and proportionate terms, the Census results show that it remains the case that both large numbers and a high proportion of the population of England and Wales continue to self-identify in some way with Christianity. Christianity continues to have a social presence and significance that goes beyond the actual numbers of those who identify with it. Especially in its established forms, it is still extensively woven into much of the fabric of the historical, artistic, cultural, legal and other aspects of the heritage of the United Kingdom and its constituent parts. An intimate relationship of this kind does not exist in the same or even a similar way between the public institutions and the culture of England and Wales and Britain and any other religion. At the same time, and perhaps counter-intuitively, it needs to be recognized that there are those, including those among religious minority groups themselves who argue (Modood, 1997) that it is beneficial for there to be an established Church to ensure a space for religion in public life.

In the light of all the above, a balanced development of policy, law and practice needs to take account of the continuing importance of the 'Christian dimension' of our 'three-dimensional' policy context. This remains so, while recognizing that society has become 'less Christian' relative to its parallel increase in both 'religious plurality' and in terms of the 'non-religious' and 'secular dimension', the importance of which is now considered.

The 'secular dimension'

In the nineteenth and during much of the twentieth centuries in England and Wales, the growth of the second dimension of the now 'three-dimensional' policy context was more in evidence than the third dimension of increasing religious plurality. Indeed, for much of the twentieth century, the overall relationships between religion, state and society, and the experience of individuals and groups of people of religion or belief within that was usually articulated in binary terms as 'Christian' and 'secular'.

Just as it is important not to underplay the continuing social significance of the Christian dimension, it is equally important not to underplay the historical and contemporary evidence for clear trends in the growth of the secular, including in relation to the place of explicitly non-religious perspectives among the population. In this, the 2011 Census data that shows a substantial rise in the non-religious population of England and Wales underlines the importance of taking account of this. As with data relating to Christian affiliation and practice, the numbers and proportions of those who explicitly self-identify as non-religious in terms of particular ethical and philosophical positions (such as atheist, humanist and so on) are smaller than the numbers and percentages of those who take a more secular view of the relationship between religion, state and society but do not have such specific positions that have been categorized in any detail. This may also include people with broadly religious, spiritual and ethical perspectives.

The 11 September 2001 attacks in the United States and 7 July 2005 bombings in the United Kingdom have led to the development of public anxieties and concerns about the perceived influence of religious 'extremism' associated with these atrocities. It is notable that in our 2011 survey, respondents from religious organizations were asked about the extent to which instances of violence and terrorism related to religion or belief had affected how their organization was perceived by others. Overall 22 per cent of (448) respondents stated that the perception of their organization had been affected. While respondents from Muslim organizations were the most likely to state they had been affected, organizations from across all the religious traditions also reported being affected. As one respondent stated: 'people seem to think that any religious belief is now anti-social'. At the same time 26 per cent of (443) respondents stated that they had been involved in activities aimed at tackling violent extremism. This included respondents from across all the religious traditions in the survey.

The 'religious plurality dimension'

The latter decades of the twentieth century have also seen the emergence of an additional 'third dimension' of the religion and belief landscape that is important to understand both in its own right and also for the way in which it will modify previous 'two-dimensional' assumptions concerning policy, law and practice. As seen in Chapters 2 and 3, people from minority religious traditions have become a growing proportion of the population of England and Wales and especially following the migrations of the post-Second World War period.

In the impact of this dimension on wider public life, the process has been gradual, but it has accelerated in the last two to three decades. *The Satanic Verses* controversy in many ways marked a watershed that has been described elsewhere by Weller (2008) as a 'mirror for our times'. Using St John Robilliard's language, in the 1960s and early 1970s, the early part of the 'struggle for existence' of predominantly migrant groups necessarily focused on their need to meet the basic needs of finding a place to live and work in order to be able to send financial remittances in support of families back home. As a consequence, during the 1970s and early 1980s the majority of social scientists, policy-makers and politicians paid comparatively limited attention to the religious characteristics of migrants, and the politics of identity and diversity were cast primarily in terms of 'race' and ethnicity. However, with prescient insight, in 1977 the Church of England Bishop John Taylor (in Wolffe, 1993: 193) argued that, 'The existence of religious minorities presents us with both problems and opportunities which are distinct from those that arise in the presence of racial and cultural minorities, and should not be lost sight of or evaded.'

In due course, however, the 'struggle for existence' among historically migrant groups developed on the basis of establishing a religious identity of their own, which then (also in St John Robilliard's words), started to become a 'struggle for equality'. In the United Kingdom, in contrast to some other European countries (e.g. Germany), this process was facilitated by the fact that the majority of those in minority religious groups have also been citizens of the United Kingdom and therefore had a legal and material position from which they could seek an appropriately equitable position within the society.

Moving forward: the next decade and beyond

The emergence and ongoing development of the 'three-dimensional' religion and belief policy context means that the calls and initiatives among Christian conservatives for Christianity to remain as central as it once was to policy, law and practice are, in practice, unlikely to be effective. This is because such calls do not take account of the realities of a growing 'non-religious' and 'secular dimension', or of the increasing religious plurality. In addition, in seeking to turn back the clock to rely on what Stuart Murray (2004) calls 'the vestiges of Christendom', such calls and initiatives may in fact run the risk of exacerbating tensions and conflicts between religion and belief groups and between the religious and the non-religious, ironically to the possible further religion or belief disadvantage also of Christians.

But it also means that strident campaigns to force through secular (and often at least perceived by religious people as ideologically 'secular*ist*') measures to be given priority relative to the religious components of the identity of individuals and groups are unlikely to find a broad enough acceptance. This is because of both the numbers of those who continue in some way to identify with a religion and because of the significance of religion for many of those, and especially so among the minority religious traditions. By contrast, an understanding of the 'secular' in which no single religion in particular, nor religion in general, nor what might be termed an ideological secular*ism* in which religion is excluded or marginalized from public life is to be privileged, but which is about a socially agreed set of institutional arrangements that can facilitate the greatest possible inclusive participation. Such an understanding of the 'secular', is likely to be able to command broad consent and to be of importance in any future 'three-dimensional' policy context.

This means that any attempt mathematically to try in an abstract way to 'equalize' all religious traditions in the public sphere (Ghanea, 2011) will run into the clearly different historical and social position of Christianity. At the same time, any attempt to form a 'united front' of religions against the secular will even more likely flounder given that the emergence of inter-faith cooperation, though significant, remains relatively fragile compared to the social embededness of the Christian tradition. Significantly for Britain in its European context, the 'third dimension' of the policy context is much more clearly marked than in other European countries where public debate still tends to take place within a more 'binary' framework or, where the 'third dimension' intrudes, is almost exclusively identified with Islam and with Muslims. This reflects the much lower proportions of people of Hindu and Sikh religious identity found in other European countries which is, in itself, of course, a reflection of the historical form and reach of the British Empire.

This difference in diversity has an even greater significance for policy, law and practice when it is mapped onto the nineteenth-century history of religion and belief. This, again, contrasts with the history of the majority of other European countries in which there has been either one very dominant Christian confessional tradition/ church (as with the Catholic Church in Austria, for example) in tension with the secular traditions of the Enlightenment or two more balanced but competing traditions (as in Germany's Protestant and Catholic Churches). In England and Wales, however, although following the Restoration of the Monarchy, the Church of England was in a legally dominant position, the position of the other Christian minority traditions was much more differentiated in terms of the continuing Catholic presence and the (itself plural) growing Free Church traditions of Christianity. These differences in both the historical and contemporary religion and belief landscapes in England, Wales and Britain in comparison with most countries in the European Union and the wider Europe should not be underestimated.

In identifying signposts for the future in policy, law and practice, it is important to take account of this distinctiveness in terms of the balance of all three dimensions of (less) Christian, (more) secular and (increasingly) religiously plural. The achievement of such a balance is necessary if the directions of travel signposted are to connect with the whole society's concerns around religion and belief, discrimination and equality, while avoiding the potential for exacerbating tensions and conflicts arising from these different perspectives on life by misplaced policy, law and practice.

In particular, this analysis should inform the action of governments and religious groups, both of which it is arguable have special responsibilities in this regard. Already in 1996, the recommendations of a report by the Council of Europe's Group of Consultants on Religious and Cultural Aspects of Equality of Opportunities for Immigrants argued that the increasing religious diversity of European societies and the intersection of this diversity with many issues of social and public life is posing many new questions and possibilities. Among their recommendations is:

> The increasing religious diversity of Europe constitutes a major challenge to both the governments of the member states and to their societies. The governments and the historical religious communities must adopt a policy which aims to establish an effective equality of rights and treatments for the new religious minorities in Europe. Failure to establish such a policy would amount to a violation by Europe of its declared principles and those of the Council of Europe. (1996: 22)

At the same time, in relation to the issues of religion or belief discrimination, it is important not to see those who report these issues simply as passive recipients of policy and/or legal processes coming from 'outside' and/or from 'above'. Rather, they are also empowering themselves by addressing these issues from 'inside' and 'below'. The dynamics and dimensions of unfair treatment and discrimination in relation to religion or belief are not new and an understanding of the past, and especially of the nineteenth century in England and Wales, demonstrates that historic discrimination was not removed simply as the product of an automatic evolutionary process based on social and economic developments. Nor did these changes come about only due to the enlightened goodwill of those who did not themselves experience such discrimination but recognized the inequity of the status quo and worked for change. Although both of these factors played a part, what was also of central importance was the struggle and campaigning on the part of those who were negatively affected by them.

Thus, alongside the role of evidence-based policy-making and of law, the element of struggle on the part of religion and belief groups within civil society remains a necessary part of bringing about social, political and legal change. However, it is of equal importance to understand that, if not challenged by a wider vision (either from within the resources of their own tradition or by external factors), religion or belief groups can start to act only in a self-interested manner that has sometimes itself led to discrimination and unfair treatment. As underlined in Belieforama's *Policy Brief for European Institutions and Civil Society Groups*, in focusing on religion or belief, discrimination and equality, the question needs also to be posed:

> How far do religion or belief groups accept the responsibility to take initiatives and find mechanisms for addressing ways in which their own traditions, teaching and/ or philosophy might lead to unfair treatment of other religion or belief groups – and/or others who see their identity partly or primarily in terms of ethnicity, gender or sexual orientation? (Weller and Contractor, 2012: 24)

At the same time, it also needs to be recognized that the European history of the relationships between religion, state and society and religion or belief discrimination and equality are not all a matter of the non-religious, the secular and the state acting as a benignly liberal force in mediating between more 'extreme' religious groups. As the historian Eric Hobsbawn's (1995) significantly entitled last volume of his series of volumes on modern history, *The Age of Extremes* points out, the recent history of

Europe also shows ample evidence of dangers to the social fabric from political forces and philosophies when implemented in ways that seek to reduce social space for the 'other' in a future social context for England and Wales that is likely to continue to become increasingly diverse in terms of religion or belief.

This means that it is very important to take account of both the experience of those who understand themselves primarily (or to a large extent) by reference to the category of 'religion' (including in all its variety) and also those who do not (and whose interests and perspectives, in current legal and policy terminology, is represented by the word 'belief'). If this is not done, then the warning issued by Gerald Parsons (1994: 154) in his essay on religion and politics in Britain becomes very pertinent. This is that, without an effort on the part of religious leaders and politicians, political parties and religious groups to '. . . understand the subtleties and complexities of the interactions to which their various commitments give rise', then, 'the alternative is the reduction of increasingly complex issues to the convenient slogans of competing religious-cum-political pressure groups – a bleak and unhappy prospect indeed'.

As expressive of democratic responsibility and accountability there remains a key role for governments to develop policy, law and practice in a way that achieves input and consent from those governed. It is in this connection that we believe what we have argued that the 'three-dimensional' approach to policy-making is of great importance. The rights for all (religious and non-religious) to question and to live according to one's freely chosen conscience, rather than as a requirement embodied in law and/or social convention, did not come about without historic struggles and these represent important social gains. Thus, when considering unfair treatment and discrimination on the grounds of religion or belief and the possible measures for tackling it and promoting equality, a balanced concern for the rights of atheists, humanists, agnostics and the more generally non-religious, as well as for those of religious believers and practitioners of various kinds, remains vital.

Pragmatically, too, if Christians, people of other religious traditions and the 'non-religious' wish to have their concerns and perspectives taken seriously as part of an agenda to create a fully inclusive plural society, then the importance of understanding and tackling discrimination and unfair treatment on the grounds of religion or belief wherever it appears and by whoever it is committed is a foundational principle for equality and equitable practice. These principles are particularly important in an era of economic crisis and growing competition for resources when fear of religious, ethnic and other groups can all too easily be generated, either from within or outside of these groups in order to set them competitively against each other with potentially disastrous consequences for inter- and intra-community, religious and cultural relations.

It is as a contribution towards the realization of that principle in the future development of policy, law and practice in this area, that the research, analyses and recommendations of this book are offered. Through the comparisons that it has been able to draw over a period of ten years, our research completed in 2011 has arrived at some unique evidence. It is our conviction that the evidence and analysis that we have presented here already provides the kind of insight on which policy-makers and practitioners and the wider religious and non-religious population can draw for the next decade and beyond.

Appendix: Selected List of Relevant Legal Cases in England and Wales, 2000–10

Across the whole period of our project (2010-12) a systematic review and analysis was undertaken of over 130 relevant legal cases using various search engines, legal directories and press reports. A list of the references for these cases follows. The cases were coded by the project according to categories reflecting different aspects of people's lives. A key to the coding of these categories is found below. In the case list, the codes follow the case references, in italics within square brackets.

The categories to which cases were coded included those to do with: abuse – physical and/or sexual; accommodation/exemption, etc.; adoption; arbitration; assets of religion/belief community; child – cases involving a child; continued existence of a church; customary law; doctrinal issues; sexual orientation; discrimination; direct discrimination; indirect discrimination; diversity; dress (head dress, hair); employment; employee definition; equality; freedom of expression; religion or belief, definitions of; observations; school; sexual orientation; and suicide. Many cases consisted of more than one element.

For non-lawyers who are interested in accessing the case, it is possible to access full details by entering the relevant reference details of the court code and case reference into an internet search engine. Thus, for the first example below – of A (CHILDREN), RE [2000] EWCA Civ 254 (22 September 2000), one takes the details RE [2000] EWCA Civ 254 (22 September 2000) and searches on this. The case records will then be identified for further reading.

Key code

Abortion
Abuse – physical and/or sexual abuse
Accom/Exemp/Diff – exemption, accommodation or differential treatment; seeking/being granted on the grounds of religion or belief
Adop – adoption
Arbitration

Assets – assets belonging to a religion or belief community
Child – childhood, case involving a child
Continued – existence of a church
Cust Law – Customary law
D-SO – Discrimination on the basis of sexual orientation
Disc – Discrimination
Disc dir – Direct discrimination
Disc indir – Indirect discrimination
Div – Diversity
Dress – Dresscode, headdress, hair
Empl – Employment
Employee def – Definition of 'employee'
Eq – Equality
FoEx – Defamation, blasphemy, limitations on freedom of expression
Health
Marriage
RoB disc – Discrimination on the basis of religion or belief
RoB – Religion or belief
RoB doct – Religion or belief, doctrinal issues
RoB def – Religion or belief, definition of
RoB obs – Religion or belief, observations on the basis of
Sch – School
SO – Sexual orientation
Suicide

A

A (CHILDREN), RE [2000] EWCA Civ 254 (22 September 2000) [*child*]

ADECCO UK LTD V F ALI [2007] UKEAT 0554_06_2302 (23 February 2007) [*Empl, RoB obs, Disc indir, dress*]

R (AGUILAR QUILA) v SECRETARY OF STATE FOR THE HOME DEPARTMENT: R (BIBI) v SECRETARY OF STATE FOR THE HOME DEPARTMENT [2010] EWCA Civ 1482 (21 December 2010) [*Disc, marriage*]

ADMISSION ARRANGEMENTS OF JFS, BRENT [2007] Determination by the Schools Adjudicator under the School Standards and Framework Act 1998 (Case Reference ada/001187) (27 November 2007) and E v GOVERNING BODY OF JFS & ANOR [2008] EWHC 1535/1536 (Admin) (3 July 2008), [2009] EWCA Civ 626 (25 June 2009) and [2009] UKSC 15 (16 December) [*RoB def, disc dir, disc indir, sch*]

AMICUS MSF SECTION, R (ON THE APPLICATION OF) v SECRETARY OF STATE FOR TRADE AND INDUSTRY [2004] EWHC 860 (Admin) (26 April 2004) [*SO, Empl, Eq, accom/exemp/diff*]

AZMI v KIRKLEES METROPOLITAN COUNCIL [2007] UKEAT 0009 07 30003 (30 MARCH 2007) [*Empl, RoB obs, Disc indir, Eq, accom/exemp/diff, dress, sch*]

B

R (ON THE APPLICATION OF BAIAI AND ORS) v SECRETARY OF STATE FOR THE HOME DEPARTMENT [2007] EWCA Civ 478 (23 May 2007) and [2008] UKHL 53 (30 July 2008) [*Disc, marriage*]

R v BRITISH BROADCASTING CORPORATION e p PROLIFE ALLIANCE [2003] UKHL 23 (10 April 2003) [*FoEx*]

BEGUM, R (ON THE APPLICATION OF) v DENBIGH HIGH SCHOOL [2006] UKHL 15 (22 March 2006) [*RoB obs, RoB disc, child, dress, sch*]

BELLINGER v BELLINGER [2003] UKHL 21 (10 April 2003) [*marriage*]

BLAKE v ASSOCIATED NEWSPAPERS LTD [2003] EWHC 1960 (QB) [*RoB doct, FoEx*]

BOUGHTON, R (ON THE APPLICATION OF) v HER MAJESTY'S TREASURY [2005] EWHC 1914 (Admin) (25 July 2005) [*RoB obs, accom/exemp/diff*]

C

CAMPBELL & ORS V SOUTH NORTHAMPTONSHIRE DISTRICT COUNCIL & ANOR [2004] EWCA Civ 409 (07 April 2004) [*Employee def, Disc*]

CATHOLIC CARE (DIOCESE OF LEEDS) v CHARITY COMMISSION FOR ENGLAND AND WALES [2009] Charity Tribunal CA/2008/0003 (1 June 2009); CATHOLIC CARE (DIOCESE OF LEEDS) v CHARITY COMMISSION FOR ENGLAND AND WALES & ANOR [2010] EWHC 520 (Ch) (17 March 2010), VARIOUS CLAIMANTS v THE CATHOLIC CHILD WELFARE SOCIETY & ORS [2010] EWCA Civ 1106 (26 October 2010) and CATHOLIC CARE (DIOCESE OF LEEDS) [2010] Ch Comm E & W final determination (21 July 2010, published 19 August 2010) [*D-SO, Eq, RoB obs, accom/exemp/diff, adop*]

CHAPLIN v ROYAL DEVON & EXETER HOSPITAL NHS FOUNDATION TRUST [2010] ET 1702886/2009 (21 April 2010); NADIA EWEIDA AND SHIRLEY CHAPLIN v UNITED KINGDOM [2011] ECtHR (No. 48420/10 738) (2 May 2011) and EWEIDA AND OTHERS v THE UNITED KINGDOM [2013] ECtHR (Nos. 48420/10 36516/10 51671/10 59842/10) (15 January 2013) [*Empl, Eq, RoB obs, RoBdisc, disc indir, accom/exemp/diff*]

CHONDOL v LIVERPOOL CITY COUNCIL [2009] UKEAT/0298/08 (11 February 2009) [*RoB disc, RoB obs, accom/exemp/diff*]

GALLAGHER (Valuation Officer) v CHURCH OF JESUS CHRIST OF THE LATTER-DAY SAINTS [2008], UKHL 56 (30 July 2008) and THE CHURCH OF JESUS CHRIST OF LATTER-DAY SAINTS V UNITED KINGDOM [2011] (no. 7552/09) EctHR, 12 April 2011 [*Accom/Exemp/Diff*]

CHURCH OF JESUS CHRIST OF THE LATTER-DAY SAINTS V PRICE [2004] EWHC 3245 (QB) (30 November 2004) [*RoB obs, FoEx*]

CONNOLLY v DPP DIVISIONAL COURT [2007] EWHC 237 (Admin) (15 February 2007) [*Empl, RoB obs, accom/exemp/diff*]

R (ON THE APPLICATION Of HM CORONER FOR EAST LONDON) v SECRETARY OF STATE FOR JUSTICE [2009] EWHC (Admin) 1974 (31 July 2009)

COPSEY v WWB DEVON CLAYS LTD [2005] EWCA Civ 932 (25 July 2005) [*Empl, RoB obs, accom/exemp/diff*]

D

DEAN v BURNE & ORS [2009] EWHC 1250 (Ch) (05 June 2009) [continued existence of a Church, assets]

DEHAL v CROWN PROSECUTION SERVICE [2005] EWHC 2154 (Admin) (27 September 2005) [*FoEx*]

DEPARTMENT OF HEALTH v INFORMATION COMMISSIONER [2009] Information Tribunal Appeal Number EA /2008/0074 (15 October 2009) [*abortion/ health/FoEx*]

DRUID NETWORK [2010] Ch Comm Decision (21 September 2010) [*RoB def*]

E

EBURY (VALUATION OFFICER) v CHURCH COUNCIL OF THE CENTRAL METHODIST CHURCH [2009] 138 (LC) LT Case No RA/33/2007 (17 July 2009) [*RoB def*]

EDGE v VISUAL SECURITY SERVICES [2006] Employment Tribunal Case No. 1301365/06 [*Empl, RoB obs, accom/exemp/diff*]

EM (LEBANON) v SECRETARY OF STATE FOR THE HOME DEPARTMENT [2008] UKHL 64 (22 October 2008) [*marriage, ROB obs*]

ENGLISH v THOMAS SANDERSON LTD [2008] EWCA Civ 1421 (19 December 2008) [*D-SO, Empl, Eq, RoB disc*]

ESTORNINHO v ZORAN JOKIC t/a ZORANS DELICATESSEN [2006] Employment Tribunal Case no. 23014871/06 [*Empl, RoB obs, accom/exemp/diff*]

EWEIDA v BRITISH AIRWAYS PLC [2007] Employment Tribunal Case No. 2702689/06 (19 December 2007) [2008] UKEAT 0123 08 2011 (20 November 2008) begin_of_the_skype_highlightingend_of_the_skype_highlighting, EWEIDA v BRITISH AIRWAYS PLC [2010] EWCA Civ 80 (12 February 2010), NADIA EWEIDA AND SHIRLEY CHAPLIN v UNITED KINGDOM [2011] ECtHR (No. 48420/10 738) (2 May 2011) and EWEIDA AND OTHERS v THE UNITED KINGDOM ECtHR [2013] (Nos. 48420/10 36516/10 51671/10 59842/10) (15 January 2013) [*Empl, Eq, RoB obs, RoB disc, disc indir, accom/exemp/diff*]

F

FUGLER v MACMILLAN–LONDON HAIR STUDIOS LTD [2005] Employment Tribunal Case No. 2205090/04 [*Empl, RoB obs, accom/exemp/diff*]

G

GALLAGHER (VALUATION OFFICER) v CHURCH OF JESUS CHRIST OF LATTER-DAY SAINTS [2008] UKHL 56 (30 July 2008) [*assets*]

GHAI v NEWCASTLE CITY COUNCIL [2009] EWHC (Admin) 978 (8 May 2009) and GHAI, R (on the application of) v NEWCASTLE CITY COUNCIL & ORS [2010] EWCA Civ 59 (10 February 2010) [*RoB obs, RoB accom/exemp/diff*]

GNOSTIC CENTRE [2009] Ch Commn (16 December 2009) [*RoB def*]

GRAINGER PLC & ORS v NICHOLSON [2009] UKEAT 0219 090 311 begin_of_the_skype_highlightingend_of_the_skype_highlighting (3 November 2009) [*RoB def*]

GREATER MANCHESTER POLICE AUTHORITY V POWER [2009] EAT 0434/09/DA (12 November 2009) [*RoB def*]

GREEN, R (ON THE APPLICATION OF) v CITY OF WESTMINSTER MAGISTRATES' COURT [2007] EWHC (Admin) 2785 (5 December 2007) [*FoEx*]

H

HALL AND PREDDY V BULL AND BULL [2011] EW Misc 2 (CC) (04 January 2011) [*SO, D-SO, RoB obs, Eq, accom/exemp/diff*]

HAMMOND v DPP [2004] EWHC 69 (Admin) (31 January 2004) [*SO, FoEx*]

HARRIS v NKL AUTOMOTIVE LTD & ANOR [2007] UKEAT/0134/07/DM (3 October 2007); 2007 WL 2817981 [*Empl, RoB obs, disc, Eq, dress, accom/exemp/diff*]

HELOW v SECRETARY OF STATE FOR THE HOME DEPARTMENT & ANOR [2008] UKHL 62 (22 October 2008) [*disc*]

HENDER & SHERIDAN v PROSPECTS FOR PEOPLE WITH LEARNING DISABILITIES [2008] Employment Tribunal (Cases nos 2902090/2006 (Hender) & 2901366 (Sheridan)) (13 May 2008) [*Empl, Eq*]

HH SANT BABA JEET SINGH JI MAHARAJ v EASTERN MEDIA GROUP LIMITED AND HARDEEP SINGH [2010] EWHC (QB) 1294 (17 May 2010) [*RoB doct, FoEx*]

HUDSON v LEIGH [2009] EWHC 1306 (Fam) (05 June 2009) [*marriage*]

HUSSAIN V MIDLAND COSMETIC SALES PLC & ORS [2002] UKEAT 915_00_0905 (9 May 2002) [*Empl, Disc indir, dress, health*]

I

I v UNITED KINGDOM [2002] ECtHR [GC] (No. 25680/94) (11 July 2002) [*marriage*]

J

JAMES v MSC CRUISES LTD [2006] Employment Tribunal Case No. 2203173/05 [*Empl, RoB obs, accom/exemp/diff*]

JIVRAJ v HASHWANI [2009] EWHC (Comm) 1364 (26 June 2009) and [2010] EWCA Civ 712 (22 June 2010) [*Empl, Eq, arbitration*]

JOHNS & ANOR, R (ON THE APPLICATION OF) V DERBY CITY COUNCIL & ANOR [2011] EWHC 375 (Admin) (28 February 2011) [*D-SO, RoB, Div, RoB disc, adop*]

K

KC & ANOR v CITY OF WESTMINSTER SOCIAL & COMMUNITY SERVICES DEPT & ANOR [2008] EWCA Civ 198 (19 March 2008) [*marriage, RoB obs*]

KHAN, MOHAMMED SAJWAL V NIC HYGIENE (unreported) Employment Tribunal Case No.803250/04 (2004) [*Empl, RoB obs*]

KHAN v ROYAL AIR FORCE SUMMARY APPEAL COURT [2004] EWHC 2230 (Admin) (07 October 2004) [*RoB obs, accom/exemp/diff*]

KHAN v VIGNETTE EUROPE LTD [2010] UKEAT 0134/09/1401 (14 January 2010) [*Empl, RoB obs, accom/exemp/diff*]

KHOJA, HASANALI V METROPOLITAN POLICE (unreported) Employment Tribunal (May 2009) [*RoB disc, RoB obs, accom/exemp/diff, disc indir*]

KINGS v BULTITUDE & ANOR [2010] EWHC 1795 (Ch) (15 July 2010) [*continued existence of a Church, assets*]

KOHN v WAGSCHAL & ORS [2007] EWCA Civ 1022 (24 October 2007) [*RoB obs, arbitration*]

K, R (ON THE APPLICATION OF) v LONDON BOROUGH OF NEWHAM [2002] EWHC 405 (Admin) (19 February 2002) [*RoB obs, sch*]

L

LONDON BOROUGH OF ISLINGTON v LADELE [2008] Employment Appeal Tribunal 20-23 May 2008 (Case no. 2203694/2007); [2008] Case No. UKEAT/0453/08/ RN (10 December 2008) and [2009] EWCA Civ 1357 (15 December 2009); LILIAN LADELE AND GARY MCFARLANE v UNITED KINGDON [2010] ECthr (No. 51671/10) (2 May 2011) and EWEIDA AND OTHERS v THE UNITED KINGDOM [2013] ECtHR (Nos. 48420/10 36516/10 51671/10 59842/10) (15 January 2013) [*Empl, Eq, RoB obs, RoBdisc, D-SO, disc dir, disc indir, accom/exemp/diff, marriage*]

M

MAGA v ROMAN CATHOLIC ARCHDIOCESE OF BIRMINGHAM [2009] EWHC 780 (QB) (April 2009) and [2010] EWCA Civ 256 (16 March 2010) [*Abuse, employee def*]

MAHMOUD v ISLAMIC CULTURAL CENTRE AND THE LONDON CENTRAL MOSQUE [2007] WL 1729857; [2007] All ER (D) 204 (27 June 2007) [*disc*]

MASIH v AWAZ FM [2009] Employment Tribunal Case Number 116403/2008 (26 August 2009 [Empl, Eq]

MAYUUF v GOVERNING BODY OF BISHOP CHALLONER CATHOLIC COLLEGIATE SCHOOL & ANOR [2005] Employment Tribunal Case no. 3202398/04 (21 December 2005) [*Empl, RoB obs, Disc indir, accom/exemp/diff, sch*]

McCLINTOCK v DEPARTMENT OF CONSTITUTIONAL AFFAIRS [2007] UKEAT/0223/07/CEA (31 October 2007); 2007 WL 3130902 [*adop, disc indir, accom/exemp/diff*]

McFARLANE v RELATE AVON LTD [2009] UKEAT 0106_09_3011 (30 November 2009), [2010] EWCA Civ B1 (29 April 2010), LILIAN LADELE AND GARY MCFARLANE v UNITED KINGDON [2001] ECthr (No. 51671/10) (2 May 2011) and EWEIDA AND OTHERS v THE UNITED KINGDOM [2013] ECtHR (Nos. 48420/10 36516/10 51671/10 59842/10) (15 January 2013) [*RoB disc, RoB obs, accom/exemp/diff, disc, disc dir, disc indir, D-SO*]

MOHMED V WEST COAST TRAINS LTD [2006] UKEAT 0682_05_3008 (30 August 2006) [*Empl, RoB obs, accom/exemp/diff, dress*]

MONAGHAN v LEICESTER YOUNG MEN'S CHRISTIAN ASSOCIATION [2004] Employment Tribunal Case no. 1901839/2004 (26 November 2004) [*Disc dir, RoB obs, accom/exemp/diff*]

MUSAWI v R E INTERNATIONAL (UK) LTD & ORS [2007] EWHC 2981 (Ch) 14 December 2007; 2007 WL 4368227 [*arbitration, RoB obs*]

N

NEW TESTAMENT CHURCH OF GOD v STEWART [2007] EWCA Civ 1004 (19 October 2007) [*Employee def, empl*]

THE NHS TRUST v A (A CHILD) AND ORS [2007] EWHC (Fam) 1696 (18 July 2007) [*RoB obs, accom/exemp/diff, health, child*]

NICHOLSON v ASPIRE TRUST [2005] Employment Tribunal Case no. 2601009/004 (21 March 2005) [*Empl, D-SO, RoB obs, disc, Eq*]

NOAH v DESROSIERS t/a WEDGE [2008] Employment Tribunal Case No. 2201867/07 (29 May 2008) [*Empl, RoB obs, disc indir, Eq, accom/exemp/diff, dress*]

O

OFFICIAL SOLICITOR TO THE SENIOR COURTS v YEMOH & ORS [2010] WLR (D) 334 [*Cust Law, marriage*]

P

PADGETT v SEROTA & ANOR [2007] UKEAT 0097 07 1712 (17 December 2007) [*Empl, RoB disc, Eq*]

R (ON THE APPLICATION OF PLAYFOOT (A CHILD)) v MILLAIS SCHOOL GOVERNING BODY [2007] EWHC Admin 1698 (16 July 2007) [*RoB obs, RoB disc, sch*]

POWER V GREATER MANCHESTER POLICE AUTHORITY [2010] UKEAT 0087_10_0810 (8 October 2010) [*Empl, RoB obs, RoB doct*]

PRETTY (R, ON THE APPLICATION OF) v DIRECTOR OF PUBLIC PROSECUTIONS & SECRETARY OF STATE FOR THE HOME DEPARTMENT [2001] UKHL 61 (29 November 2001) and PRETTY v UNITED KINGDOM [2002] ECtHR (No. 2346/02) (29 April 2002) [*suicide*]

PURDY, R (ON THE APPLICATION OF) v DIRECTOR OF PUBLIC PROSECUTIONS & ORS [2009] EWCA Civ 92 (19 February 2009); (2009) 162 *L&J* 94-95 and [2009] UKHL 45 (30 July 2009) [*suicide*]

R

RAGGETT v SOCIETY OF JESUS TRUST OF 1929 FOR ROMAN CATHOLIC PURPOSES & ANOR [2010] EWCA Civ 1002 (27 August 2010) [*Abuse, sch*]

R v ANDREWS [2004] EWCA Crim 947 (5 March 2004) [*RoB def, RoB obs*]

REANEY v HEREFORD DIOCESAN BOARD OF FINANCE [2007] Employment Tribunal Case No 1602844/2006 (17 July 2007) [*Empl, D-SO, RoB obs, disc*]

R & ORS, R (ON THE APPLICATION OF) v LEEDS CITY COUNCIL [2005] EWHC 2495 (Admin) (11 November 2005) [*Disc, sch*]

RE C (ADOPTION: RELIGIOUS OBSERVANCE) [2002] 1 FLR 1119 [*adopt, RoB obs*]

RE S (SPECIFIC ISSUE ORDER: RELIGION: CIRCUMCISION) [2004] EWHC 1282 (Fam) [*marriage, health, child*]

ROYAL MAIL GROUP PLC v JAN [2008] EWCA Civ 341 (28 February 2008) [*Empl, RoB disc*]

ROYAL MAIL LETTERS & ORS v MUHAMMAD [2007] UKEAT 0392_07_2012 (20 December 2007) [*Empl, RoB disc*]

S

SAINI v ALL SAINTS HAQUE CENTRE & ORS [2008] UKEAT/00227/08 (24 October 2008) [*Empl, Eq, RoBdisc, disc indir*]

SANATAN DHARMA MAHA SABHA OF TRINIDAD AND TOBAGO INC & ORS v ATTORNEY GENERAL OF TRINIDAD AND TOBAGO [2009] UKPC 17 (28 April 2009)

SECRETARY OF STATE FOR WORK AND PENSIONS v SISTER IS [2009] UKUT 200 (AAC) (8 October 2009) [*employee def*]

SEPET & ANOR v SECRETARY OF STATE FOR THE HOME DEPARTMENT [2003] UKHL 15 (20 March 2003) [*RoB obs*]

SOUTH LONDON HEALTHCARE NHS TRUST v AL-RUBEYI [2010] UKEAT 0269_09_0203 (2 March 2010) [*empl, disc*]

SULAIMAN v JUFFALI [2002] 1 FLR 479, [2002] 2 FCR 427 (November 2001) [*marriage, RoB obs*]

R (ON THE APPLICATION OF SWAMI SURYANANDA) v WELSH MINISTERS [2007] EWCA Civ 893 (23 July 2007) [*RoB obs, accom/exemp/diff*]

T

R v TAYLOR [2001] EWCA Crim 2263 (23 October 2001) [*RoB obs*]

TARIQ V HOME OFFICE [2010] EWCA Civ 462 (CA) (04 May 2010) [*RoB disc*]

THOMPSON, RE [2002] EWHC 2635 (Admin) (26 November 2002) [*RoB doct, RoB obs*]

U

ULLAH v SPECIAL ADJUDICATOR [2002] EWCA Civ 1856 (16 December 2002) [*RoB obs*]

UDDIN v CHOUDHURY & ORS [2009] EWCA Civ 1205 (21 October 2009) [*ROB obs, marriage*]

V

VARSANI V JESANI [2002] 1 P. & C.R. DG11 (Chancery Division) (31 July 2001) [*assets*]

W

WATKINS-SINGH, R (ON THE APPLICATION OF) v GOVERNING BODY OF ABERDARE GIRLS' HIGH SCHOOL & ANOR [2008] EWHC (Admin) 1865 (29 July 2008) [*RoB obs, RoB disc, Eq, disc indir, child, sch*]

WHITE & ORS v WILLIAMS & ORS [2010] EWHC 940 (Ch) (05 April 2010) [*assets*]

WILKINSON v KITZINGER & ORS [2006] EWHC 2022 (Fam) (31 July 2006) [*marriage*]

WILLIAMS-DRABBLE v PATHWAY CARE SOLUTIONS [2005] Employment Tribunal Case No. 2601718/04 [*Empl, RoB obs, Disc, accom/exemp/diff*]

WILLIAMSON & ORS, R (ON THE APPLICATION OF) v SECRETARY OF STATE FOR EDUCATION AND EMPLOYMENT & ORS [2005] UKHL 15 (24 February 2005) [*RoB obs, RoB def, accom/exemp/diff, sch*]

R (ON THE APPLICATION OF X) v Y SCHOOL & ORS [2007] EWHC 298 (Admin) (21 FEBRUARY 2007) [*child/Dress/RoB disc*]

Bibliography

Adhar, R. and Leigh, I. (2005), *Religious Freedom in the Liberal State*. Oxford: Oxford University Press.

Allen, C. (2010), *Islamophobia*. Farnham: Ashgate.

All-Party Parliamentary Inquiry into Antisemitism (2006), *Report of the All-Party Parliamentary Inquiry into Antisemitism*. London: The Stationery Office.

Almog, S. (ed.) (1988) *Antisemitism Through the Ages*. Oxford: Pergamon Press.

Anderson, B. (1983), *Imagined Communities: Reflections on the Origin and Spread of Nationalism*. London: Verso.

Archbishop's Commission on Urban Priority Areas (1985), *Faith in the City: A Call for Action by Church and Nation – The Report of the Archbishop of Canterbury's Commission on Urban Priority Areas*. London: Church House.

Arweck, E. (2013), '"I've Been Christened, But I Don't Really Believe in it": How Young People Articulate Their (Non-)Religious Identities and Perceptions of (Non-)Belief', in A. Day and C. Cotter (eds), *Social Identities Between the Sacred and the Secular*. Aldershot: Ashgate, forthcoming.

Asad, T. (1990), 'Multiculturalism and British Identity in the Wake of the Rushdie Affair', *Politics and Society*, 28(4), 455–80.

Atkinson, R. and Flint, J. (2001), 'Accessing Hidden and Hard-to-Reach Populations: Snowball Research Strategies', *Social Research Update*, 33. Online at: http://sru.soc.surrey.ac.uk/SRU33.pdf (accessed 5 May 2013).

Bacal, A. (1981), *Ethnicity in the Social Sciences: A View and Review of the Literature on Ethnicity*. Reprint paper on Ethnic Relations, No. 3. Coventry: Centre for Research in Ethnic Relations, University of Warwick.

Badham, P. (1990), 'The Contribution of Religion to the Conflict in Northern Ireland', in D. Cohn-Sherbok (ed.), *The Canterbury Papers: Essays on Religion and Society*. London: Bellew, 119–28.

Ballard, R. (1994), *Desh Pardesh: The South Asian Presence in Britain*. London: Hurst and Co.

Bamforth, N. (2004), *Understanding the Impact and Status of the Human Rights Act 1998 within English Law*. Global Law Working Paper, 10/04. New York: Hauser Global Law School Program.

Barker, E. (1982), *New Religious Movements: A Perspective for Understanding Society*. Lampeter: Edwin Mellen Press.

— (1989a), *New Religious Movements: A Practical Introduction*. London: HMSO.

— (1989b), 'Tolerant Discrimination: Church, State and the New Religions', in P. Badham (ed.), *Religion, State and Society in Modern Britain*. Lampeter: Edwin Mellen Press, 185–208.

Barley, C., Field, C., Kosmin, B. and Nielsen, J. (1987), *Religion: Reviews of United Kingdom Statistical Sources*, Vol. 20. Oxford: Pergamon Press.

Bates, J. and Collishaw, S. (2006), *Faith in Derbyshire: Working Towards a Better Derbyshire: Faith Based Contribution*. Derby: Derby Diocesan Council for Social Responsibility.

Bebbington, D. (1982), *The Nonconformist Conscience: Chapel and Politics, 1870–1914*. London: George Allen and Unwin.

Beckford, J., Gale, R., Peach, C., Owen, D. and Weller, P. (2006), *Review of the Evidence Base on Faith Communities*. London: Office of the Deputy Prime Minister.

Beeson, T. (1975), *Discretion and Valour: Religious Conditions in Russia and Eastern Europe*. London: Collins Fontana.

Berger, P., Davie, G. and Fokas, E. (2008), *Religious America, Secular Europe? A Theme and Variations*. Aldershot: Ashgate.

BBC (7 May 2007), 'White Fright', *Panorama*. Online at: http://news.bbc.co.uk/1/hi/programmes/panorama/6631541.stm (accessed 6 May 2013).

Bishop, P. (1991), 'Victorian Values? Some Antecedents of a Religiously Plural Society', in R. Hooker and J. Sargant (eds), *Belonging to Britain: Christian Perspectives on a Plural Society*. London: Council of Churches for Britain and Ireland, 31–52.

Bisset, P. (1986), *The Kirk and Her Scotland*. Edinburgh: Handsel.

— (1989), 'Kirk and Society in Modern Scotland', in P. Badham (ed.), *Religion, State and Society in Britain*. Lampeter: Edwin Mellen Press, 51–65.

Bruce, S. (1986), *God Save Ulster: The Religion and Politics of Paisleyism*. Oxford: Oxford University Press.

Bruce, S., Glendinning, T., Paterson, I. and Rosie, M. (2005), 'Religious Discrimination in Scotland: Fact or Myth?' *Ethnic and Racial Studies*, 28(1), 151–68.

Bruce, S. and Voas, D. (2010), 'Vicarious Religion: An Examination and Critique', *Journal of Contemporary Religion*, 25(2), 243–59.

Buchanan, J. (1994), *Cut the Connection: Disestablishment and the Church of England*. London: Darton, Longman and Todd.

Bullivant, S. and Lee, L. (2012), 'Interdisciplinary Studies of Non-religion and Secularity: The State of the Union', *Journal of Contemporary Religion*, 27(1), 19–27.

Cabinet Office (2010), *Building the Big Society*. London: Cabinet Office.

Cantle, T. and the Community Cohesion Team (2001), *Community Cohesion: A Report of the Independent Review Team Chaired by Ted Cantle*. London: The Home Office.

Cantwell Smith, W. (1978), *The Meaning and End of Religion*. London: SPCK.

Carrera, S. and Parkin, J. (2010), *The Place of Religion in European Union Law and Policy: Competing Approaches and Actors Inside the European Commission*. Religare Working Paper No. 1. Leuven: Religare.

Chaney, P. (2009), *Equal Opportunities and Human Rights: The First Decade of Devolution in Wales*. Cardiff: Equality and Human Rights Commission.

Cheruvallil-Contractor, S., Hooley, T., Moore, N., Purdam, K. and Weller, P. (2013), 'Researching the Non-Religious: Methods and Methodological Issues, Challenges and Controversies', in A. Day, G. Vincett and C. Cotter (eds), *Social Identities between the Sacred and the Secular*. Aldershot: Ashgate, 173–90.

Christians in Parliament (2012), *Clearing the Ground: Preliminary Inquiry into the Freedom of Christians in the UK*. London: Christians in Parliament.

Clark, K. and Drinkwater, S. (2009), 'Dynamics and Diversity: Ethnic Employment Differences in England and Wales, 1991–2001', *Research in Labour Economics*, 29, 299–333.

Clayton, R., Queen's Council (2012), 'Smoke and Mirrors: The Human Rights Act and the Impact of the Strasbourg Case Law', *Public Law*, 4, 639–57. Online at: http://denning. law.ox.ac.uk/news/events_files/smoke_and_mirrors.pdf (accessed 16 February 2013).

Clements, K. (1971), 'The Religious Variable: Dependent, Independent or Interdependent', in M. Hill (ed.), *A Sociological Yearbook of Religion*, No. 4. London: SCM Press, 36–45.

Cohen, S. (1984), *That's Funny, You Don't Look Anti-Semitic: An Anti-Racist Analysis of Left Anti-Semitism*. Leeds: Beyond the Pale Collective.

Cohn, N. (1973), *Europe's Inner Demons: The Demonization of Christians in Medieval Christendom*. Chicago, IL: Chicago University Press.

Comerford, R., Cullen, M. and Hill, J. (1990), *Religion, Conflict and Coexistence in Ireland*. London: Gill and Macmillan.

Commission for Racial Equality (1992), *Second Review of the Race Relations Act 1976*. London: Commission for Racial Equality.

— (1994), *Position paper on Religious Discrimination*. London: Commission for Racial Equality.

— (1997), *Religious Discrimination: Your Rights*. London: Commission for Racial Equality.

Commission on British Muslims and Islamophobia (1997), *Islamophobia: A Challenge for Us All*. London: Runnymede Trust.

— (2001), *Addressing the Challenge of Islamophobia: Progress Report, 1999–2001*. London: Commission on British Muslims and Islamophobia.

Committee on the Elimination of Racial Discrimination (2011), *Concluding Observations of the Committee on the Elimination of Racial Discrimination, United Kingdom of Great Britain and Northern Ireland*, Committee on the Elimination of Racial Discrimination, 79th session, 14 September 2011, CERD/C/GBR/CO/18–20.

Commission on Integration and Cohesion (2007), *Our Shared Future*. London: Commission on Integration and Cohesion.

Communities and Local Government (2010), *All-Party Inquiry into Antisemitism: Government Response. Three Years on Progress Report*. London: The Stationery Office.

Contractor, S. (2012), *Muslim Women in Britain: Demystifying the Muslimah*. London: Routledge.

Cotterell, R. (1984), 'Interview: Richard Cotterell MEP', *Update: A Quarterly Journal on New Religious Movements*, 8(3/4), 30–4.

Council of Europe Group of Consultants on Religious and Cultural Aspects of Equality for Immigrants (1996), *Study*. Strasbourg: Council of Europe.

Crenshaw, K. (1989), 'Demarginalizing the Intersection of Race and Sex: A Black Feminist Critique of Antidiscrimination Doctrine, Feminist Theory and Antiracist Politics', *University of Chicago Legal Forum*, 139–67.

Creswell, J. (2003), *Research Design: Qualitative, Quantitative and Mixed Methods Approaches*. Thousand Oaks, CA: Sage Publications.

Dale, A., Lindley, J. and Dex, S. (2006), 'A life-course perspective on ethnic differences in women's economic activity in Britain', *European Sociological Review*, 22(3), 459–76.

Daniels, N. (1960), *Islam and the West: The Making of an Image, 1000–1300 AD, Volume I*. Edinburgh: Edinburgh University Press.

— (1967), *Islam and the West: Islam, Europe and Empire, Volume II*. Edinburgh: Edinburgh University Press.

Davie, G. (1990), 'Believing without Belonging: Is this the Future of Religion in Britain?', *Social Compass*, 37, 455–69.

— (1994), *Religion in Britain since 1945: Believing without Belonging*. London: Blackwell.

Denham, J. and the Ministerial Group on Public Order and Community Cohesion (2001), *Building Cohesive Communities: A Report of the Ministerial Group on Public Order and Building Cohesive Communities*. London: The Home Office.

Department for the Environment, Transport and the Regions (1996), *Challenging Religious Discrimination: A Guide for Faith Communities and their Advisers*. London: Department for the Environment, Transport and the Regions.

Donald, A with the assistance of assistance of K. Bennett and P. Leach (2012), *Religion or Belief, Equality and Human Rights in England and Wales, Equality and Human Rights Commission Research Report* 84. Manchester: Equality and Human Rights Commission.

Dorey, P. and Garnett, M. (2012), 'No Such Thing as the "Big Society"? The Conservative Party's Unnecessary Search for "Narrative" in the 2010 General Election', *British Politics*, 7(4), 389–417.

Durkheim, E. (1947), *The Elementary Forms of Religious Life*. New York: The Free Press.

The Equal Rights Trust (2007), *The Ideas of Equality and Non-Discrimination: Formal and Substantive Equality*, 1–7. Online at: www.equalrightstrust.org/ertdocumentbank/The%20Ideas%20of%20Equality%20and%20Non-discrimination,%20Formal%20and%20Substantive%20Equality.pdf (accessed 16 February 2013).

Equality and Human Rights Commission (2011), 'Commission Proposes "Reasonable Accommodation" for Religion or Belief', *Press Release*, 11 July 2011. Online at: www.equalityhumanrights.com/news/2011/july/commission-proposes-reasonable-accommodation-for-religion-or-belief-is-needed (accessed 16 February 2013).

European Monitoring Centre for Racism and Xenophobia (2005), *The Impact of 7 July 2005 London Bomb Attacks on Muslim Communities across the EU*. Vienna: EUMC.

— (2007), *Muslims in the European Union: Discrimination and Islamophobia*. Vienna: EUMC.

Finney, N. and Simpson, L. (2009), *Sleepwalking to Segregation? Challenging Myths about Race and Migration*. Bristol: Policy Press.

Fischer, M., Lahiri, S. and Thandi, S. (eds) (2007), *A South-Asian History of Britain: Four Centuries of Peoples from the Indian Sub-Continent*. Oxford: Greenwood Publishing.

Fitzgerald, T. (2000), *The Ideology of Religious Studies*. Oxford: Oxford University Press.

— (2007), *Discourse on Civility and Barbarity: A Critical History of Religion and Related Categories*. Oxford and New York: Oxford University Press.

Fox, R. (1986), *Pagans and Christians: In the Mediterranean World from the Second Century AD to the Conversion of Constantine*. Harmondsworth: Penguin.

Geertz, C. (1966), 'Religion as a Cultural System', in M. Bainton (ed.), *Anthropological Approaches to the Study of Religion*. London: Tavistock, 1–46.

Ghanea, N. (2010), 'Religious Minorities and Human Rights: Bridging International and Domestic Perspectives on the Rights of Persons Belonging to Religious Minorities under English Law', *European Yearbook of Minority Issues*, 9, 497–518.

— (2011), 'Religion, Equality and Non-Discrimination', in J. Witte Jnr and M. Green (eds), *Religion and Human Rights: An Introduction*. Oxford: Oxford University Press, 204–17..

Gill, R. (1975), *Social Context of Theology: A Methodological Enquiry*. London: Blackwell.

Goldbart, J. and Hustler, D. (2005), 'Ethnography', in B. Somekh and C. Lewin Cathy (eds), *Research Methods in the Social Sciences*. London: Sage, 16–23.

Gregory, I. N., Cunningham, N. A., Ell, P. S., Lloyd C. D. and Shuttleworth, I. G. (2013), *Troubled Geographies: A Spatial History of Religion and Society in Ireland*. Bloomington, IN: Indiana University Press.

Hall, S. (1996), 'Who Needs "Identity?"', in S. Hall and P. du Gay (eds), *Questions of Cultural Identity*. London: Sage Publications, 1–19.

Hastings, A. (1991a), *A History of English Christianity, 1920–1990*, 3rd edn. London: SCM Press

— (1991b), *Church and State: The English Experience*. Exeter: Exeter University Press.

Heath, A. and Martin, J. (2012), 'Can Religious Affiliation Explain "Ethnic" Inequalities in the Labour Market?', *Ethnic and Racial Studies*, 36(6), 1005–27.

Hepple, B. (2010), 'The New Single Equality Act in Britain', *The Equal Rights Review*, 5, 11–24. Online at: www.equalrightstrust.org/ertdocumentbank/bob%20hepple.pdf (accessed 16 February 2013).

Hepple, B. and Choudhury, T. (2001), *Tacking Religious Discrimination: Practical Implications for Policy-Makers and Legislators*. Home Office Research Study 221. London: Research, Development and Statistics Directorate, The Home Office.

Hickey, J. (1984), *Religion and the Northern Ireland Problem*. Dublin: Gill and Macmillan

Hill, C. (1975), *The World Turned Upside Down: Radical Ideas During the English Revolution*. Harmondsworth: Pelican.

Hill, M. (2005), 'The Permissible Scope of Legal Limitations on the Freedom of Religion or Belief in the United Kingdom', *Emory International Law Review*, 19(2), 1129–86.

Hinton, P. (2000), *Stereotypes, Cognition and Culture*. Hove: Psychology Press.

Hobsbawn, E. (1995), *Age of Extremes: The Short Twentieth Century: 1914–1991*. London: Abacus.

The Home Office (1999), *The Stephen Lawrence Inquiry: Report of an Inquiry by Sir William MacPherson of Cluny*, Cm 4262-I. London: The Stationery Office.

— (2012), *Review of the Public Sector Equality Duty*, announced 15 May. Online at: www.homeoffice.gov.uk/equalities/equality-act/equality-duty/equality-duty-review (accessed 16 February 2013).

Home Office Faith Communities Unit (2004), *Working Together: Co-operation between Government and Faith Communities. Recommendations of the Steering Group Reviewing Patterns of Engagement between Government and Faith Communities in England*. London: Faith Communities Unit, The Home Office.

Human Rights Committee (2008), *Consideration of Reports Submitted by States Parties, Concluding Observations of the Human Rights Committee, United Kingdom of Great Britain and Northern Ireland*, Human Rights Committee, 93rd session, 30 July 2008, CCPR/C/GBR/CO/6.

Human Rights Council (2012), *Universal Periodic Review, Report of the Working Group on the Universal Periodic Review, United Kingdom of Great Britain and Northern Ireland*, respectively, 6 July 2012, A/HRC/21/9.

Huntington, S. (1993), 'The Clash of Civilisations', *Foreign Affairs*, 72(3), 22–49.

Hussain, A. (2000), *Visit to the United Kingdom of Great Britain and Northern Ireland*. Report of the Special Rapporteur on the Right to Freedom of Opinion and Expression (dates of visit: 24–29/10/1999), 11 February 2000, E/CN.4/2000/63/Add.3.

Hussain, D. (2004), 'British Muslim Identity', in M. Seddon, D. Hussain and N. Malik (eds), *British Muslims between Assimilation and Segregation – Historical, Legal and Social Realities*. Markfield: The Islamic Foundation, 83–118.

Hussain, F. (1990), *The Anti-Islamic Tradition in the West*. Leicester: Muslim Community Studies Institute.

Inter Faith Network for the UK/Inner Cities Religious Council (1999), *The Local Inter Faith Guide: Faith Community Co-operation in Action*. London: Inter Faith Network for the United Kingdom in association with the Inner Cities Religious Council of the Department for the Environment, Transport and the Regions.

Inter Faith Network for the UK in association with the Local Government Association, the Home Office and the Inner Cities' Religious Council of the Office of the Deputy Prime Minister (2003), *Partnership for the Common Good: Inter Faith Infrastructures and Local Government*. London: Inter Faith Network for the UK.

Ipgrave, M. (2003), '*Fidei Defensor* Revisited: Church and State in a Religiously Plural Society', in N. Ghanea (ed.), *The Challenge of Religious Discrimination at the Dawn of the New Millennium*. Leiden: Martinus Nijhoff, 207–22.

Jahangir, A. (7 February 2008), *Mission to the United Kingdom of Great Britain and Northern Ireland*. Report of the Special Rapporteur on Freedom of Religion or Belief, A/HRC/7/10/Add.3.

Jenkins, R. (1967), *Essays and Speeches*. London: Collins.

Jenkins, R. (1989), 'On Race Relations and the Rushdie Affair', *The Independent Magazine*. 18.3.89.

Jones, P. and Pennick, N. (1995), *A History of Pagan Europe*. London: Routledge.

Jordan, W. (1932, 1936), *The Development of Religious Toleration in England*, 2 vols. London: George Allen and Unwin.

Kaufmann, E. (2013), *Half Full or Half Empty?: How Has Ethnic Segregation in England and Wales Changed between 2001 and 2011*. London: Demos.

Kee, A. (1982), *Constantine versus Christ: The Triumph of Ideology*. London: SCM Press.

Knights, S. (2007), *Freedom of Religion, Minorities and the Law*. Oxford: Oxford University Press.

Krueger, R. and Casey, M. (2000), *Focus Groups: A Practical Guide for Applied Research*. London: Sage.

Lamont, S. (1989), *Church and State: Uneasy Alliances*. London: Bodley Head.

Larsen, T. (1999), *Friends of Religious Equality: Nonconformist Politics in Mid-Victorian England*. Woodbridge: The Boydell Press.

The Law Commission (1985), *Criminal Law Offences against Religion and Public Worship*, Report No. 145. London: Her Majesty's Stationery Office.

Lee, L. (2012), 'Research Note: Talking about a Revolution: Terminology for the New Field of Non-religion Studies', *Journal of Contemporary Religion*, 27(1), 129–39.

Lewis, J. (ed.) (2009), *Scientology*. Oxford: Oxford University Press.

Lindley, J. (2002), 'Race or Religions? The Impact of Religion on the Employment and Earnings of Britain's Ethnic Communities', *Journal of Ethnic and Migration Studies*, 28(3), 427–42.

Local Government Association (2002), *Faith and Community: A Good Practice Guide*. London: Local Government Association Publications.

Local Government Association, in association with the Home Office, the Commission for Racial Equality and the Inter Faith Network for the UK (2002), *Guidance on Community Cohesion*. London: Local Government Association.

Macey, M. and Carling, A. (2011), *Ethnic, Racial and Religious Inequalities: The Perils of Subjectivity*. Basingstoke: Palgrave Macmillan.

Madeley, J. and Z. Enyedi (eds) (2003), *Church and State in Contemporary Europe: The Chimera of Neutrality*. London: Frank Cass.

Malik, M. (2001), 'Minority Protection and Human Rights', in T. Campbell, K. Ewing and A. Tomkins (eds), *Sceptical Essays on Human Rights*. Oxford: Oxford University Press, 277–94.

— (ed.) (2010), *Patterns of Prejudice: Anti-Muslim Prejudice, Past and Present*. Abingdon: Routledge.

— (2011), 'Religious Freedom, Free Speech and Equality: Conflict or Cohesion?', *Res Publica*, 17(1), 22.

Mansur Ali, M. and Gilliat-Ray, S. (2012) 'Muslim Chaplains: Working at the Interface of "Public" and "Private"', in W. Ahmad and Z. Sardar (eds), *Muslims in Britain: Making Social and Political Space*. London: Routledge.

Marrotti, A. (2005), *Religious Ideology and Cultural Fantasy: Catholic and Anti-Catholic Discourses in Early Modern England*. N Dame: University of Notre Dame Press.

McAspurren, L. (2005), *Religious Discrimination and Sectarianism in Scotland: A Brief Review of Evidence (2002–2004)*. Edinburgh: Scottish Executive Social Research. Online at: www.scotland.gov.uk/socialresearch.

McDermott, M., and Ahsan, M. (1980), *The Muslim Guide*. Leicester: The Islamic Foundation.

McSweeney, B. (1989), 'The Religious Dimension of the "Troubles" in Northern Ireland', in P. Badham (ed.), *Religion, State and Society in Modern Britain*. Lampeter: Edwin Mellen Press, 68–83.

Modood, T. (ed.) (1977), *Church, State and Religious Minorities*. London: Policy Studies Institute.

Morris, R. (ed.) (2008), *Church and State: Some Reflections on Church Establishment in England*. London: The Constitution Unit, University College London.

Murray, S. (2004), *Post-Christendom: Church and Mission in a Strange New World*. Carlisle: Paternoster.

Nicholson, L. (2002), *Identification of Research on Sectarianism, Religious Hatred and Discrimination within a Scottish Context*. Edinburgh: Scottish Government Equality Unit. Online at: www.scotland.gov.uk/Publications/2005/01/20553/50504.

Norman, E. (1968), *Anti-Catholicism in Victorian England*. New York: Barnes and Noble.

Northwest Regional Development Agency (2003), *Faith in England's Northwest: The Contribution by Faith Communities to Civil Society in the Region*. Warrington: Northwest Regional Development Agency.

Noy, C. (2008), 'Sampling Knowledge: The Hermeneutics of Snowball Sampling in Qualitative Research', *International Journal of Social Research Methodology*, 11(4), 327–44.

Nye, M. (1996), 'Hare Krishna and Sanatan Dharm in Britain: The Campaign for Bhaktivedanta Manor', *Journal of Contemporary Religion*, 21(1), 37–56.

— (2001), *Multiculturalism and Minority Religions in Britain: Krishna Consciousness, Religious Freedom, and the Politics of Location*. Richmond: Curzon.

Nye, M. and Weller, P. (2012), 'Controversies Controversies as a Lens on Change', in L. Woodhead and R. Catto (eds), *Religion and Change in Modern Britain*. London: Routledge, 34–54.

O'Brien, J. (2010), *Discrimination in Northern Ireland, 1920–1939: Myth or Reality?* Newcastle-Upon-Tyne: Cambridge Scholars Publishing.

O'Cinneide, C. (2011), 'The Uncertain Foundations of Contemporary Anti-Discrimination Law', *International Journal of Discrimination and the Law*, 11, 7–28.

O'Connor, W. and Lewis, J. (1999), *Experiences of Social Exclusion in Scotland: A Qualitative Research Survey*. Research Programme Research Findings, No. 73. Edinburgh: Central Research Unit, The Scottish Office.

OSCE (2004), *Guidelines for Review of Legislation Pertaining to Religion or Belief*, prepared by the OSCE/ODIHR Advisory Panel of Experts on Freedom of Religion or Belief in Consultation with the European Commission for Democracy Through Law (Venice Commission). Online at: www.osce.org/odihr/13993 (accessed 16 February 2013).

Parekh, B. (2000a), *Rethinking Multiculturalism: Cultural Diversity and Political Theory*. Basingstoke: Macmillan.

— (ed.) (2000b), *The Future of Multi-Ethnic Britain: The Parekh Report*. London: Profile Books.

Parsons, G. (1994), 'Deciding How Far You Can Go', in G. Parsons (ed.), *The Growth of Religious Diversity: Britain from 1945*, Vol. 2. London: Routledge, 5–21.

Perfect, D. (2011), *Religion or Belief, Equality and Human Rights Commission Briefing Paper 1*, Manchester: Equality and Human Rights Commission.

Phillips, T. (September 2005), 'After 7/7: Sleepwalking to Segregation', *Commission for Racial Equality*, 22, n.p.

Pickering, M. (2001), *Stereotyping: The Politics of Representation*. New York: Palgrave.

Purdam, K., Afkhami, R., Crockett, A. and Olsen, W. (2007), 'Religion in the UK: An Overview of Equality Statistics and Evidence Gaps', *Journal of Contemporary Religion*, 22(2), 147–68.

Putnam, R. (1995), 'Bowling Alone: America's Declining Social Capital', *Journal of Democracy*, 2, 65–78.

— (2000), *Bowling Alone: The Collapse and Revival of American Community*. New York: Simon and Schuster.

Ravat, R. (2004), *Enabling the Present: Planning for the Future: Social Action by the Faith Communities of Leicester*. Leicester: Leicester Faiths Regeneration Project.

Rex, J. (1985), *The Concept of a Multi-Cultural Society*. Coventry: University of Warwick Centre for Research in Ethnic Relations.

Riddell, S. and Watson, N. (2011), 'Equality and Human Rights in Britain: Principles and Challenges', *Social Policy and Society*, 10(2), 193–203.

Riessman, C. (2002), 'Narrative Analysis', in M. Huberman and M. Miles (eds), *The Qualitative Researcher's Companion*. London: Sage Publications.

Robilliard, St John (1984), *Religion and The Law: Religious Liberty in Modern English Law*. Manchester: Manchester University Press.

Rubin, H. and Rubin, I. (1995), *Qualitative Interviewing: The Art of Hearing*. London: Sage Publications.

Runnymede Trust (1994), *A Very Light Sleeper: The Persistence and Dangers of Antisemitism*. London: Runnymede Trust.

Salbstein, M. (1982), *The Emancipation of the Jews in Britain: The Question of the Admission of the Jews to Parliament, 1828–1860*. East Brunswick and London: Associated University Presses.

Schratz, M. (1993), 'An Epilogue: Putting Voices together', in M. Schratz (ed.), *Qualitative Voices in Educational Research*. London: Falmer Press, 179–84.

Schratz, M. and Walker, R. (1995), *Research as Social Change: New Opportunities for Qualitative Research*. London: Routledge.

Sengaas, D. (1998), *The Clash within Civilizations: Coming to Terms with Cultural Conflicts*. London: Routledge.

Sheridan, L. (2002), *Effects of the Events of September 11th 2001 on Discrimination and Implicit Racism in Five Religious and Seven Ethnic Groups: A Brief Overview*. Leicester: University of Leicester.

Smith, G. (2002), 'Religion and the Rise of Social Capitalism: The Faith Communities in Community Development and Urban Regeneration in England', *Community Development Journal*, 37(1), 166–77.

— (2003), *Faith in the Voluntary Sector: A Common or Distinctive Experience of Religious Organisations*. Department of Sociology Working Papers in Applied Social Research, No. 25. Manchester: University of Manchester.

— (2004), 'Faith in Community and Communities of Faith?: Government Rhetoric and Religious Identity in Urban Britain', *Journal of Contemporary Religion*, 19(1), 185–204.

Spalek, B., McDonald, L. and Awa, S. (2011), *Preventing Religio-Political Extremism amongst Muslim Youth: A Study Exploring Police–Community Partnership. Religion and Society and University of Birmingham*. Online at: www.religionandsociety.org.uk/

uploads/docs/2011_04/1302685819_preventing-religio-political-extremism-spalek-april2011.pdf.

Stewart, D. and Shamdasani, P. (1990), *Focus Groups: Theory and Practice*. London: Sage Publications.

Taylor-Gooby, P. (2012), 'Root and Branch Restructuring to Achieve Major Cuts: The Social Policy Programme of the 2010 UK Coalition Government', *Social Policy and Administration*, 46(1), 61–82.

Toynbee, A. (1956), *An Historian's Approach to Religion*. London: Oxford University Press.

UK Action Committee on Islamic Affairs (1993), *Muslims and the Law in Multi Faith Britain: The Need for Reform*. London: UK Action Committee on Islamic Affairs.

Vincett, G., Olson, E., Hopkins, P. and Pain, R. (2012), 'Young People and Performance Christianity in Scotland', *Journal of Contemporary Religion*, 27(2), 275–90.

Visram, R. (1986), *Ayahs, Lascars and Princes: Indians in Britain, 1700–1947*. London: Pluto Press.

Voas, D. (2003), 'Is Britain a Christian Country?', in P. Avis (ed.), *Public Faith: The State of Religious Belief and Practice in Britain*. London: SPCK, 92–105.

— (2009), 'The Rise and Fall of Fuzzy Fidelity in Europe', *European Sociological Review*, 25(1), 155–68.

Voas, D. and Bruce, S. (2004), 'The 2001 Census and Christian Identification in Britain', *Journal of Contemporary Religion*, 19(1), 23–8.

— (2007), 'The Spiritual Revolution: Another False Dawn for the Sacred', in K. Flanagan and P. Jupp (eds), *A Sociology of Spirituality*. Surrey: Ashgate, 43–62.

Ward, P. and Dunlop, S. (2013), *Migration and Visual Culture: A Theological Exploration of Identity, Catholic Imagery and Popular culture among Polish Young People*. Online at: www.religionandsociety.org.uk/research_findings/featured_findings/photos_reveal_what_s_sacred_to_young_poles_in_britain.

Weiler, J. (2003), *Un' Europa Christiana: Un Saggio Esplorativo*. Milan: Bibloteca Universale Rizzoli.

Weldon, F. (1989), *Sacred Cows: A Portrait of Britain, Post-Rushdie, Pre-Utopia*. London: Chatto and Windus.

Weller, P. (2004), 'Identity, Politics and the Future(s) of Religion in the UK: The Case of the Religion Question in the 2001 Decennial Census', *Journal of Contemporary Religion*, 19(1), 3–21.

— (2005), *Time for a Change: Reconfiguring Religion, State and Society*. London: T&T Clark.

— (2006), ' "Human Rights", "Religion" and the "Secular": Variant Configurations of Religion(s), State(s) and Society(ies)', *Religion and Human Rights: An International Journal*, 1(1), 17–39.

— (2007a), *Religions in the UK: Directory, 2007–2010*. Derby: Multi-Faith Centre at the University of Derby and Faculty of Education, Health and Sciences, University of Derby.

— (2007b), 'Conspiracy Theories and the Incitement of Hatred: The Dynamics of Deception, Plausibility and Defamation', in M. Fineberg, S. Samuels and M. Weitzman (eds), *Antisemitism: The Generic Hatred*. Edgware: Valentine Mitchell, 182–97.

— (2008), *Religious Diversity in the UK: Contours and Issues*. London and New York: Continuum.

— (2009a), 'Roots, Developments and Issues: 19th Century Prefigurations for State, Religious and Cultural Diversity in 21st Century England', in L. Derrocher, C. Gélinas, S. Lebel-Grenier and P. Nöel (eds), *L'État et la Diversité Culturelle et Religieuse, 1800–*

1914/The State and Cultural and Religious Diversity in Canada, 1800–1914. Quebec: Presses d'Université de Quebec/University of Quebec Press, 181–214.

— (2009b), *A Mirror for Our Times: 'The Rushdie Affair' and the Future of Multiculturalism*. London and New York: Continuum.

— (2011), *Religious Discrimination in Britain: A Review of the Research Evidence*. Manchester: Equality and Human Rights Commission. Online at: www. equalityhumanrights.com/uploaded_files/research/research_report_73_religious_ discrimination.pdf (accessed 5 May 2013).

Weller, P. and Andrews, A. (November 1998), 'Counting Religion: Religion, Statistics and the 2001 Census', *World Faiths Encounter*, 21, 23–34.

Weller, P. and Contractor, S. (2012), *Learning from Experience, Leading to Engagement. For a Europe of Religion and Belief Diversity. A Policy Brief Document for the European Institutions and Civil Society Groups*. Brussels: Belieforama.

Weller, P., Feldman, A. and Purdam, K. (2000), *Religious Discrimination in England and Wales: An Interim Report, January 2000*. Derby: University of Derby.

— (2001), *Religious Discrimination in England and Wales,* Home Office Research Study 220. London: Research Development and Statistics Directorate, The Home Office.

Wengraf, T. (2001), *Qualitative Research Interviewing*. London: Sage Publications.

Wheatcroft, A. (2004), *Infidels: A History of the Conflict between Christendom and Islam*. London: Penguin.

Winckler, V. (ed.) (2009), *Equality Issues in Wales: A Research Review*, Research Report No. 11. Manchester: Equality and Human Rights Commission.

Wolffe, J. (ed.) (1993), *The Growth of Religious Diversity: Britain from 1945: A Reader*. Sevenoaks: Hodder and Stoughton.

Woodhead, L. (2011), *Recent Research on Religion, Discrimination, and Good Relations,* Research Report No. 48. Manchester: Equality and Human Rights Commission.

Woodhead, L. with Catto, R. (2009), *'Religion or Belief: Identifying Issues and Priorities,* Research Report 48. Manchester: Equality and Human Rights Commission.

Yarrow, S. (1997), *Religious and Political Discrimination in the Workplace*. London: Policy Studies Institute.

Index of Acts of Parliament and Regulations; European Court of Human Rights Legal Cases; European Union Directives; International Treaties and Conventions; UK Legal Cases

Organization Index

Organizations referred to by name in the text of the book.

Place Index

Places referred to in the text of the book.

Author and Editor Index

Authors and editors where their work is quoted and/or referred to by others in the text of the book, and specifically in their capacity as author or editor.

Named Individuals Index

Individuals identified in the text of the book by name or title, other than when quoted or referred to as authors or editors. This includes when they are quoted in publications of which they are not author or editor.

Key word Index

Key words that can frequently be found in the sections of chapters 6–7 dealing with unfair treatment in the sectors of education; employment; the media; criminal justice and immigration; housing; health care; social services, planning and other services; are *excluded* from this index.

Thus *not included* here are key words such as 'teachers', 'lecturers', 'pupils', 'schools' and 'colleges' that appear often in the section of chapter 6 that deals with unfair treatment on the basis of religion or belief in the sphere of education. However, the concentration of these words and the key themes that relate to them can be located using the lists of contents and tables at the beginning of the book.

This index therefore includes other key words that appear across the book more generally, with the exception of those already listed in the earlier indexes on 'Acts of Parliament and Regulations, European Court of Human Rights Legal Cases, European Union Directives, International Treaties and Conventions, and UK Legal Cases'; on 'Organizations'; on 'Places'; on 'Authors and Editors'; and on 'Named Individuals'.